THE NEW LEARNING AND TELECOMMUNICATIONS TECHNOLOGIES
Their Potential Applications In Education

THE NEW LEARNING
AND TELECOMMUNICATIONS
TECHNOLOGIES
Their Potential Applications In Education

Edited by

IBRAHIM M. HEFZALLAH, PH.D.

Professor of Educational Technology
Fairfield University

C H A R L E S   C   T H O M A S   •   P U B L I S H E R
Springfield • Illinois • U.S.A.

Published and Distributed Throughout the World by

CHARLES C THOMAS • PUBLISHER
2600 South First Street
Springfield, Illinois 62794-9265

© *1990 by* CHARLES C THOMAS • PUBLISHER

ISBN 0-398-05659-5

Library of Congress Catalog Card Number: 89-29813

Printed in the United States of America
SC-R-3

Library of Congress Cataloging-in-Publication Data

The new learning and telecommunications technologies : their potential
  applications in education / edited by Ibrahim M. Hefzallah.
      p. cm.
  Includes bibliographical references.
  ISBN 0-398-05659-5
  1. Educational technology—United States. 2. Learning.
3. Instructional materials centers—United States. I. Hefzallah,
Ibrahim M. (Ibrahim Michail)
LB1028.3.N5547 1990
371.3'078—dc20   89-29813
                                                                       CIP

CONTRIBUTORS

ROBERT HALE, M.S., C.A.S.
*Former President of the Association for Educational
Communications and Technology, AECT
Coordinator, Learning Resources and Technology Unit
Connecticut State Department of Education*

FRANCIS A. HARVEY, ED.D.
*Associate Professor of Educational Technology
College of Education
Lehigh University*

IBRAHIM MICHAIL HEFZALLAH, PH.D. (Editor)
*Professor of Educational Technology
Fairfield University*

STEVEN MAZZOLA, B.S. in Communications
*System Engineer
University of Lowell Instructional Network
Lowell University*

MARGARET A. McDEVITT, M.ED., Candidate ED.D.
*Instructional Network Coordinator
University of Lowell Instructional Network
Lowell University*

FREDERICK W. MIS, PH.D.
*Assistant Professor of Quantitative Analysis,
Fairfield University*

RICHARD J. O'CONNOR, ED.D.
*Associate Professor of Educational Technology
College of Education
Lehigh University*

PETER L. STONE, M.S.
*Media Specialist
Somers Public Schools System
Somers, Connecticut*

PREFACE

The ultimate goal of education is to cultivate the whole educated person for an effective and productive life. To achieve this goal and to ensure the economic vitality of our country, we must raise and enhance the quality of education on all levels.

Special attention has to be given to the design of learning environments conducive to the cultivation of the educated person. The learning environment should not be a chance environment. It should be planned and programmed to achieve designated educational objectives.

An essential element of that design is ensuring the learner's interactivity with models of excellence, both in human resources and in learning materials. Very often, access to models of excellence can be achieved through mediated interaction.

Fortunately, the technology of the information age provides students and teachers with the tools and vehicles through which models of excellence can be accessed.

This book examines the new learning and telecommunications technologies and their potential applications to enrich the learning process, and to ensure educational equity for all students.

ACKNOWLEDGMENTS

In the Spring semester of 1987, Fairfield University granted me a sabbatical leave to study the new learning and telecommunications technologies and their potential applications to education. Part of the planned activities of the leave was visitations to schools and universities which have successfully implemented some of the new information technologies to help achieve their missions.

It became clear, then, that a book written especially for educators to introduce to them the new learning and telecommunications technologies and their potential applications is needed. On presenting the idea of the book to some of my colleagues with whom I visited during my sabbatical leave, they were eager to participate.

To Fairfield University, I owe a great deal for the time I was given. To my colleagues who contributed to this book, I am grateful for their cooperation.

In developing the chapter on the learning environment, I was influenced by the writing and personal communications I had with my friend and former advisor at Ohio State University, the late Dr. Edgar Dale.

I would like also to acknowledge Southern New England Telecommunications, Inc. for allowing me to use the material on one of the most innovative telecommunications projects, SNET Links to Learning, set with cooperation with Connecticut State Department of Education to promote quality education statewide.

Also, I would like to acknowledge BRS Information Technologies, Compuserve Information Service, Dialog Information Services, Inc., Dow Jones News/Retrieval Service, Mead Data Central, Newsnet, and Vu/Text Information Services, Inc. for responding to my request to furnish basic information on their services to the reader of this book.

Furthermore, I would like to acknowledge members of the staff of Fairfield University Media Center, Barbara Coe for proofreading some sections of the manuscript, Gail Dickinson for keying the Information

Utilities Appendix, Karen Connolly and Michael Micinilio for preparing the illustrations.

Finally, to my family who had to put up with long hours of work, and for their continuous encouragement, I am grateful.

I. M. Hefzallah

INTRODUCTION

Interactive learning using computers, video, and the new telecommunications technologies of the information age has been the focus of numerous conferences during the past decade. Most of the conferences have successfully demonstrated innovative and cost-effective use of those technologies in business and in training environments.

On the education front, instructional technologists are often fascinated with the advancement in communication and computer technologies to the extent that many times they forget the focus of education: the student. On the other hand, educators and educational administrators on college and public school levels are overwhelmed with the cost needed to reap the benefits of the new technology. At the same time, they recognize the need to ensure educational excellence and equity for all students.

The prime objectives of this book are:

a. to indicate that interactivity in learning is not a new concept. It has been in practice since man thought about the best ways of communicating facts, ideas, and beliefs to the younger generation;

b. to underline the need to establish interactive learning environments whether we are using traditional teaching methods or using new instructional technologies;

c. to underline the fact that the new technologies are nothing more than new tools which can help educators achieve learner's interactivity in the absence of face-to-face communication between the student and the teacher, either due to distance or to the student's being engaged in self-teaching situations;

d. to indicate viable uses of the new technologies in helping schools and universities achieve their missions. Some of those applications include the use of telecommunications to alleviate educational inequalities, and the use of interactive data bases to expand students' learning resources; and

e. to present a sample of current practice of interactive learning technology in schools and in colleges.

The book contains three sections. Section I addresses the ultimate goal of education as that of cultivating the educated person for an effective life in our information age. To achieve this prime goal, the establishment of rich, flexible, and interactive learning environments is a must. In such environments the learner should have direct access to models of excellence. The presence of excellent teachers and community resource people is a necessary condition for the achievement of excellence in education. Very often that presence can only be achieved through mediated interaction.

Section II presents applications of mediated interaction in education. It covers the use of computers in education; the use of interactive television and interactive video in education; the applications of satellite communications in learning; and the use of interactive data bases in education.

Section III addresses the role of the school library media center in the information age, and focuses on conditions needed for the effective utilization of the new learning and telecommunications technology in education.

CONTENTS

SECTION II: APPLICATIONS OF MEDIATED INTERACTION IN EDUCATION

SECTION II—PART I: COMPUTERS IN INTERACTIVE LEARNING

THE NEW LEARNING AND
TELECOMMUNICATIONS TECHNOLOGIES
Their Potential Applications In Education

SECTION I
EDUCATION IN THE INFORMATION AGE

INTRODUCTION

The ultimate goal of education is to cultivate the whole educated person for an effective living. Chapter One, The Educated Person, examines the concept of the educated person and the environment within which the individual is and will be living at the turn of the century. Identifying the characteristics of that environment helps indicate the qualities an educated person should possess for effective living in that environment.

Chapter Two, The Learning Environment, focuses on the characteristics of the learning environment conducive to the cultivation of the educated person. The learning environment should be rich in resources and flexible. It should ensure interaction between the learner and the teacher, and the learner and the learning materials and programs.

In an effective learning environment, students should have access to models of excellence. The presence of excellent teachers and community resource people is a necessary condition for the achievement of excellence in education. Very often that presence can only be achieved through mediated interaction. Chapter Three, Mediated Interaction, addresses the reasons for mediated interaction, and its various types.

Chapter One

THE EDUCATED PERSON

Ibrahim M. Hefzallah

DEFINITION

In a 1982 report by the National Science Foundation, it was stated that:

> Across the United States, there is escalating awareness that our educational systems are facing inordinate difficulties in trying to meet the needs of the nation in our changing and increasingly technological society. We appear to be raising a generation of Americans, many of whom lack the understanding and the skills necessary to participate fully in the technological world in which they live and work. Improved preparation of all citizens in the fields of mathematics, science, and technology is essential to the development and maintenance of our nation's economic strength, military security, commitment to the democratic ideal of an informed and participating citizenry, and leadership in mathematics, science, and technology. (1)

According to Pat Ordovensky from Gannet News Service,

> The nation's business leaders ... are horrified to find the schools are teaching skills for a society that is becoming obsolete. The problem, well-documented by social researchers and even educators themselves, is that the new skills needed for the high-technology, information-based society of the '80s aren't being taught because the teachers are not qualified and the schools' facilities are inadequate. (2)

In the above references, the emphasis was on education in general, and science, mathematics education in particular. In a more recent study (1987), Hirsch addressed the concept of cultural literacy and what every American needs to know. He noted that:

> To be culturally literate is to possess the basic information needed to thrive in the modern world. The breadth of that information is great, extending over the major domains of human activity from sports to science. It is by no means confined to "culture" narrowly understood as an acquaintance with the arts. Nor is it confined to one social class. (3)

In discussing the present level of Americans' cultural literacy, he pointed out:

> What seemed an acceptable level in the 1950s is no longer acceptable in the late 1980s, when only highly literate societies can prosper economically. Much of Japan's industrial efficiency has been credited to its almost universally high level of literacy. But in the United States, only two-thirds of our citizens are literate, and even among those the average level is too low and should be raised. The remaining third of our citizens need to be brought as close to true literacy as possible. Ultimately our goal should be to attain universal literacy at a high level, to achieve not only greater economic prosperity but also greater social justice and more effective democracy. (3, pp. 1–2)

An educated person should not be judged educated simply because of the amount of information grasped, or skills mastered, or for demonstrating an appreciation of the arts. As important as the above criteria are, there is more to the educated person.

An educated person has developed a free mind willing to listen and investigate new possibilities. A mind that rejoices in discovering new facts and learning new things. A mind that is never afraid of change, but willing to examine change carefully and objectively. A mind that has learned to learn. A mind that recognizes learning as a lifelong process, and sees formal education as a foundation upon which further self-education should occur.

An educated person has also articulated his values, paramount to which is deep concern for freedom and justice for all, and love of mankind.

An educated person has compassion toward other people. He respects all individuals and finds delight in communicating with fellow men. He takes the time to express his joy for their joy, and his concern for their problems.

An educated person considers himself a member of his community, and the community as a member of the national community, and the national community as a member of the world community.

An educated person has learned that a sound mind is in a sound body, and a sound body is an active body.

If we believe that one of the main goals of education is to cultivate the whole educated person for an effective, productive, free, just, healthy, and happy life, it becomes imperative to examine the environment within which the individual is and will be living. While predictions may be fallible, certain characteristics of the present time, and of the world as it gets closer to the beginning of the 21st century, can be outlined without risk of error. Identifying these characteristics will help explain in more detail the above listed qualities of the educated person.

BASIS CHARACTERISTICS OF THE MODERN AGE

Accelerated Rate of Scientific Developments and Education for Change

At present, scientific research extends to all fields of human knowledge and activities. It advances at an accelerated rate due to improvements in research tools, and methods of storing, sorting, analyzing, and sharing information. For instance, the computer has become an indispensable tool of research in all fields of knowledge. Computers facilitate conducting research, analyzing data, and storing and retrieving information with tremendous savings of time. Consequently, more information can be gathered and developed much faster than before.

Sharing of information is greatly facilitated by advances in telecommunication and information processing and dissemination technologies. For instance, satellite, terrestrial, and telephone communications have diminished the distance between researchers. Instant interaction and sharing of information is not limited to face-to-face communication. Mediated conferences employing both the audio and visual elements surmount the geographical separation between researchers and provide channels of communication for sharing information.

Sharing information facilitates further developments. Scientific, economic, psychological, and educational theories are constantly introduced and tested. New learning disciplines and new careers are emerging. A few years back the life cycle of an individual was equivalent to preparation for and assuming a career. Today retraining and retooling are musts in the working lifetime of an individual, as Winston Hindle explained, "We can almost guarantee that a person we hire today will not be performing the same job in five years, or even two years in many cases. The problem is that the working lifetime of our employees is not very much greater than the development and support lifetimes of our products." (4) He further pointed out that, "Right now a typical employee in industry or in business can look forward to a career that consists of cycles with alternating periods of training and productive contributions." (4. p. 10)

Change is synonymous with life. When change is accelerated, our survival will depend on education which will prepare the individuals to deal with change. According to Carl Rogers:

> We are, in my view, faced with an entirely new situation in education where the goal of education, if we are to survive, is the *facilitation of change and learning*. The only man who is educated is the man who has learned how to learn; the man who has learned to adapt and change; the man who realized that no knowledge is secure, that only the process of *seeking* knowledge gives a basis for security. Changingness, a reliance on *process* rather than upon static knowledge, is the only thing that makes any sense as a goal for education in the modern world. (5)

An educated man for the 21st century should develop his ability to recognize change and to examine it. Not every change is desirable. Objective analysis of a change in terms of its total effect on human lives, human interaction, justice, freedom, and the fulfillment of a happy and content life for all can result in either fostering, diverting, or opposing that change.

An educated person also should be able to confront the unexpected and deal with it in an objective and scientific way. Years back no one thought of AIDS. Now it is a threatening disease. The present reaction of different people to the AIDS problem is a sample of how people can react to the unexpected. A reaction to the problem is not needed. However, an action to cure the AIDS victims, to immunize the public, and to eliminate the potential cause for the disease is needed. An educated person should be able to avoid emotional overreaction to a problem. Instead, he should question and investigate ways to solve the problem, and control its effects.

Serious World Problems

Today the world faces serious problems. The threat of nuclear war, environmental pollution, deterioration of values, inflation, world hunger, and military confrontation among nations of the Third World are some of the problems that need immediate attention of the world community. An educated person should be able to address these problems and exert the necessary efforts toward their alleviation. It is beyond the scope of this publication to address all of these problems as they relate to the cultivation of the educated person. For the sake of giving an example, one problem only, world hunger, will be briefly addressed in the following.

As a result of scientific developments and the discovery of antibiotics and immunization, infant mortality has decreased, and the average life span of the individual has increased. There is an alarming increase in world population, especially in Third World nations, where they need the most help in cultivating enough food and finding enough jobs to match the accelerated increase in their population.

While the above is a serious problem for developing nations, it is the responsibility of developed nations to help alleviate the problem. We are all living on one planet as the family of man. Interests of nations overlap as the human race strives for world peace. Peace cannot be built while members of poor nations are hungry for the basic foods needed to survive. Three avenues can be followed by developed nations to help solve that problem. First, help developing nations to establish a national policy to preserve and increase their national resources. Second, set an example of how they can respect national resources, and not destroy them. Third, provide food for areas suffering from a shortage.

To be able to do this, education aiming at graduating the educated person should plan to develop the young generation's:

(a) understanding of the world's hunger problem and sensitivity toward helping the unfortunate populations;

(b) concept of "a neighbor" to include all human beings on earth and not just our fellow citizens;

(c) respect for natural resources and a strong stand against any measure that might cause pollution of the environment and destruction of river and marine life; and

(d) commitment to leave the world in better shape than when they came in for future generations to enjoy. This entails developing their understanding of how natural resources can be used without harming their inherent ability to renew themselves.

Technology and the Changing Family Life Style

"Football widow" is a colloquial phrase denoting a married woman whose husband is absorbed in watching long hours of telecast football games. "Computer widow" is a relatively new phrase denoting a wife whose husband becomes a computer addict, spending a great deal of time in learning about the computer and using it for serious tasks, or for just games. Both phrases simply point to a very important fact. When technology gets into the home, especially at an early stage of that technology, family lives are affected.

As time passes by and the product proves to be apparently useful, people develop a strong, close relationship with the product. For instance, people have developed very strong ties with TV. A TV set is usually placed where it can be easily seen and comfortably watched, occupying a prominent place in living rooms, family rooms, playrooms, bedrooms, and even in the kitchen. It has become the new fireplace around which the family gathers. Watching television has become a ritual, during which certain conduct is expected of individuals viewing a program with a group of people. In some instances people watching a program together have to be quiet in order to follow the program. Comments about the program, if any, might be shared after its conclusion.

The above are just examples of how the presence of a technology product can affect family life and family dynamics. Furthermore, when a product such as television is used, its social, psychological, educational, and informational effects on the user alter his views of life, and accordingly affect family dynamics.

The expected and the unexpected changes in society and in the world as a whole will definitely have an effect on family life. For example, in some families where both spouses are working to maintain a desirable standard of living, young children might be spending less time with their parents than their parents spent as children.

It is imperative to the preparation of young people for a happy, productive life to teach them about families. When the Media Center of Fairfield University committed to the production of a six-part series on families, it was a great experience to me as the producer of the shows to look closely at a single-parent family, families with handicapped children and handicapped teenagers, a family with a mentally retarded child, a family with a learning-disabled child, and a family with a gifted child. The love and the concern that each member of those families demonstrated for each other under difficult circumstances were heartwarming. Being a family man myself, I have learned from a closer look at those families tremendous lessons. There is a need to teach young people about family life, especially when the image that television shows project for families is distorted most of the time. An educated person has developed an understanding of family dynamics, care, love, and respect for each member, and appreciation and respect for other families.

Increased Automation

Automation and Education for Leisure Time

An American home has on the average 36 motors in operation. In the kitchen alone, furnished with a can opener, an electric clock, a dishwasher, a range hood, a self-defrosting refrigerator, a garbage disposal and an oven, you can count at least eight motors. While some of the above listed appliances are not in every kitchen, it is expected that 21st century homes will be much more automated than our present homes. Automation of home chores will be only one aspect of future automated human activities. Automated offices are common now, and more routine office work will soon be automated.

Automation will help the future generation to do more in less time. The time saved from doing often mundane chores can be used for the betterment of the lives of individuals as well as the community in general. An educated person is constantly learning how to use his time wisely. There is a need to start this process as early as possible in the life of the individual. Teaching young people the effective use of leisure time will focus on the following important areas:

a. effective and productive use of leisure time;
b. physical fitness;
c. maintaining social relationships; and
d. active participation in local, national, and international communities.

Understanding the Limitation of Automation

Automation could help make life much easier. It could eliminate the mundane efforts one might spend in performing one function or another. It could speed up communication between people, and it could shorten the physical distance between people. It could increase the speed by which a service is offered, and it could increase the efficiency with which this service is offered. However, automation has its limitations, and sometimes its drawbacks.

Computers are as good as the program that runs them. Certainly the advances in computer technology are going to improve the efficiency and the ease of using computers, but they are still machines. They can break down and cause problems. Cars have made it easy to travel. At the same time they are a major cause of air pollution.

The young generation has to understand the advantages that machinery and automation can offer. At the same time, they must understand and appreciate their limitations and danger. Such dual understanding can put a lid on the shortcomings of machinery and help eliminate hazards associated with their use.

When people drive recklessly, they are putting more trust than they should in the car and in themselves. Reckless driving is an indication of a poor understanding of what the car and the driver can do under certain circumstances. Extending that capability beyond reality is stupid and accident-provoking.

In a Third World country I was visiting, an elevator accident claimed many lives. The cause was overcrowding the elevator beyond the posted load. Some passengers thought that somehow the machine could handle the overload. In another instance, a luxury ferry boat capsized because of overloading. Machines have limitations and can cause problems even when used according to the manufacturers' suggestions. The same can be said about drugs, vitamins, and dietary pills in which unwarranted use can be harmful.

Scientific and technological products can always be improved. Even after testing a product or a procedure, unexpected, undesirable, and sometimes fatal outcomes may occur. Man does not have to abandon technological development because of mishaps. Instead, the constant evaluation of a product or a procedure should be practiced with an eye to what might go wrong. Although the responsibility lies heavily with the producers and the manufacturers, the public has to avoid blind trust in a product or a procedure. Like anything in life, the critical mind of the user is a prerequisite for the advantageous use of automation and technological products.

Automation and New Careers

As a result of automation and scientific development on all fronts of human knowledge and activities, some existing careers will diminish and new ones which no one ever thought of will be introduced. The new generation has to be flexible to adopt new careers. They should be able to study emerging needs and explore new possibilities.

A free and a sound choice of career is a by-product of self-awareness, the attendant condition for a productive and satisfying life. In this sense, education addressing careers should be designed to develop a clear perspective of the student's self.

Self-awareness is a dynamic lifetime goal. As a person develops values, interests, aptitudes, and abilities, he is actually changing and developing his self-awareness. In structuring education to foster and develop self-awareness, the following five objectives were recognized by Maloney and Hefzallah as relevant:

Recognition and Articulation of Individual Differences and Similarities in Terms of Aptitudes, Values, Interests, and Abilities. This recognition includes respect for one's own individuality and accords respect to others' individuality. Achieving this objective would help develop understanding of the need for unity and diversity in a dynamic technological society.

Recognition of Changes in Self and Society. The development of new technology continuously accelerates the rate of change in all aspects of our national life. New occupations develop and create changes in the economy. Personal changes, likewise, are taking place. Therefore, there are changes within and outside of the individual. There are also three basic modes of dealing with these changes. First, the individual may seek change within himself and society. Second, he may accept change and be moved by it without active participation. Third, the individual could be passive toward change and may attempt to freeze the status quo and remain static. To exemplify these three modes, there are those who swim, and those who float, and those who stay at the beach watching swimmers and floaters without participating in the exercise.

Decision-Making Based on Critical Thinking. For too many years, educators have been advocating decision-making ability as an important objective of general education, yet the achievement of this objective is usually left to incidental development. If education is to foster self-awareness, decision-making ability based upon analytical thinking should be stressed. Continued self-awareness necessitates decisions about the self, the environment, and the interrelation between the two. Through preparation in decision-making, students are educated to identify alternatives and to make free choices based upon comprehensive, analytical, and evaluative thinking.

Thrust for Continued Learning. Self-awareness is a dynamic and continuous process that necessitates continued learning. To develop the ability for self-renewal entails the development of motivation and skills for continued learning. It is important that the individual keep pace with new technology, processes, and developments within his own area of expertise to ensure the upgrading of his competence. In addition, the individual as a responsible citizen must understand the dynamics of continued personal growth, learning, and development, which facilitate additional in-depth relationships with others and provide more self-insight and understanding.

Use of Leisure Time. More leisure time will be available in the future to working individuals. Since there is a correlation between self-awareness and purposeful use of leisure time, students today should be prepared for the constructive and purposeful use of leisure time through participation in varied activities. (6)

In summary, an educated person develops and maintains a clear perspective of self and his role for a productive and satisfying life. The emphasis in education for the 21st century, therefore, should shift from job training to developing self-awareness for all students.

The Need for a Common Shared Information

To foster communication in a society, there is a need for shared information between the citizens. Advanced technology will have a constant need for highly specialized people. If each will devote his time to a narrow field of study, communication in the society will suffer. Hirsch talks of the need of achieving a high universal literacy as the key to all other fundamental improvements in American education. In his words: "The complex undertakings of modern life depend on the cooperation of many people with different specialties in different places. Where communications fail, so do the undertakings. . . . The function of national literacy is to foster effective nationwide communications." (3, p. 2)

Hirsch believes that the amount of shared knowledge that is taken for granted in communication with fellow citizens has been declining, and that more and more young people lack the information we assumed they know. (3, p. 5) He explained:

> They (young people) know a great deal. Like every other human group they share a tremendous amount of knowledge among themselves, much of it learned in school. The trouble is that, from the standpoint of their literacy and their ability to communicate with others in our culture, what they know is ephemeral and narrowly confined to their own generation. Many young people strikingly lack the information

that writers of American books and newspapers have traditionally taken for granted among their readers from all generations. (3, p. 7)

Hirsch's claim is well-demonstrated by various studies. For instance, in a study about teenagers' heroes reported by the *World Almanac* which was based on a survey of about 4,000 teenagers in 145 cities, Michael Jackson was the No. 1 hero of high school students. Eddie Murphy ranked second, followed by President Reagan. Actors Kevin Bacon and Clint Eastwood were the fourth and fifth, followed by basketball star, Julius Erving, film stars Tom Cruise and Mr. T., rock artist Eddie Van Halen, and Katharine Hepburn. Of the ten heroes, only two, President Reagan and Julius Erving, were not in show business. (7)

Recent polls show that Americans are not well-informed. Based on some of those studies, Donna Woolfolk Cross reported that:

> Over half the population doesn't know who their senators or congressmen are and almost as many don't even know how many senators there are from their own state. Half of all seventeen-year-olds think that the President can appoint members of Congress. One survey revealed that almost 70% of the people surveyed could not identify the three branches of government, nor the Bill of Rights, and could not say what important event happened in America in 1776. (8, p. 58)

In addition, knowledge of international affairs is very limited, superficial, and incoherent.

In the well-known study, *A Nation at Risk*, it was reported that:

1. Some 23 million American adults are functionally illiterate by the simplest tests of everyday reading, writing, and comprehension.
2. About 13 percent of all 17-year-olds in the United States can be considered functionally illiterate. Functional illiteracy among minority youth may run as high as 40 percent. (9, p. 8)

The need to remedy the situation is urgent. If the problem is not addressed now, technological advances could complicate the problem in two ways.

First, increased educational inequality among the American population will be forged. Schools that can offer better teachers, advanced facilities, and administrators with vision will continue to graduate students at higher educational and cultural levels than less advantaged schools.

Second, people might tend to be narrowly trained, and lack a broad vision of life. Addressing the problem of narrow vocational training Hirsch stated:

> ... a directly practical drawback of such narrow training is that it does not prepare anyone for technological change. Narrow vocational training in one state of technology will not enable a person to read a manual that explains new developments in the same technology. In modern life we need general knowledge that enables us to deal with new ideas, events, and challenges. In today's world, general cultural literacy is more useful than what Professor Patterson terms 'literacy to a specific task,' because general literate information is the basis for many changing tasks. (3, p. 11)

Advanced technology will dictate the need for highly specialized personnel. It will also dictate the need for people from different disciplines to work cooperatively in research, and in the application of the products of technology in the daily lives of the citizens. Crossing disciplines requires the broad understanding of different disciplines and at the same time an ability of the researchers to work cooperatively with researchers from other disciplines.

To graduate students who can efficiently work in a cooperative environment should not be left to chance. Schools have to plan educational environments in which students work for the same cause, each attacking a problem or an issue from his field of interest and expertise.

The New Literacies

A few decades ago an illiterate person was one who could not read nor write, and was incapable of handling basic arithmetic operations. Literacy programs around the world aimed, then, at training the uneducated masses in basic reading, writing, and arithmetic skills. As the pace of modern life became faster, and life itself became more complex, the need to expand the concept of basic literacy to include cultural topics was recognized. Literacy programs experimented with offering cultural topics in an attempt to increase the illiterates' social awareness. The emphasis shifted from narrow literacy skills to cultural literacy.

What constitutes cultural literacy changes from one nation to another, and from one era to another. The new media/telecommunication/computer technology has introduced to us what might be defined as the new literacies. To be an educated person in this modern communication technology age, one has to possess basic information about these technologies. Most important, one has to have an open mind regarding the potential applications of these technologies, and to acquire basic skills which empower the person to use these technologies to enrich one's information. As the Libraries and the Learning Society report put it: "By knowing how to find, analyze, and use information today, they (children) certify their readiness to become reasoning, thoughtful adults tomorrow as citizens of the Information Age." (10, p. 10) The following is a brief discussion of the new literacies of the modern age.

Visual Literacy

Visual literacy is the ability to understand and use visuals in expressing oneself, and in understanding visual messages composed by others. In other words, visual literacy includes two basic competencies: competency in critical analysis of visuals perceived, and competency in communicating through the visual medium.

Critical Analysis of Visuals. Pictures play a very significant role in today's communications. Magazines, newspapers, books, posters, bulletin boards, flyers, mail advertising, television, and motion pictures use pictures to inform, to entertain, and to persuade. An educated person is capable of reading between the lines, and of analyzing the written and the spoken word. He should be also capable of interpreting the picture to reveal its intended message whether it is explicit or implied.

Even when the image looks like a real event being captured, a critical viewer understands that there is a marked difference between reality seen and reality photographed. It is that marked difference that makes photography, still or motion, and television an art. Guided by the purpose of the shot, the camera assumes the task of composing the image to magnify or reduce certain aspects of what is seen in reality. A photograph is by no means a complete and whole reflection of reality.

In motion pictures and television, the show is a continuous flow of visual images supported by sound. An action in a television program or a motion picture is conceived as a series of shots taken from different points of view. Each point conveys its own separate "picture statement." Each statement is structured to move the story of the program. Andreas Feininger explained what he meant by "picture statement." He said: "In comparison to the eye, the lens sees too much—rather than trying to say everything in one picture, subdivide complex subjects and set-ups and show them in the form of a short series in which each picture clearly illustrates only a single point." (11, p. 20)

Therefore, images, even when they look like what they represent, are interpretations of the image-maker of what he sees and wants to communicate to the viewer. Many times we are confronted with images which through the power of symbolism imply meanings, feelings, and a style of life of the characters shown in the picture. As an example, one of my early encounters with implied images in outdoor advertising was a poster advertising a menthol cigarette. As I was getting off the highway, the poster caught my attention. I felt that there was something strange about that ad. I had to go back to have a second look. The strange thing was that the poster did not have a picture of the package of cigarettes, nor were the characters smoking. It seemed that the advertiser was trying to say something through the power of suggestion. A simple analysis of the poster revealed that message. The poster depicted a healthy man and a woman in bathing suits splashing out of the water. From the big smile they had, they seemed that they were having a lot of fun. The dominant color of the poster was a cool green color. The name brand of cigarettes was printed in large enough letters to be read from a distance. The advertiser used the symbols for health, youth, beauty, happiness, fun, and coolness to make a visual statement: "Smoking brand X is healthy, clean, and fun."

Television, which is primarily a visual medium, often uses images to imply claims and statements without explicitly stating them. Studies by media scholars indicated the need to educate viewers to become critical consumers of mass media. (12) Comparing people who know how to observe with others, Arnheim, a scholar in the field of visual communication wrote:

> ... people who know how to observe and to draw conclusions from what they see will profit greatly. Others will be taken in by the picture on the screen and confused by the variety of visible things. After a while, they may even cease to feel confused: proud of their right to see everything and weaned from the desire to understand and to digest, they may feel great satisfaction. (13)

An educated person has to be able to accept or disapprove, according to his will and reasoning, a message presented through the power of visual presentations or implications. Goldman and Burnett in NEED JOHNNY READ? urged teachers to make room in the conventional established humanities curriculum for study of the visual language because:

...*without* such training, young people will get less and less from school, eventually becoming ciphers as citizens; brainwashed, manipulated, and motivated by the mindless spellbinders of films and television; whereas *with* such training, students will get more out of their normal, in-school educational experience rather than be passive passengers on a conveyor belt. (14)

Using Visuals in Communication. In today's culture, both the printed and spoken words are often integrated with visuals to maximize the impact of the message being transmitted. On almost all levels of communication the image, whether it is a graph, a photograph, or a moving image is used extensively in published work or presentations in both the classroom and the board room. An educated person should know how and when to use the visual element to enhance his message. This does not mean that each person will learn photography, video production, or graph making. If any of these skills can be developed, it is all for the good. The important thing is that the educated person should be able to identify the elements of communication that can best be communicated visually, and to request technical and professional personnel to produce the most efficient image which will help communicate.

Media Literacy

Media surrounds us all the time. Media helps shape our thinking, our attitudes, and the type of information we possess. It is a force that affects almost every phase of our lives. We are instructed, informed, entertained, and persuaded by media. It is unfortunate that many who are affected by media do not know this. For instance, many people think that they are not affected by television commercials, and that they really make up their own minds. In their view, advertising in television is irrelevant, stupid, foolish, and ineffectual. These are the people who are sold the most. They are the largest consumers without knowing why. As Wilson Bryan Key said: "... like it or not, each one of us is continuously and strongly affected by advertising." (15) It is incredible that assertions of not being influenced by a commercial is exactly what advertising intends to happen; as Key put it, "... a very necessary illusion media must perpetuate in order to succeed in making up their minds for them." (15, p. 79) He also said, "... they (audience) react to television commercials with a feeling of superiority that permits them to believe they are in control ... People are prone to trust anything over which they believe they have control." (15, p. 158)

Studies on the effects of mass media on individuals and the society as a whole are extensive. An educated person has to:

1. understand the role of media in modern society, its social, political, psychological, economical, educational effects on both the individual, the society and the world as a whole;

2. understand the advantages and limitations of different types of media, especially those that are dictated by the business aspect of media production and distribution;

3. understand the techniques of persuasion practiced by different types of media; and

4. become an activist and interact with civic and scholarly organizations which monitor the media.

In short, an educated person is a critical consumer of media.

Computer Literacy

There are two levels of this type of literacy: users' level, and programmers' level. An educated person has to develop the user's level. This entails developing a basic understanding of what can be done with computer technology in one's field, a favorable attitude toward using what is available, and basic skills in the use of computer software.

There are certain skills that many will agree are essential for computer literacy on the user's level. Heading the list are familiarity and working knowledge of word processing, use of simple spreadsheets, and graph software. Basic skills in those areas can help the user develop written documents including visual diagrams and charts.

Information Processing and Retrieval Literacy

The amount of information humankind is generating is growing almost exponentially. New information is generated every day in almost every field of knowledge. The cliche "knowledge explosion" is now becoming meaningless. We have been living in an information age.

Generation of information has a chain effect. The more the information is generated, the more new information is added to the wealth of human information, and it goes on and on. Coupled with the generation of information in almost every field of discipline are more effective methods of storing, sorting, and retrieving information. All of these phases of managing information are carried out at a very high speed as compared with that of previous years. Cross-referencing can be accomplished more efficiently and more accurately. For instance, a student using an electronic encyclopedia on a CD–ROM, such as GROLIER ELECTRONIC ENCYCLOPEDIA, can retrieve text information of items of study. Meanings of key words and related items can also be retrieved quickly. Browsing through the items he is studying can be done efficiently and with speed.

In addition to the efficiency of retrieving information from electronic publications, the expense of setting up a reference station such as a CD–ROM is reasonable. Teaching students how to use CD–ROM technology is not difficult, nor time-consuming.

In addition to the emerging digital optical disc storage technologies such as the CD–ROM, a simple personal computer and a telephone are all that one needs to access a vast number of information banks. In writing about "The Universe at Your Fingertips," Alfred Glossbrenner wrote in *The Complete Handbook of Personal Communication,*

> It is an *electronic* universe in which messages and information streak across the continent or around the world at the speed of light. A place where you can find a fact or find a job, play a game, publish a poem, meet a friend, consult an encyclopedia, or do hundreds of other things without ever leaving your office or home. It is a realm of a myriad of possibilities destined to forever change the way each of us lives, works, and plays. But most important of all, it exists *today* and is open to anyone with a personal computer. Indeed, accessing the electronic universe may well be the reason for buying such a machine in the first place. (16)

An educated person should be able to access the vast information in both print and electronic formats. In many instances, up-to-date information is available through electronic means much more readily than through the traditional printed word.

The educated person should also be capable of locating the specific information he is seeking. He should be able to evaluate the pertinency of the information gathered and weigh it against other sources. To be able to do that, the educated person should be capable of formulating questions to which he tries to find the answers. To put it in a few words, the educated person should possess the qualities and skills of an original investigator and researcher. Included in those qualities are a professional research attitude, ability to formulate questions, knowledge of data bases and sources of information which might provide the answers to the questions. However, heading those qualities is the professional attitude which dictates the need to find all the information pertinent to the problem under study, especially if that information promises to be in contradiction to previous knowledge.

CONCLUSION

One of the most disturbing observations of a visitor to a high school parking lot after the last day of examinations is the litter, mainly composed from books and note books. This phenomenon is an indication that for some students facts and knowledge recorded in books are burdens that one has to get rid of as soon as the school requirement is met by taking the final examination.

If we think that the educated person is the one who has developed the desire and the skill needed to learn more, then a school environment leading students to discard their books and notebooks is not the educational environment which will help develop the educated person. Explaining the function of the university, Alfred North Whitehead wrote,

> The justification for a university is that it preserves the connection between knowledge and the zest of life, by uniting the young and the old in the imaginative consideration of learning. The university imparts information, but it imparts it imaginatively. At least, this is the function which it should perform for society . . . this atmosphere of excitement, arising from imaginative consideration, transforms knowledge. A fact is no longer a bare fact: it is invested with all its possibilities. It is no longer a burden on the memory: it is energizing as the poet of our dreams, and as the architect of our purposes. (17)

There is a need to design, on all levels of education, exciting learning environments conducive to the cultivation of the educated person.

REFERENCES

1. National Science Board, National Science Foundation. TODAY'S PROBLEMS TOMORROW'S CRISES, A Report of the National Science Board Commission on Precollege Education in Mathematics, Science and Technology, Washington, D.C., 1982, p. 1.

2. Ordovensky, Pat. "Educators Fall Down on Jobs, Schools Failing To Teach Skills Needed in Today's High Technology Society," in James W. Brown (Ed.), EDUCATIONAL MEDIA YEARBOOK, 1983, Littleton, Colorado: Libraries Unlimited, Inc., 1983 p. 126.

3. Hirsch, Jr., E.D. CULTURAL LITERACY, WHAT EVERY AMERICAN NEEDS TO KNOW, Boston: Houghton Mifflin Company, 1987, p. xiii.

4. Hindle, Jr. Winston R. "Educational Technology, Industrial Training, and Lifelong Learning," in USING TECHNOLOGY FOR EDUCATION AND TRAINING, Silverspring, Maryland: Information Dynamics, 1983 pp. 9–10.

5. Rogers, Carl R. FREEDOM TO LEARN, Columbus, Ohio: Charles E. Merrill, 1969, p. 104.

6. Maloney, W. Paul and Ibrahim M. Hefzallah, "Career Education: The Student in Focus," *NASSP Bulletin,* September, 1974, pp. 93–96.

7. *PARADE,* May 5, 1985, p. 21.

8. Cross, Donna Woolfolk. MEDIASPEAK; HOW TELEVISION MAKES UP YOUR MIND, New Jersey: A Mentor Book, New American Library, 1984, p. 58.

9. The National Commission on Excellence in Education. A NATION AT RISK, Washington, D.C.: United States Department of Education, April, 1983, p. 8.

10. Libraries and the Learning Society. ALLIANCE FOR EXCELLENCE, LIBRARIANS RESPOND TO A NATION AT RISK, Washington, D.C.: United States Department of Education, July, 1984, p. 10.

11. Feininger, Andreas. THE CREATIVE PHOTOGRAPHER, New York: Prentice-Hall, 1955, p. 20.

12. Hefzallah, Ibrahim M. CRITICAL VIEWING OF TELEVISION – A BOOK for PARENTS and TEACHERS, Lanham, Maryland: University Press of America, 1987.

13. Arnheim, Rudolph. "A Forecast of Television," FILM AS ART, Los Angeles, California: University of California Press, 1947, p. 196.

14. Goldman, Frederick & Linda Burnett. NEED JOHNNY READ?, N.Y.: Pflaum, 1971, p. xvii.

15. Key, Wilson Bryan. SUBLIMINAL SEDUCTION, N.J.: A Signet Book, New American Library, 1975. p 80.

16. Glossbrenner, Alfred. THE COMPLETE HANDBOOK OF PERSONAL COMPUTER COMMUNICATIONS, N.Y.: St. Martin's Press, 1983 p. xiii.

17. Whitehead, Alfred North. AIMS OF EDUCATION, New York: A Mentor Book, 6th printing, 1955, p. 97.

Chapter Two

THE LEARNING ENVIRONMENT

IBRAHIM M. HEFZALLAH

SIGNIFICANCE OF THE LEARNING ENVIRONMENT

In one of the inspiring articles of Edgar Dale, "Access To Excellence," he underlined the significance of the learning environment in achieving objectives of education. He wrote:

> To learn to think we must be in the presence of thinking people—parents, teachers, principals, fellow students. To learn to love literature we must have easy and continued access to persons who are excited about literature. To become responsible citizens or parents or students we must see responsibility abundantly exemplified all around us. (1)

According to John Dewey we never educate directly, but indirectly by means of the environment. In his classic work, *Democracy and Education*, he wrote:

> ... the only way in which adults consciously control the kind of education which the immature get is by controlling the environment in which they act, and hence think and feel. We never educate directly, but indirectly by means of the environment. Whether we permit chance environments to do the work, or whether we design environments for the purpose makes a great difference. Any environment is a chance environment so far as its educative influence is concerned unless it has been deliberately regulated with reference to its educative effect ... But schools remain, of course, the typical instance of environments framed with express reference to influencing the mental and moral dispositions of their members. (2)

Addressing the importance of the environment in reforming man, Buckminster Fuller wrote, "I have learned to undertake reform of the environment and not to try to reform man." (3) He explained, "It is possible to design environments within which the child will be neither frustrated nor hurt, yet free to develop spontaneously and fully without

24

trespassing on others.... *If we design the environment properly,* it will permit child and man to develop safely and behave logically." (3, p. 70)

A learning environment has to be designed and programmed to achieve the ultimate goal of education: the educated person. Prerequisite to that design are educators who possess the attitudes, and master the information and skills of an educated person which they would reflect in the design of the learning environment.

SCHOOL PERSONNEL AS EDUCATED PERSONS

Creativity

When children interact with creative thinking teachers, they have a good chance of developing their own creativity. A creative teacher respects every student, his needs, aspirations, talents, style of thinking, and method of communicating oneself. He does not disregard an idea on the grounds that it is strange and unconventional. Instead he encourages the research of new ideas, and provides the opportunities for vague ideas to develop. He attempts to structure a flexible learning environment which leads to students achievement of information, skills, and attitudes needed for effective living; and at the same time permits the individual growth of every student. To realize such a structure, he has to build a learning environment on a continuous interaction between the learner, the teacher, other creative human resources, and rich learning materials.

It should be noted that to be able to design and implement such an environment, teachers have to experience creative learning environments in their teacher preparation programs. On the school front, teachers need the support of creative school administrators, and the diversity of creative interactive teaching/learning materials.

Learning To Learn

The educated teacher sets "learning to learn" as an extremely important educational objective. He knows that for his students to live effectively in this and the coming age, they have to master the process of learning. Dale argued that the chief product of learning may well be the process of learning. He said:

In an unpredictable world, all of us must learn to learn and develop a taste for learning. Indeed, the chief product of learning may well be the process of learning. Every learner must develop the motivation to learn— the *want-to* —and he must couple this with the methods and the materials of learning—the *know-how* and the *know-why* ... He must, in short, consciously learn how to process information, ideas, and subject matter. (4)

Carl Rogers expressed the same idea by saying: " ... if we are to have citizens who can live constructively in this kaleidoscopically changing world, we can *only* have them if we are willing for them to become self-starting, self-initiating learners." (5) In his opinion, "The significant learnings are the more personal ones—independence; self-initiated and responsible learning; release of creativity; a tendency to become more of a person." (5, p. 120)

In discussing the principles of facilitating learning, he pointed out that, "The most socially useful learning in the modern world is the learning of the process of learning, a continuing openness to experience and incorporation into oneself of the process of change." (5, p. 163)

Emphasis on the process of learning does not and should not deemphasize the product of learning. The question is not process vs. product, as Dale put it:

> ....the issue is not process versus product, form versus content, or method versus subject matter. It is rather the kinds of processes used to produce certain products. ... Indeed product and process must not be separated, any more than we would separate form and content ... the purpose of the process is progressively to create a product ... The issue is not whether there are basic facts and ideas but how they should be learned. (4, pp. 81–82)

As one masters the process of learning, he experiences the enjoyment that comes from self-discovery, the Eureka experience, and from clear understanding of a subject matter. The enjoyment of learning propels the person to pursue further learning, and thus becomes a self-motivated learner. A teacher who enjoys learning can benefit his students in two ways. First, his enjoyment of learning becomes apparent to his students. Hence, he sets up a model for the pleasure that comes from learning. Second, he is more inclined to understand and practice his teaching role as a guide and a counselor for his students in their own learning.

Critical Mind

Faced with unpredictable and accelerated change in almost every phase of our lives, and faced with alternative points of view and a vast amount of information, developing the ability of citizens to think critically becomes a condition for survival. The more choices a person has, the more he is in need of a reliable system of thinking to make the right choice. Critical thinking is a reliable system. It is an objective process which considers all possible alternatives in a situation and the consequences of those alternatives. It withholds judgment until all the facts are gathered and analyzed. It does not only evaluate the facts, but also the goals of the investigation and the methods followed to achieve those goals.

Some aspects of critical thinking are taught in traditional classrooms (mostly in science, and mathematics classes). However, such an essential educational objective should not be considered only in a specific course of study with occasional mention in other areas. Critical thinking is an outcome of intense educational situations in which critical thinking becomes the standard procedure of interacting with the situations. Accordingly, especially designed environments where critical thinking becomes the mode of operation is the only guarantee to ensure the development of that skill, and most important to develop the ability of the students to transfer those skills to diversified human activities outside the classroom, and beyond the schooling years.

Prerequisite to the implementation of learning environments conducive to the development of students' critical thinking are critical thinking teachers and administrators, and a curriculum that aims at developing students' critical thinking.

Self-Evaluation

In practice, evaluation is primarily concerned with testing the ability of the students to recite facts and to perform basic communication functions. If our interest is cultivating the total educated person, the learning environment has to employ a comprehensive system of evaluation which can test the achievement of that goal in a nonthreatening fashion.

A comprehensive evaluation system is concerned with:

1. measuring factual learning;
2. measuring the ability of the student of learning-to-learn;

3. measuring the ability of the student to practice critical thinking not only in his field of study, but also in general life situations;
4. assessing whether students have developed their ability to deal with change and to foster desirable change;
5. development of the culturally literate person, who has mastered the needed information to live in modern society;
6. development of the ability of the students to use new communication and information technology, to locate and select the needed information;
7. assessing whether students have articulated their values, and the quality and the soundness of those values;
8. assessing whether students have developed a sense of community and caring for other members of their community and the world as a whole;
9. assessing the mental, emotional and physical status of the students, and of values and habits that might hinder their growth in any of those areas; and
10. assessing the ability of the students to evaluate themselves.

A comprehensive evaluation system should be an intricate component in the design of the learning environment. A significant component of that system is fostering students' self-evaluation. Usually, traditional evaluation systems embody a threat to the students. Student participation in self-evaluation can help eliminate that threat. Moreover, student self-evaluation has two more values. First, learning is facilitated, as Carl Rogers explained: "Learning is facilitated when the student participates responsibly in the learning process." (5, p. 162) Second, it helps develop student independence and creativity, as Carl Rogers put it: "Independence, creativity, and self-reliance are all facilitated when self-criticism and self-evaluation are basic and evaluation by others is of secondary importance." (5, p. 163)

Teachers and school administrators who have developed their ability for self-evaluation can become more functional in fostering the development of students self-evaluation.

Real People

One of the big mistakes that teachers and administrators make is putting on a mask behind which they hide their real personalities before facing their students. There is nothing more disturbing for students than to detect superficiality and fakeness in their teachers. Through my experience as a student for many years, I encountered teachers who wanted to give the impression that they were "with the times," others who wanted to look serious and unapproachable, and a few who were the same people whether in class or outside the class. In one of the assignments at Ohio State University, we were asked to reflect on our past experience and write a short account of whom we considered a good teacher, and whom we considered a bad teacher. Years later, I still recall that assignment. As I reflected on my past experience, I found out that the real teachers were the good teachers, and the fake teachers were the worst.

The educated person is a real person who knows his strength as well as his weakness. He understands too that no one is perfect. Based on that understanding, an educated person is not afraid to be really known. Realness of the teacher was cited by Rogers as a condition for facilitating learning. (5, pp. 106–09) There is no need for double standards, one for the classroom, and one for outside. If we are interested in helping young people to achieve self-actualization, it becomes imperative to have them experience a learning environment staffed with real people.

In selecting persons for the teaching profession, extra care has to be taken to select teachers who can set up models of educated persons, and exemplify emotional and mental stability.

Clear Understanding of the Teacher's Role

As an educated person, a teacher finds delight in teaching others. He approaches a teaching or an information situation not with a feeling of superiority but with a drive to share and to participate in the growth of others. He recognizes his main role in the teaching/learning environment as being a learning facilitator, a counselor, and a good communicator.

As a learning facilitator, the teacher assumes a host of responsibilities to provide a rich, exciting, and enjoyable learning environment. These responsibilities are best described in Carl Rogers's guidelines for the role of the teacher as a facilitator of learning. These guidelines are:

1. The facilitator has much to do with setting the initial mood or climate of the group or class experience.
2. The facilitator helps to elicit and clarify the purposes of the individuals in the class as well as the more general purposes of the group.

3. He relies upon the desire of each student to implement those purposes which have meaning for him, as the motivational force behind significant learning.
4. He endeavors to organize and make easily available the widest possible range of resources for learning.
5. He regards himself as a flexible resource to be utilized by the group.
6. In responding to expressions in the classroom group, he accepts both the intellectual content and the emotionalized attitudes, endeavoring to give each aspect the approximate degree of emphasis which it has for the individual or the group.
7. As the acceptant classroom climate becomes established, the facilitator is able increasingly to become a participant learner, a member of the group, expressing his views as those of one individual only.
8. He takes the initiative in sharing himself with the group, his feelings as well as his thoughts, in ways which do not demand nor impose but represent simply a personal sharing which students may take or leave.
9. Throughout the classroom experience, he remains alert to the expression indicative of deep or strong feelings.
10. In his functioning as a facilitator of learning, the leader endeavors to recognize and accept his own limitations. He realizes that he can only grant freedom to his students to the extent that he is comfortable in giving such freedom. (5, pp. 164–166)

As a counselor, the teacher guides and stimulates the growth of his student. In this process he integrates well-planned teacher-student activities. In those activities, the teacher undertakes a variety of functions such as assessing learning needs, designing teaching strategies, motivating students, implementing an effective learning environment, and evaluating student progress.

As a communicator, his role becomes more than that of an authoritarian dispenser of information. He pays particular attention to the fulfillment of a successful communication process.

Lack of communication results in confusion and maladministration of even a well-designed teaching situation. Moreover, the enjoyment of teaching and learning is reduced to a mere chore. On the other hand, good communication fosters understanding and clears away confusion and uncertainty and makes the teaching/learning process enjoyable for both teachers and students.

Effective communication is not limited to teachers' classroom presentations. It includes the way in which teachers conduct a one-to-one situation, how classroom interaction is guided, and how actively and knowingly appropriate channels are used to communicate effectively with students.

Traditionally, to communicate is to convey one's feelings or ideas through verbal language, either in its written or spoken format. Traditional teacher-training programs emphasize communication through the written and spoken word. While such training is extremely essential, it is not sufficient for effective teacher-student communication. There is a need to adopt an expanded view of communication to foster successful communication in the teaching process. This view calls for considering and integrating a variety of communication forms and channels. These channels and forms include verbal communication, vocal communication—the manner in which words are spoken, the volume, rate, tone, pitch, and inflections—media communication, body language, and situational messages. (6, pp. 2–32) In situational messages, the individual manipulates his distance from others, the use of time, and the setting of the environment. For example, in a situation of a student's coming to see his teacher in the teachers' room, the manner in which the teacher conducts himself within the setting of the room and the time he gives to the student will definitely affect their interrelationship, and subsequently the effectiveness of the teaching/learning environment.

Clear Understanding of the Educational Technology Concept

To structure an effective learning environment, teachers, school administrators, and parents must have a clear understanding of educational technology. In many teaching instances, media is treated as an afterthought, or as an addition to a teaching plan that can be executed without the use of media. In other instances, use of media in instruction is considered to be a practice of a teacher who is keeping pace with the times.

Instructional media should not be an afterthought. It is not either a fad. It is firmly grounded in **educational technology**. Educational technology is a technology of the mind which may or may not use hardware or a highly technical teaching strategy to achieve the stated educational objectives. (7, p. 164–65) Its main goal is to achieve excellence in education. It requires systematic planning based on our knowledge of human learning.

It examines accessible communications and information technologies to determine those most appropriate for the achievement of the desired objective in a cost effective manner. The choice of technology of instruction is determined not only by economic considerations, but by the unique characteristics of each technology, the purpose of using it, with whom it will be used, and under what circumstances.

To be effective, an instructional program has to be designed and engineered with precision. Basic to the design of an instructional program are the following ten points:

1. Determination of clear and precise teaching objectives. In stating those objectives, vague terminology should be avoided. Instead, specific clear statements should be developed to describe precisely the intended outcome of the teaching/learning situation.
2. Identification of the target students including social, psychological, physical, and environmental factors which might hinder or foster their development.
3. Determination of the body of information, skills, and attitudes pertinent to the achievement of the stated objectives.
4. Selection of the appropriate instructional technology which will be incorporated in the teaching system.
5. Design of learning strategies taking into consideration the above points.
6. Allocation of funds needed to design and implement the program.
7. Acquisition and preparation of software and hardware needed for the implementation of the program.
8. Execution of the program keeping continuous feedback from the learner to evaluate the program's effectiveness, and to assess the learner's achievement.
9. Testing the program to identify its strong and weak points in terms of achieving the stated objectives, and of involving the learner in the program.
10. Refinement of the program's objectives, and redesigning the program if necessary for implementation with other groups.

In executing an effective teaching/learning system, information and media technology has proved to be advantageous by providing the following:

1. Well-prepared teaching materials prepared by experts in subject matter, methods of teaching, media and instructional technology;

2. A variety of learning experiences to accommodate varying needs, learning styles, and learning abilities of the students;
3. A flexible learning environment rich in learning materials and resources;
4. Learning materials which integrate various disciplines of human knowledge;
5. Expert human resources through mediated interaction;
6. Learning resources in addition to the printed page;
7. Expansion of the learning environment beyond the school physical space and time;
8. Creative visualization of abstractions and difficult concepts;
9. Extension to human senses in studying physical phenomena;
10. Effective methods of storing and retrieving information; and
11. Help for teachers in becoming better teachers by:
    (a) providing good teaching materials,
    (b) demonstrating efficient communication methods, and
    (c) giving more time to the teachers to attend to neglected aspects of the teaching/learning process.

New developments in communication technology have made the above advantages more feasible. Some of these new developments include:

1. Alternative systems of delivery of instruction focusing on the individual (e.g., video cassette vs. broadcast TV);
2. Increased use of communication media and technology in various administrative and management functions of education (e.g., use of computers in managing instruction);
3. Increased use of media technology in direct classroom instruction;
4. Expanded use of conventional technologies in new capacities (e.g., telephone teleconferencing, and the use of the television set as a display board in a telecommunication system);
5. A growing simplicity, availability, durability, affordability, and flexibility of media hardware and software;
6. A growing trend toward the development of more locally produced tailor-made and custom-designed media products targeted for needs of specialized groups;
7. A growing trend toward the development of stand-alone interactive self-learning programs which integrate computer technology with other media technologies such as the videodisc player;

8. A growing realization of information/media competencies as critical basic education skills;
9. A growing trend toward using new communications technology in homes. Home computers and videocassette recorders are on the increase, resulting in greater expectations for the use of communications technology in school settings;
10. An accelerated growth in the information industry which aims at providing the public with information on a variety of topics and issues;
11. A tangible growth in the learning industry, the thrust of which is to custom-design learning packages to meet a variety of students' educational needs; and
12. A marked increase in satellite communication for learning. Most of the educational programs distributed by satellite consortia provide participants with learning and training experience unavailable through other means.

(For more information on new developments in instructional and communications technologies, please refer to Section II of this book and references 8–24).

To summarize, media and information technology has proven to be of significant advantages to the teaching/learning process. New communications and information technology is used with great success, and promises to be a great asset to educational technology. The use of media and information technology is firmly grounded in educational technology. Teachers, school administrators, and parents should have a clear concept of educational technology to ensure designing effective learning environments. Such environments should be flexible and rich in learning resources. Also, they should be designed and maintained as interactive environments. Following is a brief discussion of these two necessary conditions of a learning environment.

TWO NECESSARY CONDITIONS
OF A LEARNING ENVIRONMENT

A Flexible Learning Environment, Rich in Resources

To meet the varied needs and interests of the learners, the learning environment has to be flexible and rich in learning resources. Individual differences exist not only in the ability to learn and the desired level of achievement, but also in the style of learning, and the preference for the media which promises to be more effective in studying a certain topic. Some might learn faster when ideas are visualized; others might find the written and spoken word sufficient for gaining information about a special topic. "We must, therefore, use varied experience in teaching." (4, p. 61)

To meet individualized differences among students some educators advocated "individualized instruction." "Ideally, individualized instruction," according to Esbensen, "means an arrangement that makes it possible at all times for each student to be engaged in learning those things that are most appropriate for himself as an individual." (25) Esbensen believed that this ideal can never be reached, and that, "The best we can do is move toward it." (25, p. 1) Robert F. Mager indicated that, "One does not simply say that a system is or is not individualized, . . . , for it is not a black or white matter. Rather, one tries to identify the *nature* and *degree* of individualization. (25, p. vii) Mager believed that an instructional system is individualized when *decisions* about objectives and how to achieve them are based on the individual student, and when the characteristics of each student play a major part in the selection of objectives, materials, procedures, and time. (25, p. vii) However, most of the individualized instructional programs produced in the sixties were composed of highly-structured learning tasks, prepared by the teacher or by an outside source. Students moved through these programs at varying speed. As Dale put it, "The diet is the same, but the spoonfuls vary in size. Time spent is individualized, but the subject matter remains the same." (4, p. 92)

Other educators advocated "Programmed Instruction." James Espich and Bill Williams gave the definition of PI as "a planned sequence of experiences, leading to proficiency, in terms of stimulus-response relationships . . . 'Planned sequence' implies that the person developing the program has determined not only what experiences the student should have but also in what order they should occur." (26) One cannot help seeing that this definition denies the participation of the individual student in planning his own instruction, as given by previous definitions of individualized instruction.

It is unfortunate when educators swing like a pendulum from advocating one practice to another. Nongraded school system, programmed instruction, individualized instruction, career education, going-back-to basics, and open education are some of the movements we have experienced within the last twenty years. It is wise to learn from each movement and adopt the most promising practices in redesigning the learning environment to graduate the educated person of the 21st century. Common among these movements are the emphasis on the individual learner, and the provision of exciting and interesting learning experiences which will prepare the student for an effective and fulfilling life.

To achieve the balance between learner-centered education and what educators, parents, and the community consider to be important, flexible teaching strategies supported by rich and diversified instructional materials are essential components in planning and administering effective learning environments.

An effective learning environment should motivate **all** students to learn. Since success is the best motivator to learn, the learning environment should be designed to help every student to experience success in learning. A flexible environment, rich in learning resources can help every student to experience success, as Dale explained: "Certainly we can provide a range of experiences wide enough to allow everyone to achieve success in learning. We know that students schooled in failure reject themselves, feel worthless, drop out of school, and become cynical, belligerent, or indifferent. (4, p. 111) He further indicated that, "Temporary failures in an atmosphere of success are inevitable, and of no lasting harm, but a daily diet of failure is a discouraging and debilitating experience." (4, p. 111)

To summarize, a flexible learning environment, rich in resources can provide exciting and appropriate learning experiences to all students involved. It also helps achieve a balance between students' individual needs and the study of systematic sequenced curricula which experts and educators consider essential for an effective and productive living.

An Interactive Environment

We learn to drive a car by being behind the wheel and actually driving the car, not by reading about it. We learn to speak a foreign language by actually speaking the language. We learn to think by actually practicing critical thinking skills. We learn to be compassionate persons by being in a situation when caring behavior can help others in their needs for affection and encouragement. We learn by taking an active role in life situations. We learn by doing. Sometimes, it is essential to motivate the learner to start. Yet the actual learning occurs when the learner assumes his responsibility and becomes an active learner.

An instructional environment has to be an interactive environment. According to Buckminster Fuller, "The instructional environment . . . is an interacting situation in which the continuity of experience and the relating of experience are critically important." (4, p. 16)

If we examine the teaching process, we find it to be primarily a communication process. If we accept Dewey's definition of communication as "a process of sharing experience till it becomes a common possession," (2, p. 9) then teaching as a communication process should emphasize interaction between the learners and the teacher.

David Berlo indicated that one necessary condition of human communication is an interdependent relationship between the source (the teacher) and the receiver (the student). "Each affects the other." (27) He identified four levels of interdependence.

At one level, communication involves only a physical interdependence. In this level both the source and the receiver require each other for its very definition, and for its existence.

At a second level, interdependence can be analyzed as an action-reaction sequence. The receiver responds to a message initiated by the source.

At a third level, the source is concerned with how others will respond to a message. The source projects himself into the internal states of personalities of others in order to predict how they will behave. "We infer the internal states of others by comparing them to our own attitudes and predispositions." (27, p. 130)

The final level of interdependence between the source and the receiver is *interaction*. Berlo explained the term interaction as follows:

> The term interaction names the process of reciprocal role-taking, the mutual performance of emphatic behavior. If two individuals make inferences about their own roles and take the role of the other at the same time, and if their communication behavior depends on the reciprocal taking of role, then they are communicating by interacting with each other. (27, p. 130)

Berlo believed that the concept of interaction is central to the understanding of the concept of process in communication. In his words, "Communication represents an attempt to couple two organisms, to bridge the gap between two individuals through the production and reception of messages which have meanings for both. At best, this is an impossible task. Interactive communication approaches this ideal." (27, pp. 130–131)

The goal of interaction in communication is "the merger of self and other, a complete ability to anticipate, predict, and behave in accordance with joint needs of self and other." (27, p. 131)

To put it in a few words, to teach is to communicate, to communicate is to interact, to interact is to learn.

Socrates realized the importance of interaction in learning. He invented the tutorial method. In this method the teacher asks questions, and the student talks. Gilbert Highet described this method in the following.

> ... the questions are so arranged as to make the pupil conscious of his ignorance, and to guide him towards a deeper truth, which he will hold all the more firmly because it has not been presented to him ready-made but drawn out of his own mind by the joint efforts of his teacher and himself. It is important here that there should be some basis of discussion, so the pupil usually does some work in preparation, which his teacher then examines, criticizes, and by constructive questioning attempts to deepen. (28)

Comparing the sophists with Socrates, Highet explained that the sophists were the first lecturers. They said that they knew everything and were ready to explain it. On the other hand, Socrates said he knew nothing and was trying to find out, and train people to think. His method stimulated his students to think. Highet explained Socrates' method in the following:

> Questions are asked, gently and almost casually. As the answers are given, Socrates draws them together and asks further questions about their apparent inconsistencies. Under his patient interrogation, irrational judgments are thrown aside and shallow ideas replumbed and discarded and objections are raised and countered and slowly, slowly, under the guidance of Reason alone, we are carried through the labyrinthine paths of learning until we arrive at a positive result, which we could by no means have foreseen when we started and could not have reached except by cool rational discussion. (28, p. 161)

Aristotle thought of research and teaching as two sides of the same coin. To him knowledge was a constant process of discovery. (28, pp. 163–165) In a more recent writing, Dale indicated that: "a good mind must do more than discover the already known; it must also *produce.*" (29) To produce, education has to choose creative interaction of the learners over "rote imitative reaction." (29, p. 24)

CONCLUSION

For decades, educators have been questioning the value of putting emphasis on memorization and neglecting the development of the total educated person. The person who can answer questions, and question answers. The person who rejoices in discovering facts and learning new things, and considers learning as a life-long process. The person who is not afraid of change and is willing to examine change carefully and objectively. The person who has articulated values and has compassion toward other people, with deep concern for freedom and justice for all. The person who respects all individuals and finds delight in communicating with fellow men.

To cultivate such a person for an effective life in the 21st century, the learning environment must be staffed with professional people who can reflect the same attitudes. It should be planned and designed as a flexible, interactive learning environment rich in learning resources.

REFERENCES

1. Dale, Edgar. "Access To Excellence," *The Newsletter,* Columbus, Ohio: Bureau of Educational Research, Ohio State University. May 1970, Vol. XXXV, No. 8.
2. Dewey, John. DEMOCRACY and EDUCATION, New York: Macmillan Publishing Co., 1916, p. 2.
3. Buckminster, Fuller. "What I Have Learned, How Little I Know," *Saturday Review,* Vol. 49, No. 46, Nov. 12, 1966 p. 70.
4. Dale, Edgar. BUILDING A LEARNING ENVIRONMENT, Bloomington, Indiana: Phi Delta Kappa, Inc. 1972, p. 51.
5. Rogers, Carl R. FREEDOM TO LEARN, Columbus, Ohio: Charles E. Merrill Publishing Company, 1969. p. 126.
6. Hennings, Dorothy Grant. MASTERING CLASSROOM COMMUNICATION—WHAT INTERACTION ANALYSIS TELLS THE TEACHER. Pacific Palisades California: Goodyear Publishing Company, 1975, pp. 2–32.
7. Association for Educational Communications and Technology. EDUCATIONAL TECHNOLOGY DEFINITION & GLOSSARY OF TERMS, Volume 1, Washington, D.C., 1977, pp. 164–65.
8. Branson, Robert K. "Instructional Systems Technology in Business and Industry," in James Brown (Ed.), EDUCATIONAL MEDIA YEARBOOK, 1984, Littleton, Colorado: Libraries Unlimited, 1984 pp. 34–43.
9. Bratton, Barry. "Changing Professional Prospects in Educational Technology,"

in James Brown (Ed.), EDUCATIONAL MEDIA YEARBOOK, 1984, Littleton, Colorado: Libraries Unlimited, 1984 pp. 44–52.

10. Bowie, Melvin M. & Robert Hart. "Coping with Technological Change," in Elwood E. Miller (Ed.), EDUCATIONAL MEDIA & TECHNOLOGY YEARBOOK, 1988, Littleton, Colorado: Libraries Unlimited, 1988, pp. 70–80.

11. Cambre, Marjorie. "Instructional Television, An Update & Assessment," in Elwood E. Miller (Ed.), EDUCATIONAL MEDIA & TECHNOLOGY YEARBOOK, 1988, Littleton, Colorado: Libraries Unlimited, 1988, pp. 37–47.

12. Clark, Richard E. "Research on Instructional Media, 1978–1988," in Elwood E. Miller (Ed.), EDUCATIONAL MEDIA & TECHNOLOGY YEAR-BOOK, 1988, Littleton, Colorado: Libraries Unlimited, 1988, pp. 19–36.

13. Ely, Donald P. & Tjeard Plomp. "The Promises of Educational Technology: A Reassessment," in Elwood E. Miller (Ed.), EDUCATIONAL MEDIA & TECHNOLOGY YEARBOOK, 1988, Littleton, Colorado: Libraries Unlimited, 1988, pp. 5–18.

14. Gentry, Cass. "Educational Technology A Question of Meaning," in Elwood E. Miller (Ed.), EDUCATIONAL MEDIA & TECHNOLOGY YEAR-BOOK, 1987, Littleton, Colorado: Libraries Unlimited, 1987, pp. 90–99.

15. Heinich, Robert, & Michael Molenda, and James D. Russell. INSTRUC-TIONAL MEDIA AND THE NEW TECHNOLOGIES OF INSTRUC-TION, Third Edition, New York: Macmillan Publishing Company, 1989.

16. Hill, Harold E. "Communication and Educational Technology," in James Brown (Ed.), EDUCATIONAL MEDIA YEARBOOK, 1981, Littleton, Colorado: Libraries Unlimited, 1981, pp. 40–49.

17. Hope, Tom. "Training—An Emerging Discipline," in James Brown (Ed.), EDUCATIONAL MEDIA YEARBOOK, 1981, Littleton, Colorado: Librar-ies Unlimited, 1981, pp. 40–49.

18. Ingle, Henry T. "Cutting-Edge Developments in Educational Technology," in James Brown (Ed.), EDUCATIONAL MEDIA YEARBOOK, 1984, Littleton, Colorado: Libraries Unlimited, 1984 pp. 14–23.

19. Johnston, Jerome. ELECTRONIC LEARNING FROM AUDIOTAPE TO VIDEODISC, Hillsdale, New Jersey: Lawrence Erlbaum Associates, 1987.

20. Kemp, Jerold E. "Significant Current Trends in Educational Technology: Some Implications," in James Brown (Ed.), EDUCATIONAL MEDIA YEARBOOK, 1981, Littleton, Colorado: Libraries Unlimited, 1981, pp. 27–35.

21. Meierhenry, Wesley. "A Brief History of Educational Technology." in James Brown (Ed.), EDUCATIONAL MEDIA YEARBOOK, 1984, Littleton, Colorado: Libraries Unlimited, 1984 pp. 3–13.

22. Ruack, Henry Clay. "Emerging Applications of New Technologies in Train-ing and Education." in James Brown (Ed.), EDUCATIONAL MEDIA YEARBOOK, 1981, Littleton, Colorado: Libraries Unlimited, 1981, pp. 17–22.

23. Silber, Kenneth. "Some Implications of the History of Educational Technology, We're All in This Together," in James Brown (Ed.), EDUCATIONAL MEDIA YEARBOOK, 1981, Littleton, Colorado: Libraries Unlimited, 1981, pp. 18–26.

24. Zimmerer, Joel W. "Computer Conferencing—A Medium for Facilitating Interaction in Distance Education," in Elwood E. Miller (Ed.), EDUCATIONAL MEDIA & TECHNOLOGY YEARBOOK, 1988, Littleton, Colorado: Libraries Unlimited, 1988, pp. 60–69.

25. Esbensen, Thorwald. WORKING WITH INDIVIDUALIZED INSTRUCTION, Palo Alto, California Fearon Publishers, 1968, p. 1.

26. Espich, James E. & Bill Williams. DEVELOPING PROGRAMMED INSTRUCTIONAL MATERIALS, Belmont, California: Fearon Publishers, Lear Siegler, Inc. Education Division, 1967, p. v.

27. Berlo, David K. THE PROCESS OF COMMUNICATION—AN INTRODUCTION TO THEORY AND PRACTICE, N.Y.: Holt, Rinehart and Winston, Inc., 1960, p. 129.

28. Highet, Gilbert. THE ART OF TEACHING, New York: Vintage Books, 1957, p. 88.

29. Dale, Edgar. THE GOOD MIND, Bloomington, Indiana: Phi Delta Kappa Educational Foundation, Fastback 105, 1978, p. 24.

Chapter Three

MEDIATED INTERACTION

IBRAHIM M. HEFZALLAH

I n Chapter Two, we have established that interaction is a must condition in an effective learning environment.

There are two basic types of interaction: face-to-face interaction, and
mediated interaction.

Face-to-face interaction occurs in the presence of both the student and
the teacher in the learning environment. Mediated interaction occurs
when the source of information or of the teaching program or material is
separated from the student by space and/or time.

Face-to-face interaction was briefly discussed in Chapter Two. This
chapter focuses on mediated interaction.

TYPES OF MEDIATED INTERACTION

Mediated interaction can take a variety of forms depending on the
technology used to bridge the space-time gap between the learner and
the instructor. The following are three basic types of mediated interaction:

Live Mediated Interaction

In this type of interaction, the teacher and the students are separated
only by space. Telecommunication technology provides them with the
means to interact live. Live interaction when separated by space has
three basic types:

Audio Interaction

Examples of audio interaction include telephone conversations, and
audio telelectures using regular telephone lines, or special audio arrangement between the originating and the receiving sites. Participants on
both sites can interact by conversing back and forth.

Visually-Augmented Audio Interaction

In this type of interaction, the parties are provided with still visuals related to the topic of discussion. The visuals could be charts, graphs, or photographic slides which are sent in advance to the receiving site; or they could be graphic material transmitted over the telephone lines by way of facsimile machines or audiographic equipment during the actual time of the conference.

Slow-scan video can also be used to augment an audio conference. A television camera is used to transmit a still image of an object from one site to the other. Transmission can take anywhere from 10 to 30 seconds. The picture can either be painted on the receiving monitors or can appear instantaneously after each scan line has been recorded in a frame-store device which will project only completed images.

Live Video Interaction

In this type of interaction, the teacher and the students interact through audio and video channels. Most of the live video interaction (video teleconferences) is conducted as one-way full-motion video. Recipients of the conference relay their feedback through call-in phones to the presenter(s). A two-way full-motion live video interaction is the most sophisticated and expensive system of teleconferencing. Both parties have television cameras, transmission and television receiving devices. The transmission lines could be permanently installed between the points of origination and reception, or two cable television channels are assigned to the event, or satellite dishes are temporarily or permanently installed to allow transmission and reception of both audio and video signals.

Computer Mediated Interaction

In this type of interaction, the teacher and students are separated by space, and cannot see or hear each other. With this type of interaction, communication takes the form of text entered by the originator and displayed on a screen, or printed on a paper at the recipient end. Usually telephone lines or satellite transmission-reception are used to connect the originating and receiving sites. In many instances, communication is rarely in real time, and usually the message is held in the computer until the intended recipient checks in.

Totally Mediated Interaction

In this type of interaction the teacher and the students are separated by both space and time. The instructional material is designed and produced based on the assumption that immediate feedback from the learner to the teacher, and vice versa, is not accessible.

Technology of totally mediated interaction varies in its degree of sophistication. On top of the list are computer-assisted instruction and interactive video programs. At a less sophisticated level are programmed instruction using simple tools from paper-and-pencil type to listen/view-respond-listen/view type. In the latter, audio, video, motion picture films, and sound/slides programs are used to display a program designed to give information, ask the user to respond to certain questions, give time to the user to respond, and provide an evaluation of the user's response before resuming the program.

MEDIATED INTERACTION
AND EDUCATIONAL TECHNOLOGY

While mediated interaction is technology-based, it is important to understand that successful mediated interaction is firmly grounded in **educational technology**. (Please refer to "Clear Understanding of the Concept of Educational Technology," in Chapter Two). In addition to the principles of designing an instructional program discussed earlier, there are guidelines for the design of mediated interactive learning programs. Following is a brief discussion of these guidelines which will be grouped under two major headings: live mediated interaction, and totally mediated interaction.

General Guidelines for the Design of Live Mediated Interaction

1. There is a need to establish a strong rapport with students in remote sites. In regular classrooms, special attention is given to encourage interaction between the instructor and the students. That attention also has to be emphasized in live mediated interaction. Lorne Parker indicated that, " 'Getting to know someone' in teleconferencing is not as easily accomplished as in a face-to-face setting." (1, p. 26). Students in remote sites should not feel that they are left out there. Some school systems experimenting with distant learning attempt to employ

different measures to encourage students' interaction. Some of the strategies used are scheduled visits by the instructor to the remote sites, arranged social gatherings between classes, addressing students in the remote sites by their first name, and acknowledging students' special occasions. (In one of Dr. Harry Wohlert's German by Satellite broadcasts from Oklahoma State University, he congratulated some of his students in the remote sites on the occasion of their birthdays.)

2. There is a need to overcome the reluctance of students to speak in a distant teaching situation. A striking phenomenon is people's hesitation to participate in a discussion when it is mediated. Being unsure of how one sounds on the system, or uncertain about the validity of one's question, people tend to be reluctant to speak in a distant teaching situation. Questions given in advance to students to respond to in class could help some students to speak during the telecast. Continuous encouragement of students to interact is vital to the success of live mediated interaction.

3. There is a need to design the teaching events in a live telecast to avoid idle time. Inactive time during a live telecast is deadly. Experience in telecasting instructional materials has indicated that more information can be presented in a telecast than in a regular classroom setting. Management of telecast time is crucial to the success of live mediated interaction.

4. There is a need to examine methods of teaching and classroom presentations and adapt the most appropriate to distant teaching. Some of the traditional classroom methods of teaching might be applicable under certain circumstances. However, use of interactive television in distant teaching provides means for developing new teaching strategies unavailable in traditional classroom environment. (Please refer to Chapter Seven.)

5. Feedback cannot be overemphasized. Immediate feedback can help change the pace and clarify points in the presentation. It can give the teacher immediate assessment of the success of his presentation. Some schools employing distant teaching installed fax machines which the students use in the remote site to send in their written assignments given during class time. (Please refer to Chapter Six.)

6. Origination and receiving sites facilities have to be designed and equipped for quality transmission and reception of signals. There is

no excuse for a bad audio transmission, or an out-of-focus and distorted television image.

7. All audiovisual and computer materials have to be professionally designed and executed to ensure clear and pleasant reception of interesting and informative displays.

8. The medium of telecast and reception in live mediated interaction has to be transparent. Teachers and students should not be distracted by equipment and personnel operating the equipment. In many school systems, the origination facility is handled by the broadcast teacher from his desk. All cameras are placed in unobtrusive positions and can be switched back and forth by a simple switcher placed on the teacher's desk. (Please refer to Chapter Six and Chapter Seven.)

General Guidelines for the Design of Totally Mediated Interaction

1. Choice of appropriate technology has to be done in terms of what it can offer to the learning tasks at hand. A hi-tech medium does not make it suitable for every teaching/learning purpose. In the early days of computer literacy movement, many computer-assisted instruction programs were poor examples of what computers can be used for. The technology has to be used to its full capacity; otherwise, other technology might be chosen.

2. The content of the program should be relevant to the tasks being learned. It should also be current. An advantage of mediated learning programs is the ability to update the information more readily than the printed page.

3. There should be a clear statement of the program's objectives. The learner has to know and understand the purpose of the encounter with the mediated interaction.

4. Learning tasks should be well-defined. The learner should be clear on what he is supposed to do. He should also be clear on the criterion of judging what he has learned.

5. The learner should have continuous access to help options. There is nothing more frustrating to a learner than to get stuck in a program without knowing how to proceed or to circumvent the snag in the program.

6. The learner should have continuous access to the exit and reentry options. The learner should be given the option to exit the program at any time he desires. He should also have the option of reentering the

program either at the point of his earlier departure, at the beginning of the program, or at a specific point in the section he covered.

7. The learner should be offered assistance in locating additional information. If the outcome of learning is the desire to learn more, mediated interaction programs should guide the students to ways of accessing more information.

8. The program should be designed to ensure active participation of the learner. In addition to the above guidelines, the following are designing criteria for the achievement of the learner's active participation:

   a. the learner should be able to learn how to use the program in a very short time. Tutorial instructions have to be concise, accurate, and clear;

   b. the program should be designed to have different entry levels to meet the different levels of students' backgrounds. Also, it should move at a pace adjustable to the learner. For instance, to slow down, the learner might have a pause option. To speed up, the learner should have the option to by-pass a section that has already been mastered in a previous setting;

   c. students should be allowed to ask questions to which the program will present the answers;

   d. the program should acknowledge the user's input. In doing that, negative feedback should be avoided. Instead gentle corrective feedback ought to be used;

   e. the program should be designed to include self-assessment tools;

   k. a modular design will help increase the flexibility of the program. It will also help the learner to achieve a sense of accomplishment when a module is mastered, and he is allowed to proceed to a second module;

   h. the program should allow the students to move between sections of the program to accommodate individual differences in style and ability to learn;

   g. the program should provide default options to prevent the crashing of the program if the learner inadvertently makes a mistake; it should also provide for help options at any time; and finally,

   i. the program should have a pleasant appearance. Graphics should be artistically executed, video portions should be professionally structured, and computer screens should be aesthetically designed. Text should be easily read, and the color and letter styles should enhance screen readability.

Mediated interaction can help meet the educational needs dictated by the information age and other economical, cultural, social, and political factors affecting our lives. The following is a brief discussion of the reasons for using mediated interaction in the modern age.

REASONS FOR USING MEDIATED INTERACTION

To Help Achieve Excellence in Education

Education has to aim at achieving excellence. Teaching for excellence helps and guides the individual to grow to maximum potential, and to become a self-generated better person.

To achieve this goal, the learner has to have direct access to models of excellence in his learning environment. The presence of excellent teachers and community resource people is a necessary condition for the achievement of excellence in education. Very often that presence can *only* be achieved through mediated interaction.

In addition to models of human excellence, rich integrated use of teaching and self-learning materials are essential to stimulate the learner, and to provide him with suitable material to meet individual needs. Addressing the effectiveness of professionally packaged instructional materials, Robert Heinich wrote:

> Our technologies of instruction were demonstrated to be effective 25 years ago. They are even more effective today. In addition to adding more technologies such as the computer, we know much more today about how students learn and how to design effective instruction. With expert teams of curricular and instructional designers planning, developing and packaging reliable instructional systems, even the average classroom teacher can achieve superior results. (2)

Learning resources of an effective teaching/learning environment include teaching materials used by the teacher, self-teaching programs used by the students, and information resources used by the teacher and the students.

To Support Evolving School Curricula

In response to advancements in knowledge, school curricula must undergo change to teach new information, and to present it in an interesting manner. New information tends to be rooted in different disciplines.

In some instances the teacher might not be well-versed in all of the areas significant to the study of a certain topic. Mediated programs prepared by scholars and specialists from different disciplines can help overcome that problem.

In addition to updating school curricula to reflect the new body of information and skills, there is a need to employ the best teaching methods which utilize information processing technology, and the most efficient presentation methods. The National Science Foundation report indicated that:

> There is evidence that many students who have an interest in mathematics, science, and technology are not being reached through instructional approaches currently used in the classroom. Whereas many students do not like school science – and form this opinion by the end of third grade – many do like the science and technology that they see on television. They also like what they encounter at science and technology museums, planetariums, nature centers, and national parks. (3)

The report recommended that innovative instructional approaches used in exhibits and television programs should be examined and, where possible, applied to the classroom setting.

To present up-to-date and interdisciplinary educational material in a creative and interesting manner requires a great deal of planning, research, and production time and effort from many creative professionals. In many instances, teachers might not have the time or the access to resources needed for the original development of quality interdisciplinary teaching/learning materials. Prepackaged mediated programs can provide the teachers with those components of the learning environment which are significantly needed for the implementation of the everchanging school curricula.

To Ensure Educational Equality for All Students

Every student has the right to an education that will foster maximum development of his talents. Mediated interaction can help implement this principle in three ways:

Provide Special Courses for Small Groups of Students

Due to lack of enough students interested in taking a course in the Russian language, for instance, a school will find it noncost-effective to offer such a course. However, if a few students in a neighboring school are interested, a two-way video connection can make offering the course cost-effective to both schools. Having a skilled teacher in one location with one group, and interacting through cable with the other group is a viable solution to offering the variety of courses needed.

Other forms of mediated programs such as computer-assisted instruction and interactive video programs can help overcome the problem by providing individualized learning situations, thus minimizing the need for the presence of a teacher all the time the students are studying.

Meet the Various Needs, Interests, and Learning Styles of Individual Students

In discussing the flexibility and richness of the learning environment, it was indicated that individual differences exist not only in the ability to learn and the desired level of achievement, but also in the style of learning, and the preference for the medium which promises to be more effective in studying a certain topic. Mediated instruction can help provide varied learning experiences presented in different formats and styles to meet the varied individual differences and interests among the students.

Achieve Educational Equality for All Students Regardless of Their Geographical Areas

It is feared that the age of information technology is widening the gap between schools with adequate funds and resources and schools that lack those resources. This gap has to be diminished to establish harmony among the members of our society regardless of social and economic background.

In discussing the use of two-way television to help overcome inequality in education as a result of school segregation, Lawrence Redd wrote:

> Where attempts to attain desegregation do not work, a new or different approach to equal educational opportunity must be developed, evaluated, and, if accepted, put into action. Current trends indicate that new communication technology might be a reasonable approach. The use of two-way television to transport minds instead of bodies across town to achieve equal educational opportunity is a relatively new concept and adds another dimension to education. (4)

Redd indicated that efforts through litigation to achieve equal educational opportunity should not be abandoned and that parents and educators should refocus on the meaning of equal education and determine ways of achieving equality. He compared busing with teleconferencing. He said, "The tradeoff between teleconferencing and travel forces that association. Teleconferencing and desegregation, however, now are mutually exclusive, whereas desegregation and busing have become complexly intertwined." (4, p. 451)

Mediated interaction will not change the racial composition of the schools, nor will it change the economic profile of the schools' population, but it will help achieve educational equality among students from different districts. Moreover, live interaction through two-way audio-video teleconferencing can help establish a common experience among students from different backgrounds.

Connick and MacBrayne described Maine's plan for a telecommunications highway system as a means to provide educational access for all Maine citizens regardless of their ability, income, or geographic location, especially since "only one-third of Maine's population lives within twelve miles of a university or vocational institute campus." (5) They indicated that research showed that "proximity to a college or university campus affects the rate of participation in higher education." (5, p. 24) They referred to an analysis which indicated that "the career choices of Maine students tend toward occupations requiring little education or training." (5, p. 23) This is happening "At a time when fundamental changes are taking place in technology, science, and the economy, creating demands for skills not yet discovered in jobs not yet designed." (5, p. 25) Telecommunications highways in Maine can "provide new opportunities for the education and retraining of the work force." (5, p. 25)

Reflecting on the future they said:

> In the future, it would be possible to connect all high schools in the state to the telecommunications network through the use of a satellite link. This electronic highway would allow for the distribution of the vast educational resources in this state in a timely and efficient manner. Approximately eighty percent of the state's population would be within a twelve mile commute to educational programs and student support systems. (5, p. 25–26)

Programs carried by the network will provide training where needed. The authors believed that accessibility to network programs and services "should improve aspirations for both young people and adults as the possibility of obtaining a higher level of education becomes a reality." (5, p. 26) Programs carried by the system will include remedial coursework, entry-level college courses, and advanced training, and education programs.

Communities, then, "can begin to look forward to economic development as a more educated work force becomes available." (5, p. 25)

To summarize in the words of the authors:

> Maine's emerging plan for a statewide community college promises to eliminate many of the barriers of geography and cost which have restricted access to learning and retraining for generations of Mainers. Recognizing the future needs of Maine society for increasing requirements for educational opportunities at all levels, it proposes a system for distributing Maine's educational resources throughout the state. (5, p. 26)

To Educate Students in the Process of Self-Learning

In the information age, learning is a life-long process. It does not end with the completion of the school day, nor the school years. The educated person continues to learn for the rest of his life. Some of that learning will be achieved within formal education and training programs, but most of it will occur on informal and individual basis. Well-designed mediated programs can be an effective teaching tool in both cases. However, unless schools educate their students at an early stage of their education, the values and the skills needed to intelligently use mediated instructional programs on their own, continuing education on the informal and individual basis will suffer. On the other hand, offering students that education can help develop their information retrieval skills. Also, it will help them experience the pleasure resulting from self-discovery and self-learning. Such a healthy environment will help develop their attitude toward self-learning and the skills associated with it. Eventually, that attitude and skills will transfer to their extended life-learning situations.

To Educate Students in the Use of New Communications and Information Delivery Systems

1. Data Banks

With the rapid technological developments in microprocessors, telecommunications, optical recording of information, technology of storing, sorting, and retrieving information, learning outside a traditional classroom will increase. The availability of alternative delivery and distribution systems of information will change the concept of the library. Libraries are no longer places for storing cataloged printed material and nonprint material. Access to a variety of data and information banks through electronic means is a common practice in many libraries. Homes, too, can have the same advantages. In a recent interview of a college sophomore who subscribes to *CompuServe,* he stated that during the last academic year he did not need to go to the library once. This is not a desirable outcome, but it points to the fact that students studying at home can have access to electronically published information. Students should be familiar with data banks, and be capable of using them to locate information they need, in addition to using the library resources.

2. Television

Educational TV programs have attracted many adult learners to tune in to improve their level of education. In England, approximately 147,350 part-time students were enrolled in the Open University in 1987–88. (6) The Open University implements the distant learning concept in which TV and radio programs, printed material, laboratory assignments (which the students can perform at home using special kits designed and distributed to the students by the Open University), summer workshops, and consultations with tutors are used in an integrated fashion.

In the United States educational television courses and programs have attracted adult learners. According to a CPB study on the use of television in higher education, 32 percent of higher education institutions offered a total of 10,594 courses over television in 1984–85, an average of twelve courses per college. Those colleges enrolled 39,921 students in the television courses, an average of 38 per course and 442 TV enrollments per college. (7) In another study by PBS, 34 percent of the population between the ages of 18 and 45 (31,000,000) who were not in college in 1981 said that they would like to take a college course via television and that they would be willing to pay for it. (8)

Schools should aim at helping students to recognize that television is more than an entertainment medium. Watching commercial television at home could be a part of a home assignment. Moreover, students should be made aware of educational and cultural programs available on various television channels.

3. Satellites for Learning and Training

The world of satellite communications is gaining ground in education especially in higher and continuing education. An alphabet soup has emerged: acronyms of satellite and distant learning consortia. A considerable amount of programming is available through consortia. Most of those programs provide the participants with learning and training experiences unavailable through other means.

In the world of work, telecommunication technology offers effective alternatives to conventional training and business meetings. Teletraining, in the words of Lorne Parker "has the ability to revolutionize the way companies train their employees, making it noticeably more effective from cost, learning, and productivity standpoints." (1, p. 1)

Most of the programs carried by telecommunication services attempt to implement interactivity between the receiving audience and the originating sites. An observer of teleconferences will notice that often participants are too shy to participate. Indicating that "discussion does not just 'happen' " in teletraining, Lorne Parker wrote:

> No matter how many students may want to make use of the opportunity to ask questions and no matter how easy it may be technically, some students are reluctant to interact at first—they may feel they are infringing on program time, other people's time, or that their questions or comments may be not worded correctly." (1, p. 26)

To overcome this problem, the designer of the telecommunication program must first recognize the importance of achieving interaction with the audience as a prime consideration. Second, there is a need to educate people on how to interact in teleconferences and teletraining situations instead of being passive recipients of information.

At present, some school districts are employing telecommunication strategies to use the expertise of available resource people in one location to reach more students in other locations. If attention is given to plan the lesson to ensure students' interactivity, they will leave high school with an ability to interact with a distant source. This ability can be enhanced further in the world of work, when the student goes through teletraining programs, or through college education, when the student becomes an active participant in a variety of teleconferences and telecourses originated by a growing number of telecommunication consortia.

CONCLUSION

To assume that conventional teaching will guarantee that students will seek electronically published information on their own after finishing their formal education is false. Unless formal education strives to educate students to effectively use electronically published information and mediated instruction programs on their own, there will be many whose continuing education will be undermined. To achieve this type of education, schools must offer their students ample opportunities to experience mediated instruction and information processing and retrieving media.

REFERENCES

1. Parker, Lorne A. TELETRAINING MEANS BUSINESS, Madison, Wisconsin: Center for Interactive Programs, University of Wisconsin-Extension, 1984. p. 26.
2. Heinich, Robert. "Legal aspects of alternative staffing patterns and educational technology," Synthesis, Southwest Educational Development Laboratory, 6(2), 3., quoted by Lyn Gubser, "Public Education in a Year of Transition," in EDUCATIONAL MEDIA and TECHNOLOGY YEARBOOK, 1985, Elwood E. Miller (Ed.), Littleton, Colorado: Libraries Unlimited, Inc., 1985, p. 6.
3. National Science Board, National Science Foundation. TODAY'S PROBLEMS TOMORROW'S CRISES, A Report of the National Science Board Commission of Precollege Education in Mathematics, Science and Technology, Washington, D.C., 1982, p. 7.
4. Lawrence N. Redd. "The Use of Two-way Television to Solve Problems of Inequality in Education: A Comment," *The Journal of Negro Education*, Vol. 52, No. 4, 1983. p. 448.
5. George P. Connick and Pamela S. MacBrayne. "Telecommunications and Educational Access: A Plan For Maine's Future," *Journal of Maine Education*, 1987 Vol. 3, No.1.
6. Europa Publications Limited. THE WORLD OF LEARNING, London, 1988, p. 1407.
7. CPB. "A National Study of the Educational Uses of Telecommunications Technology in America's Colleges and Universities," Survey Year 1984–85, *Research Notes*, September, 1986, Washington D.C.
8. PBS, PTV-3 Adult Learning Programming Department. "A Background Paper for the February 26, 1982 Teleconference on the Partnership Between Public Television and Higher Education to Deliver Adult Learning Courses.), p. 16.

SECTION II
APPLICATIONS OF
MEDIATED INTERACTION IN EDUCATION

PART I
COMPUTERS IN INTERACTIVE LEARNING

The computer is an ideal device to implement the principles of interactive learning, to upgrade the level of instruction, and to develop the students' abilities for self-learning.

Chapter Four, Forerunners to Computers in Education, surveys educational forerunners to the current use of computers in education.

During the past thirty years, use of computers in education evolved from the use of simplistic instructional programs to highly sophisticated learning systems. This has been aided by the dramatic increase and reduced costs of available computing power as well as by the enhanced sophistication of recent software systems. Chapter Five, Computer-Assisted Instruction, addresses computer-assisted instruction, and focuses on some of the recent applications of computers in education including discovery learning and the use of data bases in education.

Chapter Four

FORERUNNERS TO COMPUTERS IN EDUCATION

IBRAHIM M. HEFZALLAH

INTRODUCTION

Over the centuries, various attempts have been made by educators to increase the efficiency of the learning experience. One thought that has prevailed for centuries is using small successive steps in learning. The tutorial method, invented by Socrates, is based on this thought. In this method, he asked questions arranged so as to make the student conscious of his ignorance. The questions were asked gently and almost casually, and moved the student toward deeper understanding. (1)

At the turn of the century, educators and learning psychologists underlined basic concepts for increasing the efficiency of the learning process. These concepts can be summarized in the following:

1. the learning environment has to engage the learner; the learner has to be active and not a passive recipient of learning material;
2. the learning material can be designed in small successive steps to which the learner responds;
3. presentation of subsequent steps depends on the learner's response;
4. it is important to supply the learner with immediate evaluation of his progress;
5. an efficient learning environment should recognize students' individual differences in terms of background, interest, learning pace, and levels of achievement of the materials being learned;
6. the learning environment should lead the students to the mastery of the learning tasks;
7. since education is a life-long process, it becomes essential that the learning environment should foster the development of the learner's ability for self-learning; and
8. since education is more than imparting factual information, an

59

ideal learning environment ought to free some of the teacher's time to counsel and guide his students in their education.

With these ideas in mind, educators and learning psychologists have been examining a variety of approaches for the implementation of some or all of these ideas. Before the computer age, we lacked the technological means through which the above concepts could be implemented successfully. To fully understand the potential role of the computer in the learning process, it is imperative to trace some of the major educators' attempts to put into practice the above ideas.

PROGRAMMED INSTRUCTION & TEACHING MACHINES

A Definition

Two interrelated movements, programmed instruction and teaching machines, attempted to increase learning efficiency through emphasizing the learner's active role, use of small successive steps, immediate feedback to student response, and allowing the student to proceed at his own pace.

Programmed instruction is a planned sequence of experiences leading to the student's mastery of a topic of study. Tools for presenting the planned sequence of experiences varied from paper and pencil type to teaching machines. During late fifties and early sixties, there was a quite a variety of teaching machines. In 1960, Lumsdaine gave the following generic definition of teaching machines.

Despite great variation in complexity and special features, all of the devices that are currently called "teaching machines" represent some form of variation on what can be called the tutorial or Socratic method of teaching. That is, they present the individual student with programs of questions and answers, problems to solve, or exercises to be performed. In addition, however, they always provide some type of automatic feedback or correction to the student so that he is immediately informed of his progress at each step and given a basis for correcting his errors. (2)

This definition implied the implementation of four important teaching practices:

1. continuous student response to subsequent steps;
2. explicit practice and testing of each step;
3. immediate feedback to student's response; if the student's response

was incorrect, he was led directly or indirectly to correct his errors; and

4. the student proceeded at his own rate; faster students moved rapidly in the instructional sequence, and slower students were tutored as slowly as necessary. (2, p. 6)

Historical Review of
Programmed Instruction & Teaching Machines

In 1912, Thorndike, a professor of psychology at Columbia University anticipated programmed instructions controlled by a machine. He wrote:

> If by a miracle of mechanical ingenuity, a book could be so arranged that only to him who had done what was directed on page one would page two become visible, and so on, much that now requires personal instruction could be managed by print. Books to be given out in loose sheets, a page or so at a time, and books arranged so that the student only suffers if he misuses them, should be worked in many subjects. (3)

In the early 1920s, Sidney L. Pressey, a professor of psychology at Ohio State University, designed several machines for the automatic testing of information using multiple-choice questions. The machine advanced to the next question after the student chose the right answer for the first question. (4, 5)

Skinner explained the use of Pressey's device in the following:

> In using the device the student refers to a numbered item in a multiple-choice test. He presses the button corresponding to his first choice of answer. If he is right, the device moves on to the next item; if he is wrong, the error is tallied, and he must continue to make choices until he is right. (6)

Pressey pointed out that such machines "could not only test and score, they could teach." (6, p. 30) Skinner commented on the value of immediate report of the student's performance when using Pressey's machines. He said, "When an examination is corrected and returned after a delay of many hours or days, the student's behavior is not appreciably modified. The immediate report supplied by a self-scoring device, however, can have an important instructional effect." (6, p. 30)

Pressey's teaching machines also allowed for self-paced instruction which could increase the efficiency of instruction, as Skinner explained:

> Even in a small classroom the teacher usually knows that he is moving too slowly for some students and too fast for others. Those who could

go faster are penalized, and those who should go slower are poorly taught and unnecessarily punished by criticism and failure. Machine instruction would permit each student to proceed at his own rate. (6, p. 30)

The education world was not ready for Pressey's machines. As Skinner explained, "Pressey's machines succumbed in part to cultural inertia; the world of education was not ready for them. But they also had limitations which probably contributed to their failure. Pressey was working against a background of psychological theory which had not come to grips with the learning process." (6, p. 32)

Nevertheless, Pressey's pioneering work emphasized four important conditions for effective instruction:

(a) immediate feedback to students' responses;
(b) active student participation in learning;
(c) self-paced instructional tasks; and
(d) the need for capital equipment in realizing the above. (6, p. 32)

Edgar Dale noted another movement in education which converged with that of using self-instructional materials. The movement was developed by Franklin Bobbit and W. W. Charters. It was called "activity analysis." Activity analysis was concerned with discovering the activities performed by the individual student and with his behavior analysis. According to Bobbit (1926), "The curriculum is that performance of the activities in their earlier stages out of which the mature performance grows." (7) Bobbit also noticed that, "It is good to state each activity in terms of what the pupil will do or *experience*. One should avoid stating what he will know or be, since these latter are neither activities nor experiences." (7)

Self-instruction using teaching machines received little attention from educators until the 1950s. Two reasons for the loss of impetus were given by Lysaught and Williams:

First, no provision was made for systematic programming of materials to be used in these machines, and second, the onset of the depression and its impact on social conditions and education offered an unfavorable environment for an "industrial revolution" in the nation's schools. (8)

By the 1950s, more demand was put on education to improve its quality to graduate effective citizens in a technological world which had experienced its first attempts at space travel. In the late fifties teaching machines and programmed instruction were revived. This revival was based on the work of two Harvard psychologists, B. F. Skinner and James

G. Holland. (8, p. 6) In 1960, a comprehensive study by the Department of Audio-Visual Instruction, AECT at present, predicted the following regarding the use of teaching machines and programmed instruction in education:

> Teaching machines and programmed learning can have a major impact on education. Their use can effectively and dependably guide the student's learning-by-doing as he proceeds, as rapidly as his abilities permit, through carefully pretested instructional programs. It can thus be made economically feasible to provide every student with many of the benefits of a skilled private tutor, since auto-instructional materials can anticipate and be responsive to his needs for mastering each aspect of a subject matter. Not only do programmed materials themselves thus have the potential for producing much more efficient learning than has hitherto been generally possible, but their wise use should make possible the much more constructive use of the teacher's talents. (9)

In the 1960s, programmed instruction came into the limelight. Its promise to individualize instruction, to ensure mastery of the subject being learned, and to relieve some of the teachers' time to attend to other areas of teaching, such as counseling, challenged many educators to develop programmed materials. Basic to the development of those materials was a recognition of seven key principles of design:

a. a clear identification of the learner, his learning abilities and background as they relate to the program material;

b. well-stated objectives in measurable terms indicating what the learner would be able to perform or to demonstrate after experiencing the program;

c. a sequence of small steps which will guide the learner from introductory information to more indepth information;

d. continuous learner interaction with the program; after giving the right response to a step, the following step is revealed;

e. immediate evaluation of the learner's response to an item; a correct response is rewarded and the learner is permitted to advance in the program; a wrong response leads the learner to remedial steps until the right response is made;

f. self-instruction to allow the learner to advance in the program according to his own pace; and

g. evaluation of the program to ensure clarity of its items, as well as its suitability to the target learner and the intended objectives of the program.

Two basic approaches of programmed instruction were utilized. The first, a linear approach, was developed by Skinner. In this approach, learning material was organized in a series of successive segments called frames. After each frame, the student was required to answer a question and on the basis of that answer additional frames were presented. Each subsequent frame contained minimal additional information, and led the student a step forward toward the achievement of the program's objectives. If a frame did not lead the student forward, either by introducing new material or by expanding the use of information in previous frames, it was considered as a wasteful frame which had to be changed, revised, or discarded. (10)

The second approach developed by Norman Crowder was called branching. This approach presented to the student after each learning sequence a diagnostic multiple choice array. Depending on the student's choice, he was prompted to advance to another sequence or to branch to a corrective or remedial sequence. After the successful completion of the corrective or remedial sequence, the student was brought back to the point of his previous branching. In this approach the presentation of the learning material was adjusted to the student response. Accordingly, it allowed different students to follow different paths in learning the material depending on their background and performance.

Programmed instruction was faced with a varied degree of enthusiasm from some educators, and with skepticism from others. Proponents of programmed instruction perceived it as an instructional method which would save the teacher's time to attend to valuable and yet neglected objectives of teaching. At the same time it would help individualize instruction.

Those who opposed it thought of it as a cumbersome and mechanical instructional method which was probably more suited for training than for education environments. At the same time, there were those who viewed programmed instruction as a way to replace not only textbooks, but also the teacher.

The polarized reaction to new instructional methods and technology, such as programmed instruction, is common among educators. Usually, there are two opposing points of view. One dictates complete advocacy of the new technology, and the other is exactly the opposite. Somewhere between these opposing points of view, there are educators who can objectively examine the new technology to determine how best it can be used. In 1960, Jerome S. Brunner addressed the opposing points of view regarding teaching machines and programmed instruction. He wrote:

It is still far too early to evaluate the eventual use of such devices (teaching machines), and it is highly unfortunate that there have been such exaggerated claims made by both proponents and opponents. Clearly, the machine is not going to replace the teacher—indeed, it may create a demand for more and better teachers if the more onerous part of teaching can be relegated to automatic devices. Nor does it seem likely that machines will have the effect of dehumanizing learning any more than books dehumanize learning. A program for a teaching machine is as personal as a book: it can be laced with humor or be grimly dull, can either be a playful activity or be tediously like a close-order drill. (11)

Later, in 1969, Dale addressed the claim that programmed instruction will replace textbooks as well as the teacher. He said:

The view that programmed instruction will replace not only textbooks but also the teacher is unsound. Programmed instruction will take over some of the jobs done by teachers and textbooks, just as the textbook replaced some oral instruction by the teacher. Adjunct or supplementary programming will save the teacher time for the intangibles, for guidance in critical thinking and problem solving, for carefully planned large and small group discussion, for developing the independent learner. (7, p. 649)

In spite of the controversy about programmed instruction and teaching machines, significant learning and teaching concepts have been emphasized. It became clear that to design and administer effective learning environments the following points should be considered:

1. There is a need to examine, revise, and redesign the school curricula in the light of the goals of education and the specific objectives of school offerings, and in the light of what instructional technology can offer. The real issue in instructional technology implementation is not how it can fit into the existing curriculum, but rather how can an updated curriculum benefit from its application.
2. A new instructional technology should not be used for its own sake. The student should remain the focus of instruction.
3. Significant attention has to be given to pretesting to determine the student's background and the initial competencies he brings to a learning situation, and to posttesting to determine what the student has achieved. Accordingly, subsequent learning experiences can be planned.

4. There are individual differences among learners not only in their level of intelligence and educational background, but also in which medium of instruction one can perform better. While others can do well with oral presentations and readings, others might find visualization of concepts to be most helpful. Accordingly, learning and teaching materials, especially those designed for self-instruction, have to incorporate a variety of communication media.

5. There is a need to implement an integrated approach to teaching and learning in which a variety of teaching and learning strategies are engineered and implemented with precision. Rich varied learning experiences administered under the guidance of skilled teachers will include conventional learning and teaching materials, such as textbooks, and new material which utilizes new communications technologies.

6. Educators have to continue examining new communications and information technologies which can enhance and extend the instructional capabilities of the teacher. While programmed instruction and teaching machines of the past had certain limitations, new instructional technologies, can overcome those limitations.

In 1960, predicting new developments in technology which can improve the shortcomings of teaching machines, James Finn wrote:

> ...I see several developments. First, it is reasonable to expect that programming for teaching machines will move from the verbal Socratic-Skinner type to the audio-visual-branching type. That is, the machine will present, based upon student pretests, conceptual content using films, slides, filmstrips, tapes, and/or video tape as the medium. The presentation sequences will be longer and the student will be given an opportunity to select additional sequences for further explanation if the machine, through testing, informs him that he needs it. Records, of course, will be maintained instantaneously by miniaturized computers. (12)

Today, Finn's prediction is a reality. Prior to computers, instructional tools, including teaching machines, lacked the potential of implementing the significant teaching and learning principles discussed above.

COMPUTERS IN EDUCATION

Computers, as Dale put it, "can individualize instruction in a way never before done and it can provide valuable data about how students learn. Thus computers can make contributions both to a theory of teaching and to curriculum development." (7, p. 650) In addition, integrated use of computers with other forms of communication media can enhance the interactive learning environment to a level previously imagined by communications media educators. For instance, in 1954, projecting the teaching film of tomorrow, Robert Wagner wrote:

> Films of tomorrow will be deliberately designed to stimulate thinking, to change behavior, and to bring about that sense of participation and sharing which characterizes successful communication and effective learning. Teaching films will, accordingly, be more than an accumulation of facts. They will be provocative and challenging. There will be more "forked-road" situations, and more use of the "open ending." (13)

"Forked-road" situations and "open-ending" treatments are still difficult with the present motion pictures technology. However, transferring a motion pictures film to an optical videodisc which can be controlled by a computer provides the learners with options, including branching, depending on their responses to programs steps. Interactive video is primarily an instructional delivery system in which recorded video material is presented under computer control. Viewers not only see and hear the pictures and sound, they interact with the program by making active responses. Those responses affect the pace and sequence of the presentation. (Please refer to Chapter Eight.)

During the past thirty years, as a result of the dramatic progress in computers and their reduced cost, and the potential of integrated use of computers with other sources of information and educational media resources, the following advantages of the computer as a tool for self-learning are highlighted by many educators:

a. The computer can adjust and adapt to different learners in a way that the printed page never will.
b. The computer is a response-dependent device. It reacts instantaneously to student interaction with the programs, and keeps track of all the responses made.
c. The computer is capable of complex decision-making, and can adjust a learning environment in light of the trend of student responses.
d. The computer can serve many individual students simultaneously.
e. The computer has an extensive capacity to store and manipulate information.
f. The computer can present text information in a variety of colors and styles. It also can present audio messages, graphics, and visuals.

g. The computer can control a multimedia environment. For instance, visual information from videodiscs can be managed, controlled and presented to the student at the right teaching moment.

h. The computer can be used to access information from a variety of rich data banks available on compact discs (CD–ROM) or through information utilities. (Please refer to Chapter Nine, and Appendix II). Such access can help meet the individual needs of the student researcher.

i. The computer can accept a wide variety of input and output devices to accommodate students with special needs.

j. The computer can be used as a projection device of both text and visuals for classroom presentations and discussions.

The above advantages of the computer in teaching combined with a trend for the production of sophisticated instructional software make the computer a valuable tool for learning and education.

Current Uses of Computers in Education

Computers in education are used in a variety of applications: administration, research, and instruction. (14) Educational administrators are finding that microcomputers can help achieve many administrative tasks efficiently. One of the most important benefits of using computers in school administration "is that decisions can be based on more complete and more recent data, helping administrators to make more informed and timely decisions in a variety of areas." (15)

In research, the computer is used as a tool of research to analyze data, sort, retrieve, and interpret information. In institutions of higher learning, the computer itself becomes the object of research, refining its technology and testing its potentials.

In instruction, the computer is used as a subject students study such as in learning about programming, and as a tool of instruction. The term that describes its use as a tool of instruction is commonly known as Computer-Based Education, CBE.

CBE encompasses using the computer in instructional management, and the use of computers to assist instruction.

Computer-Managed Instruction, CMI, refers to the use of computers to manage the instructional environment. The teacher's time spent in administrative activities of the learning environment such as sequencing activities, organizing learning materials, planning and grading assignments, and maintaining students records can be saved by delegating these activities to the computer.

Usually, CMI systems are available on large computers since they require more computing power than what microcomputers can offer. The importance of CMI will increase with the growth of nontraditional forms of delivery of instruction such as in the case of distant learning.

The use of computers to assist in instruction is commonly known as computer-assisted instruction, CAI. The following chapter addresses the current and projected use of CAI.

REFERENCES

1. Highet, Gilbert. THE ART OF TEACHING, New York: Vintage Books, 1957, p. 88.
2. Lumsdaine, A. A. "Teaching Machines: An Introductory Overview," in Lumsdaine, A. A. & Robert Glaser (Editors). TEACHING MACHINES AND PROGRAMMED LEARNING–A SOURCE BOOK, Washington: National Education Association of the United States, 1960, pp. 5–6.
3. Saettler, Paul. A HISTORY OF INSTRUCTIONAL TECHNOLOGY, New York: McGraw Hill, 1968, p. 52.
4. Pressey, S. L. "A Simple Apparatus Which Gives Tests and Scores–and Teaches," in Lumsdaine, A. A. & Robert Glaser (Editors). TEACHING MACHINES AND PROGRAMMED LEARNING–A SOURCE BOOK, Washington: National Education Association of the United States, 1960, pp. 35–41.
5. Pressey, S. L. "A Machine for Automatic Teaching of Drill Material," in Lumsdaine, A. A. & Robert Glaser (Editors). TEACHING MACHINES AND PROGRAMMED LEARNING–A SOURCE BOOK, Washington: National Education Association of the United States, 1960, pp. 42–46.
6. Skinner, B. F. THE TECHNOLOGY OF TEACHING. New York: Educational Division, Meredith Corporation, 1968, p. 30.
7. Dale, Edgar. AUDIOVISUAL METHODS IN TEACHING, Third Edition, New York: The Dryden Press, 1969, p. 628.
8. Lysaught, Jerome P. and Clarence M. Williams. A GUIDE TO PROGRAMMED INSTRUCTION, New York: John Wiley and Sons, Inc., 1963, p. 6.
9. "Concluding Remarks, A Technology of Instruction," in Lumsdaine, A. A. & Robert Glaser (Editors). TEACHING MACHINES AND PROGRAMMED LEARNING–A SOURCE BOOK, Washington: National Education Association of the United States, 1960, p. 572.
10. Brethower, Dale M. PROGRAMMED INSTRUCTION: A MANUAL OF

PROGRAMMING TECHNIQUES, Chicago, Ill: Educational Methods, Inc., 1963, p. 195.

11. Bruner, Jerome S. THE PROCESS OF EDUCATION, Cambridge, Mass: Harvard University Press, 1965, p. 84.

12. Finn, James D. "Technology and the Instructional Process," *Audio-Visual Communication Review,* Department of Audio Visual Instruction, Winter 1960, pp. 5–26.

13. Wagner, Robert W. "The Teaching Film of Tomorrow," *The NewsLetter,* Columbus, Ohio: The Bureau of Educational Research, Ohio State University, Volume XIX, Number 4, January, 1954, p. 3.

14. Digital Equipment Corporation, INTRODUCTION TO COMPUTER-BASED EDUCATION, Marlborough, MA: Education Computer Systems, 1984, pp. 17–23.

15. Connors, T. Eugene and Thomas C. Valesky. USING MICROCOMPUTERS IN SCHOOL ADMINISTRATION, Bloomington, Indiana: Phi Delta Kappa Educational Foundation, 1986, p. 7.

Chapter Five

COMPUTER-ASSISTED INSTRUCTION

Frederick W. Mis

INTRODUCTION

Computer-Assisted Instruction, CAI, encompasses a wide variety of activities that attempt to apply the results of learning theory to practical classroom instruction. Teaching strategies that have been adapted to the computer include drill and practice, tutorials, simulations, and games. In addition, computerized testing, the teaching of programming as a way to improve student problem solving skills, discovery learning using LOGO, and student use or development of data bases, and expert systems can also be categorized as computer-assisted instruction.

This chapter will focus on the more traditional uses of CAI, and introduce some of the more recent adaptations, including discovery learning and the use of data bases and expert systems.

DRILL AND PRACTICE

Computerized drill and practice exercises are among the most common type of CAI. They are a direct outgrowth of programmed instruction strategies which evolved from the behavioristic research of the first half of this century. Drill and practice focuses on the simple pairing of a stimulus and response and provides the student with immediate feedback about his performance on each and every stimulus-response combination. The technique is relatively easy to program, and is applicable to a wide variety of subject areas. Examples of drill and practice exercises include basic arithmetic skills, language vocabulary drills, states and capitals, matching chemical elements with their corresponding symbols, and the matching of Shakespearean quotes with the speaker or some other aspect of the play.

Besides the ease in programming, the popularity of drill and practice can be attributed to the following:

1. Virtually all drill and practice exercises can be completed at the student's own pace, and without teacher intervention. This allows students to gain mastery of materials on an individual basis without consuming precious classroom instruction time.
2. Given the small steps of material presented during each exercise, it is easy to quantify the progress that the student is making. If the drill and practice program provides a record-keeping option, the teachers can easily monitor their student's progress and prepare classroom materials based on the student's level of mastery.
3. Most drill and practice exercises take advantage of color graphics and sound generating capabilities of microcomputers to help motivate the students to use the exercises.
4. It is possible to incorporate drill and practice exercises into a simple game, or to add some competitive aspect to the drill as a reward for mastery of some intermediate level.

Although drill and practice exercises are popular and the quality of these exercises has improved during the last few years, they are not without problems. For example, simple arithmetic drills often take advantage of the computer to randomly generate questions and answers, and determine the degree of difficulty of the problems to be presented based on the student's mastery of the material. However, no matter how sophisticated these programs are, they cannot accurately determine the cause of systematic errors that a student might make. For example, in a series of multidigit addition problems, if the student forgets to carry, the program will inform the student that he is incorrect, and might even simulate the addition process displaying the carry, but this approach does not help the student focus on the reason for his mistake. A similar problem can occur with subtraction when the student must borrow.

For other types of drill and practice exercises it is necessary for the software developer to enter all the questions and answers into data files. Although this can be a long and laborious process, it does offer the software developer complete control over the content of the course, especially if the material is presented sequentially rather than randomly. With random presentation of the materials, the programmer still has the option of grouping the questions in terms of difficulty, and randomly selecting from a particular group rather than from the entire pool of questions. Programs that allow random selection of questions can not insure that each question in a group is of a comparable degree of difficulty. Nor do they insure that questions are not repeated within a specified number of trials.

With the current availability of "expert system" it may be possible to develop intelligent computer-assisted instructional, ICAI. (1) For example, a simple expert system used in libraries guides the user in selecting appropriate reading materials. The system prompts the user to enter his age, gender, and interests. After processing the user's response, the system presents to him an appropriate list of reading material.

Usually, an expert system consists of a set of rules which specify what actions should be undertaken given that a particular set of events has occurred. Expert systems have two major components. The first component consists of a list of rules, specified as a collection of "what-if" relationships, and an "inference engine" which acts to process the data presented to the systems to determine which rules apply. One unique feature of expert systems is a component which extracts the rules that were invoked and applies these rules to the data that was entered to "explain" why a particular action was suggested. It may be possible to incorporate this explanation feature of expert systems with traditional drill and practice exercises in order to help students come to an understanding of the errors they are making in the exercise, and thereby facilitate their mastery of the materials. (2)

TUTORIALS

Tutorials focus on the presentation of material in small steps, frames, that are easily comprehended and assimilated by the student. This frame-by-frame approach to tutorials is also an outgrowth of programmed instruction techniques that were developed in the 1950s and 1960s.

Efficient development of tutorial materials requires the courseware author to either use sophisticated authoring systems, or develop the necessary programming tools to create the components of the tutorial. Some of the most recently developed authoring systems such as Laserworks, Hypercard, and Quest allow the author to interface videodisc with the computer. (3) With these authoring systems, the author has the options of a unified or separate displays for the video and computer-generated material. A unified option allows superimposing of computer text on the video display. (3) In this option one monitor is used. The separate-display option uses two monitors, one to display the computer material and the second to display the video material from the videodisc. The computer controls and coordinates the presentations on both monitors. (For more information on authoring systems, please refer to Appendix I.)

When a course authoring system is not available, the author must develop a suitable substitute. For example, in the early 1980s, the computer center at Fairfield University developed a CAI system to teach APL programming using a DECSystem 20 and the Digital Equipment Corporation's GIGI color graphics terminals. (4) During the early development of the course the authors focused on developing subroutines to generate graphics, randomly generate questions, format text on the screen, keep records, and switch between sections of the course. Only after these tools were developed could the authors begin the actual frame-by-frame layout of the course. These tools provided a potential environment for the development of additional CAI materials, and were refined and later incorporated into a computer-assisted module for the introductory chemistry course at Fairfield University. (5)

Regardless of the sophistication of authoring system employed, it is the overall design of course material that determines the effectiveness of the tutorial. Some of the major design principles that an author should employ are:

1. posing various types of questions—such as multiple choice, true and false, or free-form response—and either matching the answer, or scanning the input for a character string;
2. branching to a different section of the program is based on the user's response;
3. keeping records of the student's performance, and allowing the teacher to easily examine the student's performance; and
4. integrating appropriate features such as full screen graphics, simple animation, or alternative input devices such as touch-sensitive screens to maintain student's interaction with the program.

Steinberg suggested that the development of CAI materials follows a three-phase plan. (6) The first and most important stage is the planning stage. It is here that the author comes to understand the target audience, their needs and their basic skills. During this stage, the course developer formulates the overall goals of the course and develops an initial set of evaluation materials.

In the second stage, the presentation of the materials is generated, evaluation materials are expanded, and the choice of user interface (input device) is made.

During the last stage, details which will allow for the efficient operation of the courseware are added. They might include the development of menus, special introductory and concluding graphics displays, and testing and revision of the evaluation materials. Before the course is ready for general use, the author must document the course and finalize any noncomputer materials and activities that make up the course.

SIMULATIONS

Computer simulations enable the student to examine and manipulate a representation of the real world in a controlled situation. Simulations allow the student to experiment with and experience situations which might otherwise be dangerous or impractical to manipulate directly. With the advent of the computer, the flexibility and quality of simulations have greatly improved. We can mimic activities such as driving a vehicle of some type, examining the results of pollution, traversing the Oregon Trail, or controlling a nuclear power plant.

Recently, Reigeluth and Schwartz concluded that the overall effectiveness of a simulation is determined by three factors: the scenario, the logical model used to represent the situation being simulated, and an instructional overlay which is designed to optimize the student's learning. (9) The instructional overlay is an instructional component which focuses on the teaching of facts and concepts, or principles and procedures.

In general, tutorials provide an effective medium for the presentation of large numbers of facts. However, the strength of a good simulation lies in how well the principles that govern a process or a procedure are presented.

Ideally, the simulation should present a realistic portrayal of the situation being mimicked. However, in some cases it may be more appropriate to simplify the situation to maximize the effectiveness of the instruction. (10) To decide how close the simulation will match the real world situation, we must consider how complex the real world situation is in terms of available stimuli. Then, determine if it is necessary to reduce the number of stimuli in the simulation for the novice user. For example, a flight simulator used by a novice would contain many fewer variables than one used to train Air Force or Navy pilots. On the other hand, the instructional designer of a simulation would like to maximize the amount of transfer from the simulation to the real world, and that makes it necessary for the simulation to mimic the real world as much as possible.

The motivational qualities of a simulation help to determine whether or not the students will actively use it. For example, a simulation filled with action and high resolution graphics might easily entice students to participate in the simulation. On the other hand, a simulation of the economic stability of a corporation which consists of manipulating parameters to generate extensive financial reports might require some external motivation to encourage student participation. For example, the students completing the simulation might receive an additional five points on their final grade.

Simulations can teach new material by employing one or all of following approaches:

1. They may provide the students with the steps and decisions necessary to perform a skill such as driving a car, flying an airplane, or performing basic arithmetic skills.
2. They may allow the student to observe, examine or manipulate the process involved in a situation. For example, a simulation of a gasoline engine might allow the student to control the various cycles involved in the operation of the engine.
3. They may allow the student to manipulate a variety of factors which control some particular outcome. For example, students may manipulate the water temperature of a pond to observe how this affects the oxygen content of the water, hence the survival of its marine population.

Regardless of the approach a simulation employs, there are some general characteristics that are common to all simulations.

Before a student can actively engage in a simulation, he must acquire the basic knowledge required to use the simulation. For example, before one can use a joy stick to guide a plane off a simulated flight deck, the student must orient himself with the controls and dials which provide feedback about the current status of the airplane.

Also, a student must be able to easily restart the simulation, or reduce its complexity so that he can practice as often as he wishes at a comfortable level.

The input device used by the student, or as it is often called, user interface, must be appropriate to the student. For example, if a young child does not possess typing skills needed to use the simulation, the designer could reduce the number of keystrokes necessary to operate the simulation, use a keyboard designed for young children such as the Muppet Keyboard, or use game paddles or a joy stick as the input device.

In using the simulation, immediate feedback is essential. Simple feedback messages displayed on the computer screen can act as a guide for a young student's successful completion of the simulation. With an older student, it may be useful to present additional expository material. This can be accomplished in the form of on-line help. The on-line help could present background information on the real world situation, description of the simulation rules, or special features of the simulation.

When designing a multilevel complex simulation, the developer must include measures to ensure that the student has mastered the current level before allowing him to move on to a more complex and sophisticated level.

With any situation, the designer of the simulation must specify the path or paths that allow the student to successfully complete the simulation, and also specify each and every alternative path that the student may take as a consequence of making a decision. For example, the initial stocking of the student's covered wagon in the *Oregon Trail* simulation can have a dramatic effect on the student's progress to Oregon as the simulation unfolds.

In conclusion, the creative design of a simulation provides students with some of the most innovative and motivational instructional experiences.

GAMES

Playing games is a natural, motivating, and entertaining activity. Before educational software became available on microcomputers, the microprocessors, which make up the heart and soul of a microcomputer, were used to control simple, competitive arcade-style games either between two players, such as in PONG® game, or between a player and the computer, such as in Space Invaders® game. The first software that was readily available on the early microcomputers was variations of video arcade games. For example, when the Apple II was first introduced, the software that was bundled with the computer was a package of simplified video arcade games written in BASIC. When the IBM PC was first introduced, a number of simple games were included on the DOS disk to help demonstrate the features of the machine. More recently, games packaged with the computers have been designed to instruct the user on some aspect of the computer's operation. For example, simple games were included with the first Macintosh and Apple IIGS computers to help the novice user become accustomed to using the mouse as an input device.

Games make their way into the classroom with little or no effort. Some of these games are merely entertaining and are used by the teacher as a reward for performance in other classroom activities, while other games help teach the students something about the real world. For example, *Lemonade Stand,* is a popular game with children and adults. It helps teach the players about the relationship between demand for a product and the price that can be charged for that product. During the past year, the author demonstrated that game to inservice teachers enrolled in an introductory course on computers in education. It was difficult to get the class away from the game. Before the end of the course some teachers decided to introduce the game to their classes.

Other software, initially introduced to the public as a game, has been found to be useful as an instructional tool. For example, Chris Crawford's *Balance of Power* has been used in politics courses to help students come to an understanding of the many factors that influence global politics in the nuclear age.

Often, the competitive nature of games is incorporated into many drill and practice exercises. *Math Blaster* incorporates the features of a game to teach simple arithmetic skills. The student is presented with a math problem, and five possible answers. A missile moves back and forth across the bottom of the screen, and when the missile is below the answer that the student thinks is correct, the student launches the missile, and receives immediate feedback as to whether he is correct or not.

Similarly, *Math Baseball* provides the student with an arithmetic problem that he must solve. With *Math Baseball* the student selects the degree of difficulty of a problem by choosing whether he wishes to swing for a single, double, triple, or home run. There is a time limit placed on the student, and if he answers the problem correctly in the allotted time he will be allowed to advance around the baseball diamond.

With the recent advances in hardware capabilities, and the subsequent development of games that make use of this new hardware, we are finding that the games being developed today have taken on a new level of sophistication. Mastery of these games is no longer contingent on the development of good eye-hand coordination or quick reflexes. Although these attributes are still helpful, the new games require the player to learn a variety of complex strategies. For example, in *Super Mario Brothers*, the player advances through eight worlds in an effort to rescue the princess. The degree of difficulty is increased by adding new obstacles, and increasing the number of options open to the player. In this and similar games, the player's problem-solving capabilities are challenged along with his reflexes.

Characteristics of Games

1. The game must be easy to learn. Yet, it must challenge even the most proficient player. For example, the ideal game should entice a six-year-old child, as well as his teachers or his parents.
2. Success in the game must depend on the player's skill and not on chance. This should hold true both for recreational as well as educational games.
3. Ideally, the player must be able to successfully complete the game by following the rules, and not by taking advantage of some particular peculiarity in the logic of the game. For example, some of the newer and more complex arcade games allow the player to continue where they left off, even though the stated object of the game is to reach the goal in one play.

DATA BASES & EXPERT SYSTEMS

Student-Developed Data Bases & Expert Systems

A data base consists of information about a topic and its related field. An expert system goes beyond that to include a set of rules to prompt the user in making use of that information.

Student development of data bases provides an alternative approach of the standard tutorial approach to CAI. Rather than providing the student with information, the student develops, refines, or expands a knowledge base. This approach to the use of computers in education emphasizes the student's knowledge of a subject, and his ability to apply this knowledge to appropriate situations. The student becomes a "knowledge engineer." A knowledge engineer is a person who gathers all the relevant information available on a topic, and formulates the rules which specify how that knowledge is applied to a particular situation. According to Lippert, the student knowledge engineer follows the process described below.

1. Define the problem and its particular characteristics.
2. Gather all the information they can about the topic.
3. Organize this information into concepts.
4. Generate rules for applying the concepts.
5. Validate the rules that were generated. (1)

Although this process does not guarantee that the students develop a usable expert system, most educators feel that the process helps the students develop problem solving and other higher order thinking skills. (7) For example, the students will develop a thorough understanding of the knowledge required to solve a problem, and the relationships between the individual pieces of information. In addition, by allowing the students to choose the expert system they will develop, they will perceive their endeavors as a fun activity, (7); and ones that have a purpose. (1)

Lippert has suggested that the results of recent advancements in artificial intelligence, AI, research have provided educators with the tools (expert systems) for the development of intelligent computer-assisted instruction, ICAI. (1) These tools can be incorporated into CAI as decision aids, an explanation component of an intelligent tutoring system, or as an adjunct to a student's refinement of his understanding of a topic by having the student act as a knowledge engineer to develop an expert system. (See also 7.)

This approach tends to focus on the student and his or her ability to solve problems. It is a departure from the usual CAI model where the courseware mimics the teacher as lecturer and grader. Lippert envisions a new classroom situation where the teacher is a coach and a project designer, and does not necessarily possess all the answers. (1) (See also 8.)

Teacher-Developed Data Bases & Expert Systems

Data or knowledge bases and expert systems can be used as resources which students explore to locate additional information they need to fully understand a topic of study. For example, one of the objectives in a course focusing on Shakespearean plays could be to come to an appreciation of a particular play or plays. Often, students might find a difficulty in:

1. understanding the relationships between the characters;
2. understanding the history or geography of the play's location;

3. determining how that play relates to other Shakespearean plays; and

4. appreciating and focusing on particular quotes given the incredible number of quotes that are brought up in class discussion.

Lynch developed a Shakespearian plays data base. It presents an overview of each play, a detailed summary of each scene, and a tree-structured description of the relationship between the characters in each play. It links quotes with characters, and presents a variety of historical and geographical information that allows the student to come to a better understanding of the play. (11) The students can study the data base in any order that they wish moving freely from identifying a particular quote, to reviewing a scene, or examining the relationship between the characters.

In social studies, we often try to get our students to understand how a group of people become assimilated into a particular culture. The history of the United States is filled with examples of various ethnic groups trying to become assimilated into the mainstream of American life. Getting students to understand what these people went through in their struggle to "make it in the new world" is difficult. One approach is to have students pretend that their families have just arrived from a foreign country and must find work and set up a household. The students would then research the era during which the ethnic group arrived in the United States and specify the level of education, type of job training, quality of housing available to the new immigrants, and their home culture which they carried with them to this country. Given a sufficient supply of resource materials, each student might eventually gather enough material to come to an understanding of the era.

Alternatively, the teacher could create a data base which would link a series of files that would describe a large number of different families, the housing stock available to the ethnic group, a job bank and any other information that might constrain the immigrants' assimilation into the "new world." After creating this data base, the student searches it to extract information relevant to his family, and then asks a series of "what if" questions, to determine what it would take for his family to make it in the "new world."

At the end of his explorations the student would then summarize the history of his "family" as it becomes assimilated into the new culture. (12)

In both of these examples, the teacher has put together the data base which the students explore. However, the extent to which the students explore the data base, and the path that the students follow in this exploration are not completely under the control of the instructor. In comparing Drill and Practice programs with these new approaches we are seeing a movement toward more student control over the acquisition of new material. Papert suggested that the student learns best when he identifies the material being studied as his own. (13)

DISCOVERY LEARNING

Most of the skills that we acquire prior to entering elementary school are learned not through formal instruction but through self-discovery learning. During the first five years of our lives we learn language, basic numerical skills, basic interpersonal skills, and a foundation for our moral standards. To paraphrase Fulgham, we have discovered a great deal of what we need to know before we finish kindergarten. (14)

It is this discovery aspect of learning that is often missing from most of our formal education. Papert and his associates at the Massachusetts Institute of Technology had initially been concerned with how children master the fundamental concepts and operations of mathematics. As they developed LOGO, they came to understand that both the process by which we acquire knowledge, and the knowledge itself must be linked. When a skill is essential for our day-to-day existence, it is acquired relatively easily. For example, preschool children are rarely given formal language instruction, yet they learn to speak, and they learn most of the grammatical rules which govern how they put words together to form sentences.

Papert believed that through the use of LOGO we can make learning mathematics, logic, elementary computer science, and some basic concepts of artificial intelligence as natural as the preschool learning of language.

Papert stated that LOGO has no floor and no ceiling. However, the limits of personal computers that we find in the classroom have placed limits on the ceiling. It is easier, however, to bring down LOGO to a level where almost any student can benefit from interacting with it. At the kindergarten level, teachers can easily modify LOGO so that a single keystroke can evoke an elementary turtle graphic command. For example, the system can be set up so that pressing the keys F, B, R, and L makes the turtle move forward, backward, turn right, or turn left. As the children become familiar with these commands and discover how they can be used to draw familiar shapes, additional single keystroke commands to draw circles and triangles can be added easily.

Before the children reach middle school they would be able to use and understand the structure of LOGO commands and write simple procedures that draw geometric figures. As they proceed through middle school, the children can be introduced to the other aspects of LOGO which allow them to manipulate numbers, words and lists of numbers or words. Later, they can be introduced to more complex problem solving situations and the fundamentals of programming. In general, LOGO makes it possible for students to develop and apply mathematical principles and problem-solving skills to other areas of study.

During the past few years, LOGOWRITER was introduced. It added simple word processing capabilities to LOGO. A student can use LOGO-WRITER to write a story, then illustrate it using turtle graphics.

Recently, an interface was introduced which allows LOGO to control motorized LEGO constructions. A child can now create a motorized LEGO vehicle and use LOGO commands to control its movements. The vehicle can be made to go forward, backward, turn right, turn left, and/or follow a geometric path. In addition to these movements, the child can write commands which will turn on or off headlights, sound horns or buzzers of the mechanized LEGO vehicle.

The above features allow LOGO to enhance other instructional activities such as understanding robots, linking language skills with graphics, developing educational games, and introducing young students to the application of artificial intelligence.

CONCLUSION

Computer-assisted instruction may finally make a substantial impact on the way we teach. Until recently, the best materials could only be found on large mainframe computers. With the advent of the first microcomputers, educators attempted to develop courseware that would meet the needs of their students. However, these machines were expensive and limited in their capabilities. The new Apple IIGS, Macintosh, IBM PS2, and NeXT computers bring many necessary features of a powerful and sophisticated computer to the desk of the individual.

The development of new software such as Hypercard, and recent advances in artificial intelligence have made sophisticated programming tools available to both the courseware developer and individual user. The combining of new hardware and software gives the teacher and student the opportunity to make the computer an integral part of the educational experience.

REFERENCES

1. Lippert, Renate C., "Expert Systems: Tutors, Tools and Tutees," *Journal of Computer-Based Instruction,* 16:11–19, 1989.
2. Brown, J. S., Burton, R. R., and de Kleer, J., "Pedagogical, Natural Language and Knowledge Engineering Techniques in SOPHIE I, II and III," In Sleeman, D. and Brown, J. S. (Eds): INTELLIGENT TUTORING SYSTEMS. New York: Academic Press Inc., 1982.
3. Phillipo, John, "An Educator's Guide to Interfaces and Authoring Systems," *Electronic Learning,* Vol. 8, 42–45, January, 1989.
4. Schurdak, John J. and Mis, Frederick W., "The Use of Color in CAI at Fairfield University," *EDU,* 20:218–219, 1982.
5. Lisman, Frederick, An Interview with the Author, 1989.
6. Steinberg, Esther R. TEACHING COMPUTER TO TEACH. Hillsdale, N.J.: Lawrence Erlbaum Associates, 1984.
7. Knox-Quinn, Carolyn, "A Simple Application and a Powerful Idea: Using Expert System Shells in the Classroom," *The Computing Teacher,* 16:12–15, 1989.
8. Watt, Molly, "A Reflective Teacher's Interventions With a Tentative Learner of LOGO: A Case Study," *The Computing Teacher,* 16:51–53, 1989.
9. Reigeluth, Charles M. and Schwartz, Ellen, "An Instructional Theory For the Design of Computer-Based Simulations," *Journal of Computer-Based Instruction,* 16:1–10, 1989.
10. Alessi, S. "Fidelity in the Design of Instructional Simulations," Paper presented at the Annual Meeting of the American Educational Research Association, Washington, D.C., 1987.
11. Lynch, Donald, "The Shakespeare Library," Paper presented at Brown University, March, 1989.
12. Honeycutt, James, An Interview with the Author, 1989.
13. Papert, Seymour. MINDSTORMS. New York: Basic Books, 1980.
14. Fulgham, Robert. ALL I REALLY NEED TO KNOW I LEARNED IN KINDERGARTEN. New York: Villard Books, 1988.

DISKOGRAPHY

Oregon Trail
MECC
3490 Lexington Ave. North
Saint Paul, Mn 55126-8097

Lemonade Stand
Apple Computer,
1020 Bandley Drive,
Cupertion, Ca. 95014

Balance of Power
Mindscape, Inc.
3444 Dandee Road,
Northbrook, Il. 60062

Math Blaster
Davidson & Associates
La Crescenta, California, 91214

Math Baseball
Educational Activities Inc.
P.O.B. 392 Freeport, N.Y. 11520

Super Mario Brothers
Nintendo of America, Inc.
Included with the Nintendo Entertainment System.

PART II
INTERACTIVE TELEVISION

Interactive television is an instructional delivery system which allows for student interaction with the teacher, and/or with the teaching program.

In the first case, a two-way delivery system is used. The teacher and the students interact through audio and video channels. There are different configurations for the achievement of live-interaction between the students and the teacher through interactive television. A two-way full-motion live video is the most sophisticated system of delivery. In this system both the teacher and the students at the remote sites have television cameras, transmission, and television receiving devices. Some school systems have been able to arrange with cable television operators the leasing of two channels on the cable system for this purpose. One channel carries the television signal from the teacher to the students, and the second channel carries the signal from the students at the remote site to the teacher at the originating site. This allows both the teacher and the students to see and hear each other.

Other configurations include using one-way video, from the teacher to the students, and two-way audio. Others include, in addition to two-way audio and one-way video, the use of slow-scan video to carry the students' feedback to the teacher. Some schools found out that the use of fax machines to send in assignments to and from either direction can augment the interactive television environment.

Chapter Six, The Cable Classroom Project, describes the cable connection between three towns in Northeastern Connecticut which utilizes two cable television channels.

Chapter Seven, The University of Lowell Instructional Network, Using Technology to Expand Learning Opportunities, addresses the work being done at the University of Lowell Instructional Network, ULIN. ULIN seeks to build on existing knowledge of how teaching with media affects the learning environment. Its focus is not on the glorification of the medium, but the implications of the technology on school organization, school curricula, student learning, and staff development.

In the second case, interactive video programs are centered upon computer-controlled, random-access optical videodiscs. Students interact with the program by making active responses which will affect the pace and sequence of presentations. Chapter Eight, Interactive Video, describes an approach for schools to make effective use of the two of the most powerful communication technologies of our age: the computer and television.

Chapter Six

THE CABLE CLASSROOM PROJECT

PETER STONE

INTRODUCTION

The Cable Classroom Project is a distance learning project that makes use of the two educational access channels on the local cable TV system to share instruction between high schools in the towns of Somers, East Windsor, and East Granby in Connecticut. The activities of the teacher and students at the origination site are seen and heard on one channel, while the students at the receiving site are seen and heard over the other channel. Thus, a two-way video conference is possible. (See Figure VI-1, and Figure VI-2.)

At different times during the regular school day, the three schools

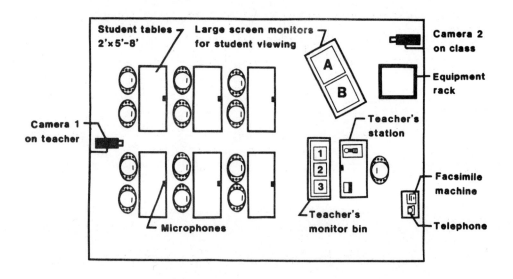

Figure VI-1 The Cable Classroom Design

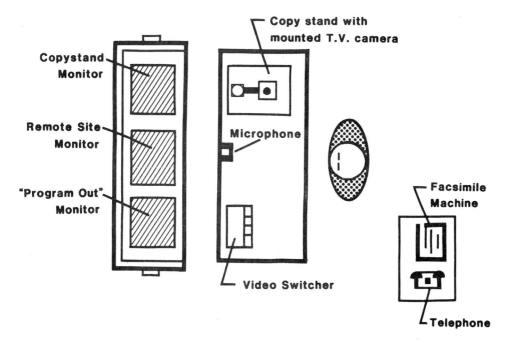

Figure VI-2 The Cable Classroom Teacher's Station

share classes in different two-site combinations. Each site is equipped with video cameras, TV monitors, microphones and speakers to provide a fully interactive setting. In addition, there is a separate phone line at each site with a facsimile machine that makes it possible to distribute and collect written work during class.

The system makes it possible to share a variety of classes depending on the program needs of the participating schools. To date, cable class offerings have included Advanced Composition, Stenography 1, Stenography 2, French 4 and Music Theory 1.

RATIONALE AND PURPOSE

In each of the school districts participating in the Cable Classroom Project, the educational program at the high school level has come under a great deal of pressure due to low enrollment. Enrollments in grade 9–12 in each district are small, under 400 students, and student numbers are expected to decline further over the next five years. With fewer and fewer students enrolled in some classes, the assignment of staff to teach these classes becomes more difficult to justify.

Participating school districts have to drop or restrict course offerings, which has had a direct and negative impact on the educational program. Especially when compared to the course offerings at larger high schools in the area, it is obvious that there is a growing inequity in educational opportunity for students in the smaller school districts. This is happening at the time when boards of education at the state and local level are advocating higher academic standards and increased graduation requirements. This trend is a reflection of higher expectations from the public in general.

In response, school administrators have actively explored different arrangements for sharing programs between school districts. Busing students to another district for part of the school day was explored. Mounting costs of transportation, the class time that students miss while in transit, and a certain reluctance that students show to be parted from their friends and familiar surroundings are negative aspects of the busing option.

Video conferencing was proposed as an alternative means of sharing instruction between schools. The development of this technically-based system offers distinct advantages over the busing option and at the same time opens the door for other types of programs in the future.

PROJECT PREREQUISITES

Within a year and a half of receiving the first grant award, the Cable Classroom Project was up and running with four full-semester courses. The rapid development of the program was largely due to a number of significant local circumstances that were happily exploited:

1. All of the participating school districts are in the same cable franchise area.
2. The two educational access channels on the local cable system were available for the asking.
3. The general manager of the local cable company had personal experience with distance learning at the university level.
4. The business philosophy of the cable company genuinely fostered the development of the cable system as a community resource.
5. The state department of education had just implemented two new grant programs that were intended to promote cooperative pro-

grams between school districts and to develop pilot projects that used technology to address school program needs.

6. Enough grant funding was available over a three-year period to purchase and install most of the equipment needed to establish the cable classroom sites.

7. The high school principals involved were well established, had a very good relationship with their staffs, and were ready to work together to see the program evolve.

8. The candidate for project coordinator possessed the necessary background and initiative to assume responsibility for moving the project along.

This is more than a list of fortunate circumstances. For the Cable Classroom Project these were essential preconditions. If any one had been missing, then the project probably would not have been attempted at all.

Of all these circumstances, access to the cable delivery system was the most critical. Because the delivery system is such a critical part of distance learning, it may be wise in the planning stages of a similar project to consider the technology "cart" before the program "horse" and seek to enlist program partners that will have easy access to the same delivery system from the start.

THE COOPERATING AGENCIES

There are seven major cooperating agencies involved in the Cable Classroom Project with additional subgroups in each school district. Each group has a contribution and role to play in the project.

1. The State Department of Education

The Connecticut State Department of Education was the first and foremost cooperating agency in this project. Two grant programs sponsored by the DOE provided more than $66,000 over three years in support of the pilot phase of the Cable Classroom Project.

In addition to the considerable financial support, state officials provided personal encouragement. As the members of the project advisory board, the cable class teachers, the teacher aides and the students worked to develop the project, there was a sense that they were pioneers in the field. What they were doing would have important ramifications in the state. Their progress was being watched with great interest and their accomplishments were viewed with pride by those state officials charged with overseeing the grant program.

The DOE went to great lengths to convince the legislature that a grant program was needed to address a particular shortcoming. The proof of that claim comes with the development of a successful project at the local level that the participating schools rave about, and that serves as a model site for other districts in the state.

2. The Local Cable Company

Continental Cablevision proved to be a full partner in the development of the project. At every juncture, the general manager, the programming director and the technical staff worked to find solutions to the problems that were encountered. Much of the technical work was not directly required of them by the franchise agreement, but they took it on just the same because it was a challenge and because they wanted to establish themselves as an important resource for the communities they serve.

The cable system now has two educational access channels, in addition to other public access channels. The up-to-date technical system that was installed incorporates sophisticated technical features that the cable classroom project takes advantage of. The cable classroom districts were the first to come forward with a proposal for the regular use of the educational access channels.

In a project like this, the payback for the cable company comes from good media coverage, good relations with the community and from recognition as a pioneer in distance learning. These are not insignificant and intangible commodities for cable companies because of a number of critical challenges the cable operators face. For instance, there is a general perception that cable companies are taking advantage of the monopoly they are granted when franchise areas are awarded. As a result there might be considerable political pressure to shorten the term of the franchise agreement so that cable operators will be more responsive to community needs.

In the foreseeable future, optical fiber technology will be used by telephone companies to provide phone service to individual homes and businesses. Optical fiber has the capacity to transmit much more information at the same time than do standard phone lines and cable TV lines put together. In the past, phone companies have only provided the transmission conduit. It seems that now they might be looking to provide content services, including cable TV types of programming, to individual homes as well. In the future we may be using video-phones, participating in "distant learning classes" without ever leaving home, choosing among 100 TV channels and never be aware of the computer transmissions passing over a single optical fiber cable to each home. The monthly bill for all of this may come from the phone company alone.

At present, a reasonable arrangement with the cable company would cover the basic technical requirements for video conferencing between different school sites in the cable area, including:

1. Educational access channel space. One channel per town would be ideal. Two channels to serve all towns in the franchise area is the minimum that will allow video conferencing.
2. The capability of originating a cable broadcast from any public institution in the cable area.
3. Assistance with information and possibly the acquisition of the equipment required to match the technical specifications of the cable system.
4. Assistance with the installation of switching equipment at the head end facility which will allow different "upstream" signals to be routed onto regular "downstream" TV channels at different times of the day.
5. The general maintenance of the cable delivery system up to the cable drop at each site.

It is probably unreasonable to ask a cable company to provide or maintain any equipment inside the cable classroom sites or any equipment that is installed at the headend facility that is for the exclusive use of the project. Once the technical pieces are in place, the only obligation of the cable company should be to maintain the quality of the broadcast signal over the cable system in the same way that they do for all channels.

3. The Local Cable Advisory Group

Citizens advisory groups to the cable company are required as a part of the franchise agreement. Each group will have its own scheme for representative membership that is written into bylaws. Membership will often include an appointed representative from each school district in addition to at-large representation from each community. The ability of advisory groups to affect change varies considerably from franchise to franchise. In areas where customer service is poor and the cable company is unwilling to provide for community access, the advisory groups seem to be the most active. Regardless of the strength of the advisory group, it is an important participant. It bestows legitimacy to the use of the educational access channels. If any individual or organization is going to question that use or propose another use, the cable advisory council is the group that can hear the arguments and make the final determination—provided that it is properly prepared for that role ahead of time.

The Cable Advisory Council was formally approached for its support of the project. The reaction of the group was very favorable and there was little objection to allowing the use of the educational access channels. There were several points raised in the discussion, however, that were significant. There was a concern that the three participating school districts would be setting up an exclusive operation and that the project would not be open to all school districts. How would scheduling conflicts be resolved when other groups wanted to make use of the same educational access channels? It was always the intention of the project to be open for expansion with the option for additional partners joining in the future. Realistically, the number of sites that could participate in a seven-period day with two channels available is limited. In addition, the $18,000 cost of equipping a cable classroom site without grant support is prohibitive. For these reasons, taking on additional partners has not been likely to pose a problem.

The issues of jurisdiction and procedures to handle potential conflicts can be resolved by the education committee of the advisory council. The membership of the education committee consists of representatives from all the school districts in the cable area. There are three members, one from each of the cable classroom towns, who are sure to attend all meetings. Formal proposals from that group serve to establish that the education committee will consider all proposed uses of the educational access channels, and that any scheduling conflicts will be resolved according to written procedures.

The best way to maintain a good relationship with the cable advisory council is first, to make sure that a representative from the school district attends meetings regularly, and second, work to develop the use of the cable system for the benefit of all the school districts in the cable area.

4. The Regional Education Service Center

On the grant application to the state DOE, it helps to include the regional education service center, RESC, as a participant in the project. The state-wide organizational scheme for regional service is reinforced when the area RESC is involved in an interdistrict project, and there is a greater level of confidence in the proper management of the program. RESC executive directors have more contact with state officials than do local superintendents and they can often provide valuable information about DOE interests and priorities. RESC directors have experience with the issues involved in cooperative programs. If meetings bog down they can often raise the discussion above immediate local concerns. A RESC staff member below the rank of executive director may not have the same contribution to make.

The Capital Region Education Council is the area RESC that has been a partner in the Cable Classroom Project from the start. The influence and the supporting role that the executive director has had on the project have been highly significant to the success of the project.

While listing the area RESC as a participating agency is worthwhile, it may not be a good idea to have the RESC sponsor the grant application. When the RESC serves as the fiscal agent, 10 percent of the grant total automatically goes to the RESC for administrative overhead costs.

The fiscal procedures established by the RESC can be agonizingly slow and inflexible. For the person who is actually doing the work of ordering and installing equipment to meet program deadlines, dealing with the RESC business office can be very frustrating. One suggestion is to use the Other Purchased Services budget line to make all equipment purchases through a vendor who will forward monthly bills to the RESC, rather than try to forward individual purchase order requests for equipment to the RESC.

The RESC may not be the logical agency to coordinate and manage the project overall. Unless there is a RESC staff member who has the required technical expertise or has specific experience with distance learning, there is no advantage in taking day-to-day responsibility for the project out of local hands. The project coordinator is most effective when he or she is on the scene, knows the staff members involved and can tend to details in a timely manner.

5. Local School Districts

A formal vote of the board of education is required in order to take part in a grant program. As a group they need to be convinced that the project is well conceived, that it will benefit students, that teachers won't go on strike because of it, and that ongoing costs will be reasonable. While regular progress reports to the board serve to maintain interest, outright enthusiasm for the project can be generated if cable course offerings include a favorite subject like Latin, Calculus, or AP French. Positive publicity from the local press also helps to win the support of board members.

The superintendents of the participating school districts meet at several points in order to assure each other that there is a serious commitment to the project for the following year and beyond. From these meetings the principals receive the word to go ahead with planning and scheduling. If major obstacles come up, superintendents are called upon to intercede in order to get the project moving again.

The principals make the decisions about which classes will be offered over cable, which teachers will be assigned to teach them and when they will meet during the school day. Planning is made more difficult because all of this must be coordinated between participating schools. It can happen that the entire school schedule must be switched around in order to accommodate a very few people.

When the Cable Classroom Project first started, there were three veteran principals managing events at the three high schools. Within nine months, two out of the three principals resigned and their positions were filled by new principals. It takes time to gain control of everyday events and to build relationships with staff members, and it is exactly those aspects of the principal's job that are required by the project. The net result was that the same cable class offerings were repeated in the second year, and the program did not expand to include other subject areas or other types of uses. As it stands now, the program is underutilized and does not address the most important program needs at each school.

Teacher unions are most concerned with protecting teacher jobs and working conditions. A distance learning project could be perceived as a threat to both concerns. Classes that combine the enrollment from two schools could conceivably leave one teacher short a teaching assignment. Technophobic teachers could be forced to conduct class in a room surrounded by equipment for students, whom they have never met, over an open cable channel that can be viewed in several thousand homes.

The level of trust between teachers and administrators is a key element. In school districts where there's a history of angry battles between the union and administrators, the program should be presented in a careful and nonthreatening manner. The presenter should be prepared for a barrage of "what if . . . " questions from staff members. The superintendent and the board of education should be willing to address teacher concerns in contract language.

For the Cable Classroom Project, an addendum to the teachers' contract was developed and adopted in two of the three towns participating in the cable classroom project. Once it was in place, all anxiety about the project seemed to fade away. A more detailed discussion of the provisions of the contract follows in another section.

6. The Project Advisory Board

The composition of the Cable Classroom Project Advisory Board is determined by the different agencies involved in the project. Formal membership includes representatives from:

The board of education (one per district)
The high school administration (one per district)
The teaching staff (two per district)
The high school student body (two per district)
The community-at-large (one per town)
The Capital Region Education Council (the area RESC, one)
Continental Cablevision (one)
The Area 25 Cable Advisory Council (one)

Nonvoting membership on the project advisory board includes the project coordinator, the project evaluator, all past and present cable class teachers, and representatives from other towns in the cable area. At the insistence of one teachers' union, there are two teachers per district with voting power equal to the board member and the administrator from each district.

In the pilot phase, the project advisory board met on-the-air four times a year to discuss project developments, address the various issues that arise, plan future activities and forward recommendations to boards of education and other participating groups. For the most part, the project coordinator used the meetings to inform the members about progress and problems, and to propose different policies for consideration and adoption.

Bringing members up to date on the status of the project and upcoming decisions is as important as the discussion of project issues. Each member is serving as a representative to another group, and the importance of relaying information back to the constituent group was emphasized. In turn, the advisory board provides a forum for the participating agencies to bring forward any concern that they may have for discussion.

7. The Project Coordinator

A rare individual is needed to coordinate and manage a distance learning project in the implementation stage. The want-ad for the job would read: "Strong self-motivation and personal initiative required, willing to put in a great deal of extra time, is comfortable dealing with several private and public agencies at the same time, is sensitive to the concerns of the different subgroups within the agencies, has a solid background in the audiovisual field and is willing to learn much more, prepares budgets and generates purchase orders, writes grant proposals, newsletters and project updates, conducts video conference meetings, entertains visitors, and trains teachers and aides—all with no assistance and never enough time in the day."

The coordinator of a distance learning project is a true technocrat. This person can function most effectively with some appreciation for the juggling act involved in coordinating all the details, unrestricted use of a telephone, occasional help with mailings, and a generous allotment of time during the school day to pursue project business.

STAFFING PATTERNS

The project manager and the school principals will be doing most of the work that is required during the implementation phase of the project. Once the program is fully up and operating, many of the tasks performed by the project manager can be spread comfortably to others in a staffing pattern that will ensure that the project operates smoothly on a day-to-day basis.

1. Cable Class Teachers

The primary task of cable classroom teachers is to conduct class for two groups of students at the same time in a setting that is generated electronically. Though the cable classrooms are set up to allow the teacher to conduct class in as normal a manner as possible, there is still an array of equipment that teachers have to learn to deal with. Teachers turn on equipment and flip switches at the start and at the end of class. Controls are arranged so that the whole process takes less than ten seconds. Teachers receive about two hours of training when they first start, and each year they get a refresher workshop. Each teacher is provided with a full operations manual as well as a reference sheet listing the steps for start-up and shutdown.

Teachers receive informal coaching from other cable teachers, from the local program manager and from the program coordinator. If the teacher aide cannot resolve the difficulties when technical problems arise, the local program manager can be called upon. If technical problems prevent the class from continuing, assignments are faxed to the remote site and both groups of students continue working on their own.

The cable class has become one of the regular teaching assignments for a teacher, with no extra pay or planning time provided. The staff members that volunteer to teach over cable usually display a poise and self-confidence that comes across well on TV.

2. Cable Class Teacher Aides

The teacher aides do a number of things to ensure that cable classes run smoothly. The remote cable classroom sites are always supervised by aides who assist the teacher with the exchange of student papers, make adjustments to equipment if needed, keep teachers informed of upcoming inservice days and special events that may interrupt class, remind teachers about grade reporting deadlines, see that remote site students get extra help if they need it, follow through with assignments when the teacher is absent and deliver fax messages to people in the building so that project business can proceed.

Teacher aides also receive two hours of training that includes some time with the teacher that they will be assisting. In training, the emphasis is on equipment operation and technical troubleshooting. After a few months in the cable classroom, teacher aides are able to solve most technical problems on their own.

In many high schools there is already a teacher aide on the staff who can be assigned to duties in the cable classroom. Teacher aides are usually receptive to the idea, given the choice between the cable classroom and some other duty assignment.

3. Local Program Managers

Each site needs someone on hand who knows how the technical system works, can troubleshoot technical problems, looks after the upkeep of the facility and plans for improvements, sets up for nonregular uses of the cable classroom facility, and trains, assists, and coaches cable teachers and aides. The local program manager is the primary contact person in the building for project business and should also serve as a voting member of the project advisory board and the cable advisory council.

The local program manager should be paid an extra stipend similar to that paid a faculty advisor to a student club. This person would be trained initially by the program coordinator and continues to work with the coordinator to ensure that the program runs smoothly.

4. High School Principals

In most ways, the role of the principal doesn't change for the cable classroom project. Principals are still involved in the scheduling of cable classes and the assignment of staff. They evaluate their teachers' performances in person and they handle the serious discipline problems. Principals are expected to attend the meetings of the project advisory board, and at other meetings they are expected to explain and defend the project.

The cable classroom project also brings some new twists to the role of the principal. Scheduling cable classes requires a great deal of coordination within and between high schools. Principals are put in the position of recruiting staff volunteers to teach cable classes. The staffing patterns required to manage the program need to be developed, supervised and evaluated.

5. Program Coordinator

Once all the equipment is installed, and the technical system reaches a final configuration, the job of the project manager becomes that of an overall program coordinator. In addition to serving as the local program manager at one of the schools, the program coordinator continues to serve as chairman of the project advisory board and chief liaison with the different cooperating agencies as well as the technical service. The coordinator provides training for local program managers, teachers and aides, and generally supervises the ongoing technical aspects of the program, including research into possible improvements to the system.

6. The Technical Support Service

Technical support for the project is provided through a contract with a local technical service company. The contract covers the regular maintenance and repair of equipment housed in each cable classroom site and at the cable headend facility. When an assortment of equipment is interconnected in a system, there are additional system maintenance requirements as well. The contract also provides for emergency service as well as technical research into equipment requirements for project expansion.

PROJECT OUTCOMES

At the end of each school year, an extensive questionnaire is completed by all the cable class teachers, teacher aides and students. Their responses provide the best insight into the strengths and weakness of the program. A sampling of the questionnaire results follows:

1. Teachers and teacher aides did not feel that it was overly difficult to teach a lesson and operate equipment at the same time.
2. To the students, it seemed as though the teachers and aides knew how to operate the equipment, and when technical problems did occur, they were minor and infrequent and quickly resolved.
3. Teachers, aides, and students were satisfied with the facsimile machine as a means of exchanging papers.
4. The teachers and aides felt that students at both sites could be seen and heard, and that all students were free to interrupt to ask a question at any time.

5. The technology does obstruct communication to some degree. Teachers felt that they had to work harder to create a more personal atmosphere. Teachers got to know the students academically, but not well enough personally.

6. The students missed the opportunity to get to know each other better. The teachers planned social gatherings early in the fall so that both groups of students could meet face to face. At least two other gatherings were planned at other times of the year.

7. Student suggestions for improving communication included class visits, chatting on the air, and open class discussions.

8. 75 percent of the students liked being on TV, and 90 percent indicated that it did not bother them and that it took less than two weeks to get used to it.

9. Teachers and aides felt that student behavior was constructive and attentive, and that students learned as much or more than they would have in a regular class.

10. Teachers felt that the students at both sites learned equally and that the remote site students were generally not at a disadvantage.

11. Teachers said that they did not change their approach or teaching style to suit the TV medium, though they did some things differently in class.

12. Before cable classes started, teachers were most concerned about the equipment, the interaction between teacher and students, how good a job they would do and how they would appear on TV.

13. After a full year of cable classes, teacher concerns included matching school calendars and daily schedules, and the amount of prep time it takes to do a good job on TV.

14. All teachers and aides felt that cable teaching was an enjoyable experience overall, and that it seems to work well with some limitations.

15. Advice for new cable teachers included these suggestions; relax and be yourself, observe a cable class underway, the equipment is easy to operate, be prepared, and it does take extra energy and effort.

16. 85 percent of the students indicated that they would be willing to take another cable class.

Questionnaire results indicate that the cable classroom provides an effective way to deliver instruction. Both teachers and students are often better prepared than they would be for a regular class. Teachers have to work harder to get to know the remote site students and keep them involved in class. Special on-air activities and face-to-face gatherings during the school year help to overcome the barriers of the technology.

With advanced level classes, it is necessary to make sure that remote site students have a comparable background in the subject before the class gets underway. Because the teacher is not readily accessible outside of class, it can be more difficult for remote site students to catch up.

TEACHER CONTRACT ISSUES

When the idea of experimenting with distance learning was first introduced to the high school staff in Somers, the reaction was both emotional and extreme. In order to satisfy the teachers' union that the project was not intended to eliminate teachers or radically alter working conditions, a contract addendum was prepared.

Much to the credit of the board of education and the leadership of the teachers' union, a working document evolved that fairly addressed the concerns voiced by teachers. Since it was adopted, the specific language of the contract addendum has not been altered significantly, and almost all of the initial concerns have subsided. The specific provisions of the contract addendum follow, along with some notes about the intention of each paragraph:

Paragraph 1 — Project Intention

"It is agreed that the intention of the Cable Classroom Program is to make available to students courses and other learning opportunities that would not be available otherwise, and not to take teachers' jobs or reduce teacher assignments."

The need for some assurance that the project would not cause teacher jobs to be eliminated was the top of the priority for the teachers' union. What this paragraph does not say is that the program may cause some teaching assignments to be shifted around.

To date, the classes selected for cable delivery were already scheduled to run at one location, and were not available at the remote site. In this situation there is no conflict about which school will provide the teacher for the cable class. In one case, the program worked to preserve a teaching assignment that would have been dropped due to a lack of enrollment at the origination site.

Paragraph 2—Teacher Participation

"Teacher participation in the Cable Classroom Program shall be strictly voluntary."

Voluntary participation works two ways. Certainly no teacher will be forced to teach over cable. At the same time, administrators will not be forced to put someone on the air who they don't feel will do a good job. When principals get together to discuss cable course possibilities, they compare notes on prospective cable teachers as well as course needs. The principal is often the one who approaches particular staff members about teaching on cable, rather than the other way around.

Paragraph 3—Teacher Evaluation

"For the purpose of regular evaluation of performance, the cable teacher shall be observed and evaluated 'live.' No videotape of a teacher will be used for teacher evaluation. Policies and procedures already in force for each school district for teacher evaluation shall be followed."

Teachers were concerned that they would be evaluated on how well they came across on TV, which is far from a standard criteria for assessment of teaching performance. If in the future a teacher is hired to teach exclusively over cable, then other criteria might apply.

Paragraph 4—Off-Air Recording

"Any off-air taping of class sessions shall be done only with the permission of the cable teacher."

If the intention of the project is to provide real-time fully interactive instruction, then there is no need to video tape the class except in certain situations. The school does not own the copyright to the teacher's on-air performance and the course is not being "canned" for later use. In addition, if a parent comes storming into a board meeting waving a videotape and claiming to have proof of a teacher's incompetence, the "evidence" is inadmissible.

Paragraph 5—Student Absence

"Class sessions will be recorded whenever a student is absent and the tape retained under the control of the cable class teacher for the purpose of student makeup work. The minimum length of time that a makeup tape is kept will coincide with the local school policy for makeup work."

There are three situations when off-air recording is allowed—whenever the teacher may give permission, in the case of student absence, and for project promotion. In each case the teacher retains as much control of the recording as possible.

Paragraph 6—Teacher Absence

"In the case of teacher absence, the teacher will provide lesson plans at both sites. Class will not be televised. An attempt shall be made to provide a substitute at the originating site and the teacher aide will follow through with lesson plans at the remote site."

As straight forward as this sounds, a contract question may arise when a teacher aide at the remote site substitutes for a certified staff member at the origination site. If school districts allow aides to substitute for the teachers they assist, then it may be possible for the teacher aide to conduct the class when the teacher is absent.

Paragraph 7—Video Taping for Project Promotion

"By the end of the course, cable teachers shall provide video tapes of two cable classroom sessions. These two video tapes may be edited and will be used for project evaluation or project promotion, not teacher evaluation. Teachers may videotape the two sessions of their choice."

This paragraph covers a special situation when video taping is allowed. Again the teacher retains as much control of the recording conditions as possible.

Paragraph 8—Class Size

"The recommended limit for cable class size at the originating site is sixteen students. At the remote site, the recommended class size is six students."

In any instructional situation, class size affects how much attention the teacher can give to individual students. Because the technology creates an additional barrier between teacher and students, special consideration should be given to the number of students at both ends of a distance learning class. If there are more than six students at the remote site who want to take a particular class, then a school district may want to consider offering that class in normal form.

Paragraph 9—Responsibility for Instruction and Discipline

"The cable teacher is responsible for instruction at both sites, but not liable for damage to equipment or injury to students at the remote site. Supervision and discipline shall remain the responsibility of the local school."

This paragraph addresses a major concern about personal and institutional liability. The business of issuing grades is completely in the hands of the instructor.

Paragraph 10—Local Contract

"All provisions of each district's local contract shall still apply. Nothing is superseded by this Memo of Understanding, including but not limited to grievance procedure, prep periods, duty assignments, compensation for training, etc . . . "

Paragraph 11—Precedence

"This Memo of Understanding sets no precedent, nor establishes any past practice for future negotiations."

The provisions of the local teachers' contract are usually carefully crafted over a number of years, and represent an investment of many hours of work. The paragraphs dealing with local contract and precedence are intended to assure that nothing about the project will be at odds with the existing contract.

It is a good idea to present distance learning as nothing more than an alternative way of providing instruction when no other options are available. The project does create some new circumstances, and these are addressed in the specific provisions of the contract addendum.

Paragraph 12—Informing Staff

"School administrators shall make information about the Cable Classroom Project available to all staff through contractual posting procedures so that all eligible teachers have the opportunity to express their interest in participating."

This paragraph is intended to assure that teachers will be informed about cable class offerings and that the opportunity to teach over cable will be available to all teachers. This paragraph suggests that cable course offerings are determined before staff assignments are made. In reality, decisions about cable class offerings and the volunteer staff members to teach them are not separate matters.

PROJECT ISSUES FOR ADMINISTRATORS

1. Scheduling

In order to make it possible for 20 students to participate in cable classes, the entire school schedule may have to be modified or switched around. After decisions about cable course offerings and teachers comes the designation of a time slot when the bell schedules of the two participating schools match up. Because class time is very valuable, it may be necessary to change the entire bell schedule by a few minutes or make special provisions for the cable class students and teacher so that they can all start at a time that doesn't coincide with the normal daily schedule.

First-time cable teachers will feel the need for extra time for class preparation. If it isn't possible to provide extra free time in a cable teacher's schedule, it may at least be possible to schedule a free period immediately before or after the cable class. This may be necessary if the cable class will be meeting at an odd time outside the normal bell schedule.

There is likely to be a limited number of time slots that match up between schools. For this reason, cable classes may have to be scheduled first, and all other classes filled in around them. The teaching assignments of cable teachers may have to be determined first, which can easily affect the schedules of other teachers.

If school calendars do not match up, teachers will have to prepare special assignments for students to work on independently when one or the other group of students is on vacation. Inservice days pose another problem, as do periodic school-wide assemblies. When mid-year and final exam schedules don't match up, it's possible to lose two weeks of classes.

The best that an administrator can do is to work toward a common schedule and calendar year-by-year. Bell schedules can be modified by a few minutes for the coming year; a plea can be made to the board of education for a match up of the winter and spring vacation weeks; it may be possible to suggest certain dates for inservice activities and for mid-year and final exams. School-wide assemblies can be held during periods when cable classes do not meet.

Decisions about the schedule and calendar are made at predictable times of the year, and usually at about the same time in each district. If the superintendents and high school principals in the participating districts can agree ahead of time on the schedule and calendar options that will best suit the project, then steady progress in this area can be made.

2. Relationship to Staff

A project of this nature relies heavily on a good relationship between administrators and staff. Principals have to be able to approach individual staff members to teach over cable, and they should be ready to offer whatever "compensations" are possible for the extra work. In the pilot phase especially, the reactions of teachers is critical to the future of the program.

There should be a recognized staffing pattern within and between schools to manage the project (described in a previous section). The high school principal is a member, a supervisor, and an evaluator of that management group. It is good practice to reinforce the different roles and expectations, to examine and resolve problems and to let staff members know when they are doing a good job. As with any new program, a distance learning project needs a good show of support from administrators.

3. The Costs

Two different grant programs provided a total of $66,000 over three years to develop the Cable Classroom Project. In each year the participating school districts contributed a greater percentage of the total project budget. This in-kind local contribution consisted primarily of the salaried time that cable teachers and the project coordinator spent in connection with the project.

In addition to equipment purchases, grant money covered the costs of phone installations and monthly bills, office supplies, the printing of meeting notices and a project newsletter, mailing costs for all project correspondence, travel reimbursement for the project coordinator, the formal training of teachers and aides and the rental of facsimile machines. Grant money also covered the services of the project evaluator, an acoustical engineer and the technical support service.

Most of the grant money was used to purchase equipment for the three cable classroom sites. At the end of the pilot phase of the project, two sites are completely equipped to originate and to receive cable classes, and one site is equipped to receive only. The approximate equipment cost for a complete site is $18,000. It costs $7,000 to set up a remote site, and it is possible to purchase and install equipment over a number of years so that a remote site is able to originate a full cable class. The ongoing costs of the program include:

Half-time teacher aide, half benefits	5,750.00*
Extra duty pay for local project manager	500.00
Shared cost for project technical support service	2,500.00
Supplies for FAX machine	500.00
Yearly cost of the phone line at each site	500.00
	$9,750.00*

FUTURE EXPANSION

Future plans for the Cable Classroom Project include additional sites in different towns, combining two or more sites on one channel in a "split-screen" arrangement and college credit courses originating from the local community college.

Access to the local cable system opens the door for a number of future uses. Instruction for home-bound students could be offered over cable. With a satellite dish located at one of the cable classroom sites, a wide range of satellite programming could be made available, copyright permitting, to the ten towns in the cable area when cable classes are not

*Because a teacher aide who is already employed may be assigned cable classroom responsibilities, this position may not figure as an additional project cost in some districts. Accordingly, the total cost will be $4,000.00 in stead of $9,750.00.

in session. Professional development workshops could be offered over the cable system, with teachers in all ten school districts able to respond to the presenter over the telephone. A guest speaker on a timely topic could be shared between districts in a similar way. Presentations or panel discussions about the school program could be presented to the community with an opportunity for people to call in with their comments and concerns.

It is likely that the cable classroom represents the first of series of projects that will make more extensive use of the local cable system to enhance the educational program for all districts in the cable area.

Chapter Seven

THE UNIVERSITY OF LOWELL INSTRUCTIONAL NETWORK USING TECHNOLOGY TO EXPAND LEARNING OPPORTUNITIES

MARGARET A. McDEVITT
STEVEN MAZZOLA

INTRODUCTION

With each advance in technology comes a new hope for solutions to problems in American education. Since the early days of radio and television, technology/media specialists have celebrated the potential of electronic media to bring real world experiences to classrooms, provide expertise in the content areas, and promote the cause of equity and excellence in education for all students. However, the promise of technology has, in most cases, yet to be realized. (1)

The University of Lowell Instructional Network seeks to demonstrate the potential of telecommunications technology to expand and enhance educational opportunities for elementary and secondary school students and teachers. The Network uses a full-motion, two-way television system which allows students and teachers at remote locations to both see and be seen, hear and be heard by participants at other locations. This simultaneous interactivity is achieved through a system designed and built on existing public and private cable networks. The resulting hybrid system demonstrates the successful combination and utilization of coaxial cable, fiber optic cable, microwave, and satellite technologies. (See Figure VII-1).

The Instructional Network, a project of the Center for Field Services and Studies of the College of Education, University of Lowell, evolved in response to the needs expressed by local area superintendents of schools for an appropriate telecommunications system model and link to the University's varied resources.

In addition to facilitating negotiations with local cable companies and aiding the communities as they plan the configuration of the network,

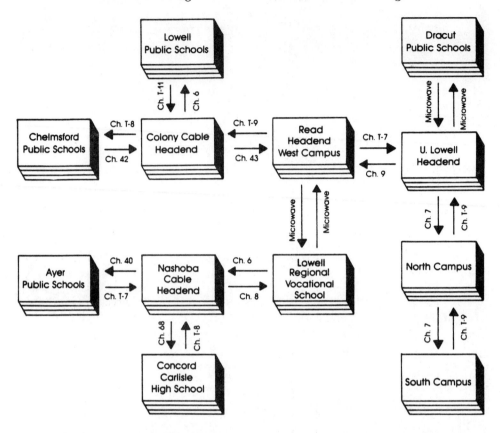

**Figure VII-1 Transmission Paths of Television and Data Signals
Along the Instructional Network**

the Center for Field Services and Studies has four additional and on-going
roles with respect to the Network:

1. Demonstrate instructional strategies appropriate for and unique
   to the use of two-way television.
2. Develop and deliver inservice courses and establish other forms of
   professional collaboration between educators at distant sites.
3. Provide unique instructional opportunities for students utilizing
   the various facilities and faculty of the University.
4. Facilitate course sharing opportunities between schools where declining enrollments or lack of qualified teachers threaten advanced
   level or special interest courses.

To date the University of Lowell Instructional Network, which was
established in 1984, has successfully linked eight Northeastern Massachu-

setts communities. Similarly, six school systems can access any room or laboratory of the University's four campuses and two high schools are linked to each other. (See Figure VII-2.)

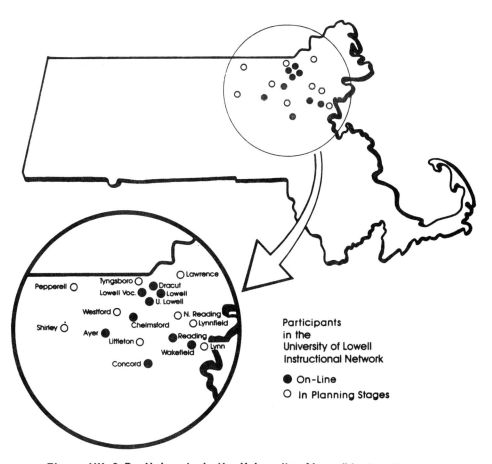

Figure VII-2 Participants in the University of Lowell Instructional Network

PROJECT HISTORY

As noted, the University of Lowell Instructional Network evolved in response to the needs expressed by area superintendents of schools who were faced with new challenges resulting from declining enrollments, an aging teaching staff, and severe fiscal constraints. This need-based development, coupled with the Networks's link to the Center for Field Services and Studies at the College of Education, University of Lowell, focused the project not only on geographic connections but on improvement of instruction. Thus, the Instructional Network has a dual agenda: educational access *and* excellence, goals that shape much of its operation.

Educators here, as elsewhere, saw two-way television primarily as a means of solving such problems as declining rolls in high schools, teacher shortages in critical areas, and the loss of specialized courses. By linking schools via two-way television, a teacher based at one school site is able to instruct small groups of students at distant sites, thus consolidating expertise and preserving courses which might not otherwise be offered.

The opportunity to share instruction among school districts provides the rationale throughout the country for the participation of most urban and suburban school in two-way television networks. (2) However, schools linked to the University of Lowell Instructional Network have the added advantage of participating in special courses conducted by faculty from one of the seven colleges at the University, by consultants, or by advanced graduate students. Through such classes, precollege teachers have an opportunity to observe varied teaching techniques, update their own content knowledge through participation in lessons delivered by experts in the field, and observe their own students interacting with teachers and students in other settings.

As a result of University originated courses, the Instructional Network has been able to demonstrate that two-way television encourages teachers to expand and alter their repertoires of teaching strategies, and that the medium is not limited in value to teaching small groups of advanced students. The application of two-way television to a variety of courses, across grade levels, and with diverse teaching strategies as illustrated by the University of Lowell Instructional Network, is in marked contrast to other documented reports on teaching via the medium. Hagon reported that teachers can easily replicate the traditional teacher lecture format used exclusively by most teachers and do not need to change teaching strategies for lessons conducted via two-way television. (3) Additionally, a study of dropouts from two-way television courses in Minnesota concluded that the system is not well-suited for students experiencing academic difficulty or for those who were not self-reliant learners. (4) It is our contention that two-way television provides the means to develop new teaching strategies not available in face-to-face lessons. Moreover, to limit the use of two-way television technology to small group lecture formats or to advanced classes is to waste the potential of the medium for improving instruction and enhancing learning for a wide variety of students.

PROGRAM DESIGN

The two-way television instructional design model employed by University and school faculties is consistent with the Network's goal to improve the quality of instruction. The seven-point model is a collaborative planning process between school and University faculties to:

1. **identify** program curriculum areas
2. **contact** expert instructors
3. **generate** ideas for lessons
4. **design** instruction
5. **organize** resources
6. **schedule** lessons
7. **evaluate** process

1. Identify Program Curriculum Area

Each school year classroom teachers and school curriculum department heads meet with University and school system Instructional Network staff to identify areas of the curriculum that can benefit from two-way television programs or the areas of expertise schools would be willing to share. These meetings, conducted via the two-way television network in an effort to sensitize teachers to the medium, expose teachers to the wealth of resources available to them through the Network. Subject areas are identified on the basis of the following criteria:

1. lack of teacher content knowledge in rapidly changing subject areas, usually science
2. lack of teacher pedagogical knowledge and methodological skills
3. willingness to share expertise in a subject area
4. school or system professional development goals
5. equity issues
6. cultural awareness issues

2. Contact Expert Instructor

Contacting an expert instructor is the task of the University's Instructional Network coordinator. Acting as a liaison between the University and the schools, the coordinator is able to facilitate a meeting with a faculty member working in the area identified by the school. University of Lowell faculty work voluntarily on school curriculum projects as part of the University's overall commitment to improving the quality of life in the community surrounding the University.

3. Generate Ideas for Lessons

The goal of school and University faculty meetings is to generate ideas for lessons appropriate for precollege students. Ideas focus on lessons that require active student involvement or provide experiences students and teachers would not have under any other circumstance. In some instances, teachers identify areas where student skills may be weak so that a proper review of prerequisite knowledge is included in the first lesson. Both University and school faculties have described the program planning meetings as professionally rewarding.

4. Design Lessons

A review of the literature on teaching on two-way television did not identify an instructional design model specifically for teaching via two-way television. However, further research identified the work of Gagne and Briggs on instructional design, specifically the **events of instruction** as an appropriate model for two-way television lesson development. The events of instruction are:

1. Gaining attention
2. Informing learner of objectives
3. Stimulating recall of prerequisite learning
4. Presenting the stimulus material
5. Providing learner guidance
6. Eliciting the performance
7. Providing feedback about performance correctness
8. Assessing the performance
9. Enhancing retention and transfer (5)

These nine events provide the framework for modifications of face-to-face lessons required by the television medium. For example, visual displays must conform to the requirements of television. Handwriting on a chalkboard is not easily seen on a television monitor by students at remote sites. Another consideration is providing adequate and personal student feedback. Use of facsimile machines to collect and return homework, electronic mail to send personal messages and confer with students, and use of traditional telephone services are the ways in which a variety of technologies mitigate against the loss of personal contact during telecommunicated lessons.

5. Organize Resources

Once the lesson is planned, school and University staff organize personnel and equipment necessary for the project. In some cases supplies and demonstration materials need to be ordered and delivered to one or more sites. In other cases, television equipment needs to be temporarily assigned to a different location. In all cases, Instructional Network administrators or technicians, *not teachers,* are responsible for this step.

6. Schedule Lessons

Scheduling the transmissions often proves to be one of the hardest aspects of planning. In general, when the transmission originates from the University, University faculty have conducted classes at a time chosen by the schools, but when scheduling involves more than one school and the University or when schools share instruction, it becomes necessary to negotiate a mutually convenient time.

7. Evaluate Process

Teachers evaluate their experiences with two-way television during interviews with Instructional Network staff. When appropriate, student learning outcomes are evaluated by the teachers and students' attitudes toward the technology are evaluated by Instructional Network staff.

SAMPLES OF PROGRAMS—VIGNETTES

The following vignettes will illustrate the seven-step instructional design model in detail. The spotlighted programs reflect issues of concern to educators in Northeastern Massachusetts and, as such, are a valid representation of the University of Lowell Instructional Network program schedule.

Vignette—Science Teachers Accessing Resources
STAR

Two high school science teachers, intrigued by the possibilities of two-way television links with the College of Pure and Applied Science at the University, identified polymer chemistry as a weak area in their science curriculum. After a preliminary discussion with the Instructional Network coordinator, a meeting was arranged between the teachers and a chemistry professor. As the high school and University chemists talked, they began to identify experimental procedures using sophisticated University equipment that might be appropriate and exciting for high school students. Through the two-way television connection, professors at the University could use equipment, too expensive or dangerous to be found in high schools, to conduct experiments while students at the high school observed and participated in discussions led by the professor. Using facsimile machine technology, students could receive hard copies of charts or graphs generated during the experiment.

Experiments were selected that had the potential to actively engage students procedurally and educationally. It was decided then, that the first experiment would have students test the caffeine levels of popular soda using High Performance Liquid Chromatography, HPLC, and students would prepare the sample in the high school laboratory to be tested at the University. The growing concern in the scientific community of the need to attract high quality students entering college to study science motivated the professor to serve as a role model for students by leading them in the prelab class held at the high school.

Lesson plans, guided by the instructional design model described above, reflected the collaborative expertise of high school teachers and university researchers. Care was taken to meet the needs of adolescent learners while exposing them to "real science."

Various instructional aids, laboratory equipment, and chemical substances needed to be brought to the high school for the sample preparation laboratory and, in turn, the prepared sample was brought back to the University to be run in the experiment the next day. Dates and times for both prelab and experiment were determined by the students' class schedule.

Students were able to properly prepare the sample materials and the experiment was successfully conducted. The full motion video capabilities of the system allowed students to take readings from the sophisticated instrumentation, ask questions of the professor at the University during the processing time, and examine charts and graphs transmitted via facsimile machine throughout the transmission. The experiment concluded with University and school faculties setting an assignment that required analysis of the data collected. High school teachers assumed responsibility for evaluation of student learning according to existing class standards.

Vignette—Bilingual Instruction Through the Eyes of Children
BI-TEC

An elementary school principal, concerned about a lack of cultural awareness among students in his predominantly white, middle class school, contacted Instructional Network administrators in his school system to ask if two-way television programs were possible between multi-cultural and multi-ethnic urban schools and suburban schools at the elementary level. The answer was yes.

A program was designed to replicate a Spanish/English two-way bilingual program piloted by the Instructional Network the previous year where two-way television was used to link native English-speaking and native Spanish-speaking students in a team teaching situation. As a first step, the Instructional Network coordinator arranged a preliminary meeting between an experienced two-way television, bilingual first grade teacher in the city of Lowell and a first grade teacher doing whole language instruction in the suburb of Chelmsford.

The teachers established an immediate rapport, and began planning activities appropriate for their first grade students. The instructional design reflects the importance of language skills, both in the native and second languages; an appreciation for our multicultural society; and use of technology with a variety of teaching strategies. Music, dance, counting games, and ethnic holiday celebrations are activities that have been successfully incorporated into this team teaching, two-way television program. Several social events are planned during the course of the school year to provide an opportunity for students to meet their television classmates and practice their new language skills face-to-face.

A suburban first grader's admission after the first class, that he was surprised the Spanish students' did not wear big hats, gave proof to the medium's potential to challenge the stereotypes that sometimes grow in racially homogeneous school communities. (6)

THE TECHNOLOGY

Getting From Here to There and Back

Signal paths chosen for transmissions from any site at the University to remote school locations adhere to a single distribution principle: utilize existing facilities whenever possible. For example, the University of Lowell provides channel space to the video network on its fiber-optic broadband cable system, used previously for computer data only. Additionally, subscriber cable companies, bound by franchise agreements and with approval from local cable commissions, provide channel space for two-way telecasts using previously designated educational or public access channels. In some cases, individual cable companies have provided the technical linkages necessary to join school systems served by different cable companies. In other cases this level of cooperation from the cable companies was not forthcoming and the school systems were forced to install microwave dishes to pass the signal relatively short distances.

Surprisingly, installation of dedicated telephone lines to studio/ classrooms has been the most difficult component in the system design; a problem caused by existing school administrative policy concerning telephone installations. Telephone links are necessary to provide dependable communication with every classroom in the system to: troubleshoot technical problems, add a measure of security for remote site students and teachers, and utilize other technologies via telephone lines, i.e., facsimile machines, electronic mail, and computer conferencing facilities.

Classroom Configurations

Once a signal path has been designed and constructed, the schools need to consider equipment purchases required to send and receive televised lessons. Schools in the University of Lowell Instructional Network are responsible for purchase and maintenance of classroom video and audio equipment, thus classroom equipment configurations vary according to budget and room constraints. The ideal situation is equipment standardization across the Network to ensure the integrity of the signal and equal opportunities for all sites to transmit as well as receive courses. While this ideal has yet to be realized, schools are asked to purchase equipment selected on the basis of minimum industry standards and recommended by the Instructional Network's system engineer. Two designs are found in two-way television systems across the country, a complete studio/classroom design or a basic start-up classroom design. The complete studio/classroom, costing approximately $15,000 to $20,000, requires a dedicated room and allows total teacher control of the transmission with no technician needed. The basic start-up model costs approximately $5,000 to $10,000. It is primarily a portable system and requires minimum time from a technician to set up and operate in regular classrooms.

The University maintains a model studio/classroom at the University's Center for Field Services and Studies. This configuration, Figure VII-3, is a three-camera operation controlled by a special effects generator. During transmissions, the cameras are preset by the teacher: one on the students, another on the teacher, and the third on a podium used to display visuals or demonstrations. The special effects generator allows the teacher to select the camera to be transmitted, and to create interesting special effects like split images or "wipes." To achieve a split screen, two cameras can be selected simultaneously with half the screen showing the instructor and the other half showing demonstration materials. Omnidirectional microphones placed on floor stands and a lavelier microphone worn by the teacher provide clear audio interaction. A minimum of three monitors is used to show the output of the special effects to the teacher and students at the transmission site and to receive the return transmission from the remote site.

The University also utilizes the basic classroom design when programs originate from laboratories or classrooms in other locations around the University. A single camera, monitor, microphone, and modulation equip-

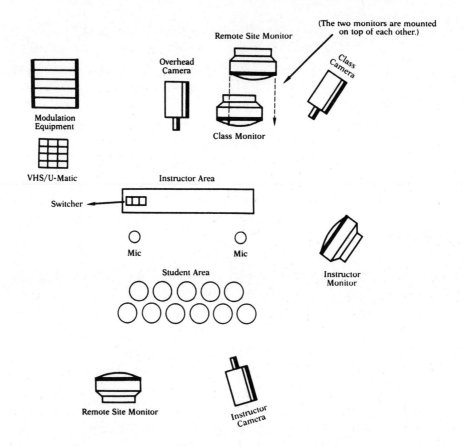

Figure VII–3 The Origination Classroom at the University of Lowell

ment are temporarily set up and operated by Instructional Network staff. Both models appear to be effective when instruction is designed to exploit the unique capabilities of the medium.

PERSONNEL

Telecommunications networks require knowledgeable personnel to ensure high quality production values and educationally sound programs. The University of Lowell Instructional Network currently operates with support from the University's Department of Telecommunications and two full-time people at the Center for Field Services and Studies: a coordinator for curriculum issues and a system engineer for technical issues. Additionally, several independent contractors are needed for construction, wiring, and physical plant maintenance. In this Network, most of the transmission path is owned and maintained by local cable companies.

School systems need to consider dedicated personnel as well. Exact job descriptions differ from one school system to another and are defined by school policy and the demands of the technology. Each school system's director of media services coordinates efforts for the entire district. In some cases, classroom teachers assume total responsibility for transmissions; in others, teachers are assisted by library/media aides. Apart from technical responsibilities required during the video and audio transmission, school and University personnel videotape each class whenever possible for archival purposes.

SCHEDULING

Because the Instructional Network depends on the cooperation of separate University departments, individual schools, and private cable companies, precise broadcast scheduling is critical. The scheduling process, however, is dictated by the nature of the programming so there is no standard operating procedure. For example, if two high schools are sharing one or more courses, school people must find a mutually convenient time; when high school students take University courses, students' schedules must conform to the University's schedule; special events and ad hoc programming is done on a case specific basis. In all cases, availability of channel space on private cable company lines is a prerequisite.

FUNDING AND MANAGEMENT

Funding

Unlike other telecommunications networks found throughout the country, the University of Lowell Instructional Network is not a project directly funded by the State Board of Education. Initially, the Massachusetts Board of Regents School/College Collaborative program was the sole funding source for the programs and projects of the Center for Field

Services and Studies of the College of Education, University of Lowell. As the Instructional Network began to expand to include more school systems, identification of additional funding sources became a priority. Funds were needed to assist local schools pay line connect charges demanded by cable companies to link individual school systems to the Instructional Network and to purchase transmission and classroom audio/video equipment. Several school systems received grants sponsored by state and federal agencies to supplement existing local resources and enable the schools to join the Network.

Initial costs vary dramatically among the school systems involved in the Network. For example, the Center for Field Services and Studies is located on the West Campus of the University of Lowell which is physically in Chelmsford, Massachusetts whose cable contract provides for the inclusion of every public building on the town's institutional television system. Thus the Chelmsford Public Schools and the University of Lowell Instructional Network were linked free of charge. Additionally, a fully equipped public access studio is housed at the high school and no additional equipment needed to be purchased.

Another town, bordering the City of Lowell which is the site of the University's three other campuses, was not able to negotiate the joining of two different cable company lines that would have provided the link to the Network. Thus, two microwave dishes needed to be purchased to provide the necessary signal path. One was funded by the Center for Field Services and Studies' School/College collaborative grant, and the other was funded by the Dracut Public Schools. Dracut High School also houses the public access studio, thus eliminating additional equipment costs.

Several other communities paid line connect charges to their local cable companies, varying in price from a few hundred to multiple thousands of dollars with monies secured from a combination of technology grants, school improvement funds, and local equipment budgets. In most cases, total costs were shared by the Center for Field Services and Studies and the school systems. Three school systems purchased the equipment specified by Instructional Network staff in the complete classroom/studio design. The remaining schools utilize existing equipment in several variations of the basic classroom configuration model outlined above.

School systems are not required to pay any subscription or tuition fees to the University of Lowell or any other state or local agency to participate in Instructional Network programs. University of Lowell faculty, consultants, and graduate students do not receive stipends for their work in courses specifically designed for the Instructional Network. Assisting elementary and secondary schools to provide learning opportunities for students is part of the University's mission to improve the quality of life in surrounding communities. The only exception to this no-cost policy is when high school students or inservice teachers take graduate or undergraduate courses for University of Lowell credit. In these cases, tuition must be paid to the University. Special arrangements are usually made for high schools to pay the students' tuition in an effort to provide a challenging curriculum for all students in public school settings.

Management

The University of Lowell Instructional Network Advisory Board provides a forum for anticipating, discussing, and resolving issues related to Network programming. The Network coordinator and system engineer meet bimonthly with representatives from the University and public school superintendents, to share progress and collaboratively plan programs.

Meeting agendas include: school spotlight, system update, policy issue discussions, and brainstorming sessions. The school spotlight is a presentation by one of the school-based Instructional Network coordinators, usually the media specialist, to highlight successful two-way television projects or classes in one school system. The system update focuses on expansion and technical upgrade of the Network, in terms of additional school systems coming on-line or new equipment purchases that may expand services.

Policy issues include schedule alignment among schools, collective bargaining, and staff development. Similarly, brainstorming sessions have included curriculum topics, potential funding sources, and innovative use of the Instructional Network.

EFFECTS ON TEACHING CONDITIONS

Our experiences at the University of Lowell Instructional Network suggest that two-way television can have significant positive effects on the conditions of teaching. These effects are centered around issues of staff development and professional collegiality.

Staff Development

Staff development opportunities available for teachers through the Instructional Network include a wide variety of topics such as instructional design methods, hands-on seminars for teaching with two-way television equipment, new topics in the content areas, and techniques for teaching critical thinking skills. Utilization of the University's satellite downlink capabilities allows school personnel to participate in teleconferences available nationally via satellite technology. Because programming can originate at one site and be distributed to all sites in the Network, schools are able to share teleconference costs or to share expert consultant fees and receive needed services in local school buildings for a fraction of the total cost.

The Instructional Network staff consider instructional design issues key to effective use of the medium in educational settings. Teachers are taught to plan lessons that take advantage of the unique capabilities of television. Included in the staff development program are sessions on basic storyboarding techniques, preparation of interesting and effective visual materials, questioning strategies to involve students at remote locations, and provision of substantive learner feedback.

Additionally, Instructional Network staff offer workshops and seminars for school-based media coordinators and technical support staff. Technical workshops are offered to keep school media specialists up-to-date with new trends in the educational technology industry, including product advances, purchasing strategies, and system layout and design. Grant writing workshops provide an opportunity to share knowledge of potential funding sources and collaborate on submitting proposals.

Professional Collegiality

Instructional Network programs that access the resources of the University of Lowell provide a vehicle to initiate school/college collegial relationships. University and school personnel collaboratively plan, develop, and produce two-way television programs that expand educational opportunities for teachers and students. School teachers and University faculty alike report the opportunity to meet their colleagues in different levels of the educational process as one of the most beneficial aspects of the project. These school/college relationships have been described by high school science teachers as a way to keep current with new developments in rapidly changing areas of math and science.

Similarly, teachers involved in team teaching situations across school districts enjoy the opportunity to share expertise, discuss common concerns, and observe their students working with other teachers.

CONCLUSION

The work being done at the University of Lowell Instructional Network seeks to build on existing knowledge of how teaching with media affects the learning environment. The Instructional Network focus is not on the glorification of the medium, specifically two-way television, but rather the implications of the technology on school organizations, school curricula, student learning, and staff development.

Clearly, the University of Lowell Instructional Network is an experiment. We hope to show that educational innovations that employ technology and media should have improvement of teaching and learning as their primary goal. There is much work to be done, for historically, most technologies were adopted by educational administrators before their efficacy in schools was tested. (7)

Telecommunications technology has the ability to expand the limits of classrooms to teachers and students alike. It is our responsibility to provide schools the tools they need to educate our young people for the challenges of the new century and to fulfill the promise of public education in the American democracy.

REFERENCES

1. Cuban, L. TEACHERS AND MACHINES, New York: Teachers College Press, 1986.
2. Kested, W. "Two-way Instructional Television," *Phi Delta Kappan*, 1985, 67, 315.
3. Hagon, R. "Two-Way Cable TV Links Rural Schools." *Techtrends*, 1986, January, 19–21.
4. Dronka, P. Educators Tune in to Interactive Television. *ASCD Update*, 1987, January, pp. 1,6,7.
5. Gagne, R. M., Briggs, L. J., Wagner, W. W., PRINCIPLES OF INSTRUCTIONAL DESIGN, New York: Holt Rinehart and Winston, Inc. 1988, 3rd ed.

6. Redd, L., "The Use of Two-Way Television to Solve Problems of Inequality in Education: A Comment." *Journal of Negro Education,* 1983, 52, 446–453.
7. Solomon, G., Clark, R. E., "Media in Teaching." In M. C. Wittrock (Ed.) HANDBOOK OF RESEARCH ON TEACHING, 3rd ed., (pp. 464–478). New York: Macmillan Publishing Company, 1986.

Chapter Eight

INTERACTIVE VIDEO IN EDUCATION

Richard J. O'Connor

WHAT IS INTERACTIVE VIDEO

Interactive video is an instructional delivery system in which recorded video material is presented under computer control. Viewers not only see and hear the pictures and sound, they interact with the program by making active responses. Those responses affect the pace and sequence of the presentation. (1)

Generally, interactive video programs are centered upon either random-access videocassettes or optical laser videodiscs. In industry and business applications of interactive video, the use of videotapes has diminished substantially since the advent of videodisc technology, with one industry observer recently noting that "Interactive videotape systems seem completely dead. Panasonic dropped its line in 1986. Expect no resurgence in 1988." (2) However, some schools might find the use of computer-controlled videcassette programs as the most financially feasible entry into the field of interactive video.

By convention, interactive videodisc programs are described as falling within one of three "Levels of Interactivity."

A Level I videodisc instructional program usually is a consumer videodisc player used to play videodisc programs with a minimum of user interactivity. Still-frame access may be possible at Level I, but generally the recorded video is played back by the user with no, or only minor, interruption.

Level II industrial videodisc programs are characterized by on-board programmable memory and improved access time. Level II videodiscs are different from Level I in that they have digital coding data integrated into the videodisc itself at the time of mastering. This digital information is then "dumped" into the videodisc player's temporary memory storage area so that when the player is started (initialized), an effective random-access capability is provided on a stand-alone basis.

Level III videodiscs do not contain the embedded digital control data of Level II programs but, rather, are controlled entirely by an "outboard" microcomputer. This use of a microcomputer rather than internal control data embedded on the disc itself gives more flexibility in constructing effective interactive video programming and is therefore the preferred approach of most educators today.

The roots of interactive video extend to two formative elements: instructional television and programmed instruction. Each of these elements emerged as important educational developments in the early 1960s. The major impetus to the growth of interactive video since then has been the introduction of videocassette and optical videodisc technology and the development of microcomputer technology.

Videocassettes and videodiscs introduced "off-line," "on-demand" access to instructional television materials. Microcomputers provided the learner with a reliable and efficient mechanism to access any specific segment of a TV program. The use of the computer for this purpose overcomes three major deficiencies of TV as an educational medium: (1) lack of active learner participation, (2) lack of instructor-student interaction, and (3) lack of recordkeeping for formative evaluation of learning gain.

Video, on the other hand, brings dynamic color, sound, and motion to a static, text-oriented computer screen. This synergistic effect was recognized early as an important characteristic of interactive video (3, 4), and continues to account for much of the interest in interactive video today.

In addition, the potential of interactive video has been increased greatly with recent development of CD–ROM, compact disk-read-only memory, technology as well as increased power and versatility of microcomputer authoring systems. (5, 6)

CURRENT APPLICATIONS

Interactive videodisc programs in the United States are characterized by two common features: (1) difficult to produce and (2) highly-expensive. Accordingly, most interactive videodisc programs now in use have been produced by large industrial organizations such as General Motors, International Business Machines, and government agencies such as the U.S. Department of Defense. Estimates vary, but most observers would quote a figure in the area of $100,000 as the minimum amount of investment required for production of a Level III videodisc program. It is not difficult, therefore, to understand why there has not been more of a penetration of videodisc technology into the school systems of the United States. Less than 4 percent of the total number of videodisc applications in the United States are identified specifically as "education" applications. Most videodisc players now in use are devoted to coin-operated arcade applications (38,718), point-of-purchase programs (9,863), and military uses (7,957). (7)

In a June, 1987 national survey of 169 school districts with at least 25,000 students (50% response rate to mailed survey), 28 percent of the districts reported current use of interactive videodisc, with 52 percent of the districts planning to use interactive videodisc by 1990. (8)

With regard to conventional instructional TV use in schools, the Corporation for Public Broadcasting reports 81 percent of all teachers have access to video recording and playback equipment and 29 percent of all teachers actually use at least one ITV series regularly. (9)

The installed base of microcomputers in education at the end of 1987 was just over 6 million, with 2.1 million in schools, 3.2 million in colleges and universities, and 700,000 in industry and government training centers. (10)

Some attempts have been made to increase utilization of videodisc technology in the classroom by production of "generic" videodiscs, consisting largely of visual data bases in areas such as art history, biology, earth sciences, astronomy, and other subjects. (11) Repurposing, or interactivating, fixed-pace linear videotapes represents another approach of this type. (12) Although excellent educational resources, generic videodiscs and videotapes are used by only a small percentage of teachers and, in most instances, are used for group teaching as opposed to microcomputer-controlled, individualized study.

Despite attempts to use existing videotapes and generic videodiscs in educational applications, however, the major thrust of interactive videodisc technology unquestionably has taken place outside of mainstream education.

Can this situation be rectified? If there is recognized potential in interactive video technology as an effective educational tool, is its future use to remain restricted to only those organizations large and affluent enough to afford hundreds of thousands of dollars for in-house videodisc productions? Is it practical, even possible, for the average classroom teacher to take advantage of interactive video as a viable teaching method for his or her own students? And, if so, how is this to be accomplished?

To achieve this goal two important steps are needed. First, there is a need to develop a new conceptual approach to the use of television and computer in teaching; and second, there is a need to facilitate the implementation of interactive video in instruction through strategic planning and organizational development.

I. NEW CONCEPT OF TELEVISION AND COMPUTERS IN EDUCATION

The key to more widespread use of interactive video in the schools lies in the need to change our basic approach to the design and production of instructional television programming. To use television effectively in teaching, we must alter our production approach; in essence, we must change our fundamental perception of television as a "viewing" medium to that of a random-access "information storage and retrieval" mechanism. This simple change of perception regarding instructional television, now possible because of the powerful data storage and branching capability of the microcomputer, will allow a paradigmatic change to take place in the use of television in our schools. To understand why this change of perception is appropriate, it is helpful to consider a few basic problems related to the use of film-making techniques in instructional television and why, because of emerging technology, such problems may now be avoided altogether simply by altering our production approach. These problems are:

1. Linear Approach

In embryology, there is a popular adage: Ontogeny recapitulates phylogeny, meaning that the growth and development of the individual often mirrors the growth and development of the entire phylum or species. This phenomenon is true in the arts as well; for example, the early movies closely mimicked stage productions and, more recently, television production methods have closely followed those of the film-making industry. Accordingly, most instructional television programs resemble teaching films, characterized by a linear format, fixed-pace, single main theme, and emphasis placed upon smooth scene transitions and continuity of storyline. Theodore K. Rabb, Professor of History at Princeton University, recently discussed the difficulty in using film as a teaching device:

After more than 10 years of involvement in a television series on the Renaissance . . . I have concluded that the major problem is a fundamental division of purpose between scholarship and television. No film producer can fully share the aims of a scholar, except in the case of preparing a specific, technical program for a limited audience.

The differences begin at the most basic level: Academics deal in nuances, qualifications, and subtle distinctions, while film makers seek broad strokes, drama, and simple, vivid ideas . . . Unless scholars can adjust to the special requirements of television—the insistence on drama, on the visual, on two-to-three minute sequences, and relentlessly simple ideas, transitions, and stories—there will be little serious factual film making. (13)

Budd Schulberg, author of the On The Waterfront, makes a similar point in a recent article that contrasts the differences between film-making and writing a novel:

The difference between a novel and a film is more qualitative than quantitative. Film is an art of high points. It should embrace five or six sequences, each one mounting to a climax that move the action onward to its final crescendo.

The film does best when it concentrates on a single character. It tells "The Informer" superbly. It tends to lose itself in the ramifications of "War and Peace." It has no time for what I call the essential digressions— the digression of complicated, contradictory character; the digression of social background. The film must go from significant episode to more significant episode in a constantly mounting pattern. It's an exciting form. But it pays the price for this excitement. It cannot wander as life wanders, or pause as life always pauses, to contemplate the incidental or the unexpected. The film has a relentless form. Once you set it up it becomes your master, demanding and rather terrifying. It has its own tight logic, and once you stray from that straight and narrow path the tension slackens, the air is let out of the balloon. (14)

2. Production Values

A second important problem of using a film-making approach in instructional television has to do with production values. Essentially, film is an entertainment medium and relies heavily on high production values such as talented actors, dramatic episodes, special effects, and other extrinsic motivational devices. This approach invariably results in high production costs, thereby forcing the producer to appeal to the widest possible audience in order to ensure maximum distribution of the film. Thus, in the case of an educational film, the content of the program would be purposely kept on a general level so as to attract the broadest number of viewers. Educationally, however, the effect of this production approach often is dysfunctional since it does not allow the degree of specificity required for the particular instructional application at hand. Indeed, such high production values should not be necessary to promote interest on the part of the viewer; the learning experience itself is, or should be, intrinsically motivating, thereby eliminating the need for such expensive and even distracting extrinsic motivational devices. As put by one experienced industrial television producer:

> Before you invest in expensive design, strategy and media, analyze the viewer's need-to-know level and weigh that against the resources to be invested. Quite often, because of the viewer's desire and need to receive the information, a very simple presentation may serve just as well as a sophisticated, expensive videotape production. (15)

3. On-Camera Performance

In addition to the need for random-access rather than linear approach, and emphasis upon program content rather than production values, a third major distinction between film and instructional television production methods exists in the area of on-camera performance. In films, actors should perform a role; in interactive television, teachers should teach. The reason to employ the teacher as the primary on-camera performer rather than a professional actor goes to the heart of the television process as a communication medium and is a critical consideration in utilizing interactive video as a teaching method. An excellent explanation of this interesting characteristic of the television medium is provided by Hefzallah:

> Due to the relatively small size of the TV screen, the TV maker relies heavily on close-up shots of performers. Watching the performers from a very close distance, we come to recognize TV stars, newscasters, and masters of ceremonies as people we know.
>
> To depict a scene or shot from the performer's point of view, subjective angle shots are used. In these shots, the viewer is placed in the position of the performer as the camera reveals to the viewer what the performer is visually experiencing in the scene. This technique tends to increase the viewers' interaction with the events of the program and reinforces his/her identification with the performer.
>
> Using close-up and subjective angle shots to present soap-opera characters, for instance, in their daily life tragedies, hopes, and dilemmas

helps establish those characters as personal acquaintances of some soap-opera fans. In talk shows, a similar relationship is usually established between the master of ceremonies and the viewer. Donald Horton and Richard Wohl called this relationship a "para-social relationship." (16) It is so called because the relationship is "based upon an implicit agreement between the performer and viewer that they will pretend the relationship is not mediated—and that it will be carried on as though it were a face-to-face encounter." (17)

This "para-social relationship" established between television performer and viewer is an exceedingly important characteristic to exploit in producing an instructional TV program. In effect, the television/computer delivery system provides the student "on-call" access to his or her own teacher discussing an issue or topic of immediate interest and direct relevance to the student. This type of programming cannot be done with conventional, film-style, television production methods. The only practical way for this to be accomplished is for the teacher to become directly involved with the TV production process itself, including microcomputer control of random-access videorecordings.

II. STRATEGIC PLANNING
AND ORGANIZATIONAL DEVELOPMENT

Although in the past interactive video has been a time-consuming, complex, and expensive undertaking, emerging technology is rapidly changing this picture and, today, there is no reason why any teacher should not be able to make effective use of interactive video as an effective instructional method.

Emerging television and microcomputer technology now provide a practical opportunity to teachers to complement classroom teaching with individualized instruction programming. For instance, today it is possible to purchase a portable television camera for less than $2,000 that will provide an ITV recording capability that, only five years ago, would have cost up to ten times as much. This has come about largely from development of CCD, charge-coupled device, television cameras and digitized processing of the television signal. The end result, however, is that a classroom teacher may now have direct access to a low-cost, reliable, very powerful video production capability. Some of the professional production features include fades to black or white, built-in character generator for titling, macro lens for extreme close-ups, frame accurate edits, variable playback speeds, 400 lines of horizontal resolution, and other sophisticated features.

This high-quality recording and editing capability can be used by individual teachers to place selected teaching material in a format readily accessible either directly through random-access videocassettes or videodisc, including microcomputer control of either the videocassette or videodisc player. In addition, even the interfacing of the videodisc player with a microcomputer has been greatly simplified and microcomputer authoring systems designed for interactive video production are increasingly becoming more effective and less expensive. (18)

To obtain the advantages associated with interactive video, it will be important for educational leadership to design an organizational strategy, or operational plan, to facilitate adoption of the technique by individual teachers. To ensure effective utilization of interactive video as an instructional method, it must be planned, produced, and presented with direct participation and direction of the teacher. In this sense, television and the computer are viewed no differently than the classroom blackboard or overhead projector. Media production and computer programming specialists may be available to assist the teacher in the production of interactive video materials, but only to assist. It is essential that the teacher be in direct control of the entire production process, both in master recording and editing of the video footage as well as in microcomputer programming.

To do this, three primary support mechanisms must be provided for the teacher:

1. Teacher Training and Preparation Time

Adequate in-service training and preparation time must be available for teachers interested in learning how to create and utilize interactive video technology. Such training need not be extensive in the early stage of development; what is more important is to have technical support available to the teacher on a continuing basis as he or she is acquiring practical experience in this regard. For example, the fundamentals of interactive video production could be provided in a three-day workshop to initiate the program. However, it would be essential to ensure that the workshop participants have back-up consultation available on a regular basis, such as weekly or monthly consultations throughout the school year.

Interactive video production is a skill, learned primarily through hands-on experience by the individual teacher. To learn this skill most efficiently, the teacher will need:

(a) a resource person for technical consultation available on a continuing basis, particularly in the early stages, and

(b) an adequate amount of preparation time for the conversion of classroom teaching materials into an interactive video format.

Production of interactive video materials requires a large front-end investment of time and energy. Expenditure of such time and effort will later be amply justified with improved student performance as well as increased availability of time on the part of the teacher to interact personally with students on an individual basis. With incorporation of interactive video programming, much "information-giving" activity can be transferred to video for individualized viewing outside of class, thus allowing more classroom time to be devoted to discussion and analysis of such information.

2. Individualized Study Carrels

A second important planning consideration for implementation of an interactive video program is provision of adequate self-study areas that contain appropriate video and microcomputer equipment. Essentially, this would entail an extension of present self-study facilities in the school library to include interactive video units as well. Existing procedures for video and microcomputer software distribution could be used to incorporate teacher-produced materials for the students, including checkout of software for use on home videocassette players and microcomputers. Many schools already have self-study carrels of this type in place; the important planning consideration would be to increase the number of such units to accommodate a greater number of students and frequency of usage. Scheduling availability of self-study units would also be an important planning consideration.

3. Equipment Standardization

A third major planning issue necessary for successful implementation of an interactive video production program would be standardization of video and microcomputer production and playback equipment. Such decisions, of course, will be based upon a number of local factors and no specific recommendations would be appropriate for every school. However, within each school, or school district, some degree of standardization is desirable; for example, the format size of videorecorders may be standardized on either the three-quarter or half-inch size videotape. In addition, it would be helpful to standardize on use of industrial-level video production equipment rather than less-expensive, but limiting, consumer videorecorders and monitors. Color microcomputer monitors should be specified. Such decisions should be made in close consultation with the teachers involved with interactive video production and, as much as possible, are based upon the teachers' own television production and microcomputer needs.

SUMMARY

In summary, contemporary communications technology, particularly television and the microcomputer, offers a powerful tool for today's teacher to dramatically improve his or her ability to communicate with each student. To make efficient and effective use of interactive video will require a new perspective on current use of instructional television, however. Television can be much more effectively used in teaching with a random-access, personalized approach rather than with conventional, fixed-pace generic programs produced for broad distribution. The microcomputer can be used by teachers to present their own teaching content to students. Microcomputer programming and video programs created by the teacher may be combined into an interactive video format, thereby vastly increasing the educational effectiveness of such material.

Such use of educational technology does not represent a paradigmatic change in how the teaching process is carried out. Good teachers have always used available tools to help students learn; good teachers have always recognized the importance of individualization in learning. Contemporary computer and television technology, in essence, represent only tools that can be used to mediate good instruction. As suggested in a recent review of interactive technology in education, "It may be more sensible to approach interactive video as an extension of our capacity to present and to manage instruction rather than as a technology that dramatically redefines the process of learning." (19) Furthermore, there is no reason to believe that teachers cannot make effective use of interactive video, just as professionals in other areas are making effective use of television and microcomputers. This is particularly true with respect to the potential of interactive video to enhance the opportunity for individualized instruction.

Educational technology is not a panacea and there remains much to learn about the most effective ways of utilizing it in the educational process. However, when placed in the hands of a competent, dedicated teacher who, in turn, is encouraged and assisted with strong institutional support, there is a strong expectation that educational technology can significantly improve the teaching/learning process. Why not give it a chance?

REFERENCES

1. Heinich, R., Molenda, M. and Russell, J. INSTRUCTIONAL MEDIA AND THE NEW TECHNOLOGIES OF INSTRUCTION, 2nd Ed, New York: John Wiley & Sons, 1985.
2. Stalos, S. Industry Update. *AV Video*, Vol. 10, No. 1, January, 1988.
3. DeBloois, M. (Ed). VIDEODISC/MICROCOMPUTER COURSEWARE DESIGN, Englewood Cliffs, N.J.: Educational Technology Publications, 1982.
4. Nurnberger, R. The Effect of Active Response to ETV Instruction. *Journal National Soc. Prog.*, Vol. VIII, No. 3, March, 1969.
5. Lambert, S. and Sallis, J. (Eds.). CD–I AND INTERACTIVE VIDEODISC TECHNOLOGY, Indianapolis: Howard W. Sams & Co., 1987.
6. O'Connor, R. "Integrating Optical Videodisc and CD/ROM Technology to Teach Art History," *Journal Educational Technology Systems*, Vol. 17(1), 1988.
7. *The Videodisc Monitor*, Vol. VI, No. 4, April, 1988.
8. QED LARGE DISTRICT SURVEY. Denver, Col.: Quality Education Data, Inc., June, 1987.
9. Riccobono, J. AVAILABILITY, USE, AND SUPPORT OF INSTRUCTIONAL MEDIA, 1982–83, SUMMARY FINAL REPORT OF THE SCHOOL UTILIZATION STUDY. Washington, D.C.: Corporation for Public Broadcasting, 1984. As reported by [5].
10. *The Videodisc Monitor*, op. cit., p. 30.
11. Jonassen, D. "The Generic Disc: Realizing the Potential of Adaptive, Interactive Videodiscs," *Educational Technology*, January, 1984.
12. Allen, B. "A Theoretical Framework for Interactivating Linear Video," *Journal of Computer-Based Instruction*. Vol. 13, No. 4, Autumn, 1986.
13. Rabb, T. "Opinion," *The Chronicle of Higher Education*. October 7, 1987.
14. Schulberg, B. *New York Times Book Review*, April 26, 1987.
15. Cartwright, S. TRAINING WITH VIDEO. White Plains, N.Y.: Knowledge Industry Publications, Inc., 1986.
16. Horton, D. and Wohl, R. "Mass Communications and Para-Social Interaction:

Observation on Intimacy at a Distance," *Journal of Psychiatry*, Vol. 19, No. 3, August, 1956. As quoted in [17].

17. Hefzallah, I. CRITICAL VIEWING OF TELEVISION—A BOOK FOR PARENTS AND TEACHERS. Lanham, MD.: University Press of America, 1987.

18. Schwartz, E. THE EDUCATORS' HANDBOOK TO INTERACTIVE VIDEODISC. Washington, D.C.: Assoc. for Educational Communications and Technology, 1985.

19. Hannafin, M., et al. "Keeping Interactive Video in Perspective," Miller, S. and Mosely (Eds.), EDUCATIONAL MEDIA AND TECHNOLOGY YEARBOOK. Denver: Libraries Unlimited, 1985.

PART III
SATELLITE COMMUNICATIONS

Business, industry, and education are discovering the benefits of satellite communications. Speed, cost-effectiveness, and flexibility of satellite communications have intrigued professionals in training and development in corporations, and in continuing education in schools and universities. Educators on campuses around the country are studying and experimenting with the potential uses of satellite communication to enhance universities' missions. Public schools with installed satellite reception antennas reap the benefits of receiving staff development programs and special courses for their students from satellite consortia.

Schools and universities cannot afford to neglect the state of satellite communication and what it can offer to help them achieve quality education and educational equity for all students in our country.

Chapter Nine, Satellite Communications for Learning, addresses the basics of satellite communication, reviews major educational satellite consortia, and discusses some of the potential and innovative uses of satellite communication in learning.

Chapter Nine

SATELLITE COMMUNICATIONS FOR LEARNING

IBRAHIM M. HEFZALLAH

INTRODUCTION

In 1982, Elliot Richardson said, "There was a time when the seas seemed endless and the skies vast enough to swallow any of the mistakes and errors of man. The world used to be big and men could afford to be small. Now the world is small and men must be big." (1) Today, satellites are making the small world even smaller. Satellite systems provide the fastest, cheapest, and most efficient ways of sending and retrieving information to and from any location on earth. Business, industry, and education are discovering the benefits of satellite communications. Speed, cost-effectiveness, and flexibility of satellite communications have intrigued professionals in training and development in corporations, and in continuing education in schools and universities. Educators on campuses around the country are studying and experimenting with the potential uses of satellite communication to enhance universities' missions. Public schools with installed satellite reception antennas reap the benefits of receiving staff development programs and special courses for their students from satellite consortia.

Satellite programming is quickly becoming another source for widespread access to global communication, entertainment, and education. Schools and universities cannot afford to neglect the state of satellite communication and what it can offer to help them achieve quality education and educational equity for all students in our country.

Prior to the planning for effective use of satellite communication in education, educators have to develop basic understanding of satellite communication, become familiar with a variety of satellite consortia and the kind of programming and services they offer, and learn about some innovative use of satellite communication in enriching students' learning experiences.

142

This chapter addresses these points. Specifically, the following focuses on the:

1. Basics of Satellite Communication
2. World-Wide Satellites
3. Educational Satellite Consortia
4. Potential Uses of Satellite Communication in Learning
5. Innovative Use of Satellite Communication in Learning

1. BASICS OF SATELLITE COMMUNICATION

Just a few years ago laymen were not accustomed to terms like "VCR" and "cable television." Today, however, they are household words because the consumer and educator soon recognized and began to take advantage of the enormous potential of both. Likewise, the satellite and all that it promises will usher us into an age when words like "downlink" and "KU–Band" become part of our everyday vocabulary. We are on the brink of a new age in which satellites are going to shrink the distance between people, and facilitate the interaction among them. Common understanding of the basics of satellite communication, and knowledge of the basic terms often used in talking about satellite communications are essential to the achievement of that goal.

Satellite

In 1945, Arthur Clarke, author of 2001: A Space Odyssey, introduced the idea of satellite communications. Clarke theorized that if a satellite were positioned high enough above the equator and its speed controlled to match that of the earth's rotation, it would appear stationary in the sky. Such a geostationary orbit, however, would be possible only if the satellite were positioned directly above the equator at a distance of 22,300 miles. (2)

A satellite's main function is to receive the signal from an earth station and rebroadcast it on a new channel. From its position high in space it can see one-third of the earth's surface. (3, p. 148)

Satellite Transponders

Every satellite has 24 channels or transponders. Each of these transponders can transmit one television signal or thousands of simultaneous telephone calls.

C–Band; KU–Band

Satellite signals use a high frequency band ranging from 3.7 to 4.2 GHz. This band is called the C–Band; however, a new generation of satellites is using a higher frequency ranging from 11.7 to 12.2 GHz called the KU–Band. It is expected that more and more satellites will be operating on the KU–Band.

Footprints

The satellite's antenna directs its signal to all designated reception areas on the ground in a particular shape called a footprint. (2, p. 16) The signal is strongest at the center of that area, which makes it possible to use smaller dishes for reception. The signal diminishes in its intensity as one moves away from the center, so larger dishes are needed.

Uplink; Downlink

An uplink is simply a ground station that sends a signal up to the satellite. The satellite changes the signal's frequency and retransmits it to a downlink. A downlink is a ground receiving station.

TVRO

Television-Receive-Only refers to satellite-receiving stations or homes. The two primary components of this system are the dish and the receiver. By directing the dish toward the satellite and tuning the receiver, it is possible to receive one channel at a time.

The Satellite Dish

The satellite dish is mainly an antenna that collects and focuses the satellite signal. Satellite signals are weak signals, almost as weak as a CB radio signal. For this reason, the satellite dish must be relatively large in diameter for good reception.

Clarke Belt/Satellite Parking Lot

The band of outer space above the equator at a distance of 22,300 miles is called the "Clarke Belt" in recognition of Arthur Clarke's pioneering vision. (2, p. 13) Spacing between satellites in the Clarke Belt, or as it is also called the "satellite parking lot," is crucial. Satellite spacing is calculated in degrees. One degree, as measured from the earth, is equivalent to 460 miles between satellites. How far apart satellites are "parked" from each other depends on the transmission power of the satellite and frequency used. For example, C–Band satellites are spaced two degrees apart, while higher frequency KU–Band satellites are spaced three degrees apart. (3, p. 157)

Direct Broadcast Satellite

DBS refers to a soon-to-be-used technology in which the satellite signal will be much stronger allowing the use of smaller dishes. Smaller dishes mean lower cost for individuals to receive satellite signals directly in their homes.

2. WORLD-WIDE SATELLITES

Mark Long's *World Satellite Almanac, The Complete Guide to Satellite Transmission & Technology,* (4) is a comprehensive guide and an informative reference on domestic, international, and eastern block satellites. This reference contains valuable information on the status of satellite communication technology. For the purpose of providing the reader with basic information on the fleet of satellites orbiting the earth, the following is a list of some of the world's major satellites. In compiling this list, the author used *World Satellite Almanac,* and Mark Long & Jeffrey Keating, *The World of Satellite Television.* (2) Two other references which the reader will find helpful in gaining more information on the status of satellite communication are: Mark Long's *The Down to Earth Guide to Satellite TV,* (5) and *Satellite Communication Research's Satellite Earth Station Use in Business and Education* (6).

U.S.A. Domestic Satellites

Galaxy I

Galaxy I provides cable television services to cable operators including: HBO, Cinemax, Showtime, CNN, ESPN, The Disney Channel, Spanish International Network, The Movie Channel, C–Span, People That Love (PTL, Christian religious and entertainment programs), WTBS, and Galavision.

Satcom F3R

Satcom F3R relays cable television services and educational video programming including: Nickelodeon, Fun And News Network (FNN), Cable Sports Network (CSN), USA, MTV, The Learning Channel, Lifetime, Eternal Word Television Network (EWTN, Catholic religious and entertainment programming), National Jewish Television (NJT, religious and educational programming for the American Jewish Community), Black Entertainment TV (BET), The Weather Channel, The Arts & Entertainment Network (AEN).

Satcom F4

Satcom F4 relays cable television services including: Bravo, Madison Square Garden (MSG), Biznet, National Christian Network, American Movie Classics, The Playboy Channel, Oddysey.

Westar IV

Westar IV provides several telecommunication services including: PBS, Catholic Telecommunications Network (CTNA), and occasional video feeds. In addition, it relays National Public Radio (NPR) signals to member stations nation-wide.

Westar V

Primarily used for voice and data transmission to Western Union customers, and video transmission on an irregular, non-scheduled basis.

Satcom F1R

Some of the uses include: video feeds by the networks and the Armed Forces Radio Television Service (AFRTS); audio feeds for RKO, ABC, NBC, and CBS radio networks; occasional video, and digital high quality audio programs relayed to affiliated radio stations.

Satcom F5

It acts as a long distance telephone carrier within Alaska and between Alaska and North America. It also carries the Alaskan Rural Area Network, the Alaskan Television Network, and an emergency medical network.

Telestar 301, 302, 303

AT&T Telestar series transmits AT&T "Skynet" family of business services which includes a data transmission service, Skynet Television and Skynet audio broadcast services for television and radio signals, and Skynet Transponder Service which allows customers to lease transponders on a part-time basis. Major customers of the Skynet Service include ABC and CBS television networks, Meadowlands Communications, Inc., and Hughes Television Network teleconferencing.

Spacenet & GStar Satellites

Owned and operated by GTE/Spacenet Communications. The GTE family of satellites incorporates more than 100 satellite transponders. Some of those transponders are used for long distance telephone service, SPRINT, operated by GTE. Customers of this family of satellites include the Baptist Telecommunications Network (BTN) and the American Christian Television Service (ACTS). In addition, Occasional Order service allows customers to lease transponders when need arises.

Canadian ANIK Satellites

Among the Canadian ANIK Satellites is ANIK D1, which was launched in 1982. Some of the services it carries include: French language programming from Montreal and Quebec; CBC Parliamentary Network (English and French); occasional news feeds; and a 24-hour-a-day Canadian sports programs.

International Satellites

Intelsat

The International Telecommunication Satellite Organization (INTELSAT) has over a hundred member countries. It began service in 1965 with Intersat I (Early Bird) to relay telephone and television services between Europe and North America. INTELSAT I, II, and III are no longer operational. The services are carried by INTELSAT IV, IVA, V, and VA satellites. Programs that can be viewed from North America on INTELSAT systems come from England, Portugal, Brazil, Columbia, Peru, Venezuela, Argentina, Mexico, Chile, and from the Armed Forces Radio Television Service (AFRTS) which transmits American television programs to military installations abroad. Since foreign television programs use different television standards than the American NTSC, conversion equipment is needed to view the program in full color.

The Soviet Satellite System

There are two types of Soviet satellites: stationary and nonstationary. Geostationary satellites provide domestic relay of voice, data, television and radio services throughout the Soviet Union. The most famous satellite in this group is GHORIZONT.

The second nongeostationary satellites, MOLNIYA series provide video services to the northern part of Russia. For about six hours every day, a MOLNIYA satellite maintains its position above the Hudson Bay. During that time, it is possible for earth stations in North America to pick up the satellite signal. However, since the Russian television signal is different from the American television system, conversion equipment is needed.

Intersputnik

This is the international satellite corporation of the Communist countries providing similar service to that of INTELSAT.

European Communication Satellites, EUTELSAT

In 1983, the first of a series of EUTELSAT satellites was launched. EUTELSAT satellites are owned and operated by the European Telecommunications Satellite Organization, representing 21 nations including Austria, Belgium, Cyprus, Denmark, Finland, France, Germany, Greece, Ireland, Italy, Luxembourg, the Netherlands, Portugal, Spain, Sweden, Switzerland, Turkey, the United Kingdom, and Yugoslavia.

3. EDUCATIONAL SATELLITE CONSORTIA

The world of satellite communications is gaining ground in education especially in higher and continuing education. A considerable amount of programming is available through satellites. Most of those programs provide the participants with learning and training experience unavailable through other means. An alphabet soup has emerged: acronyms of satellite and distant learning consortia. Following is a brief summary of the principal objectives of seven consortia.

CTNA, Catholic Telecommunications Network of America

Headquartered on Staten Island in New York, CTNA was established in 1982 to produce, acquire, and distribute programming of specific interest to the dioceses of the U.S. to Catholic colleges and institutions of higher learning, and to hospitals and health care centers. While some programming is religious in nature, other programs cover a wide variety of subjects.

NTU, The National Technological University

NTU is a nonprofit institution located in Fort Collins, CO. It was established in 1985. Its main objective is to serve the continuing education needs of engineers, scientists, and technical managers. NTU's satellite delivery system incorporates a network of 22 participating universities to offer accredited Master of Science degrees in computer engineering, computer science, electrical engineering, engineering management, and manufacturing systems engineering.

NUTN, National University Telecommunications Network

NUTN was founded in July, 1982. Its coordinating office is located on the campus of Oklahoma State University in Stillwater, Oklahoma. It is a coalition of 257 two- and four-year colleges (60% two-year colleges and 40% four-year colleges) joined to develop a telecommunications system for higher education. About 50 percent of the programming comes from those colleges. The other 50 percent NUTN contracts from other sources. NUTN provides full teleconference services for members and external groups. It provides primarily three major categories of programs:

- Programs originated by member institutions;
- Programs originated by a variety of external groups, such as federal agencies, corporations, and associations, and
- Commercial programs whereby the client pays the member sites for the use of facilities and equipment to reach a selected audience.

NUTN established a computer conference system for use by its members. Up-to-date announcements of coming programs can be obtained through that system.

AMCEE, The Association for Media-Based Continuing Education for Engineers

AMCEE is a nonprofit educational consortium. Its main objective is to offer noncredit continuing education courses in various engineering fields by satellite and by videotape. The consortium was originally formed in 1976 by 12 universities. At present, it has 33 member institutions with 16 uplink sites across the nation. AMCEE and NTU share a satellite network. Both consortia agreed to consolidate their efforts. As a result, NTU administers the AMCEE satellite operation, while the main office of AMCEE in Atlanta, Georgia, concentrates on videotaped courses.

PBS–NNS, National Narrowcast Service

NNS is a satellite service which was launched by PBS in 1985. Its mission is to offer education and training services designed specifically to meet the needs of American business. It delivers video-based education and training directly to work-sites, campuses, and community centers across the country using satellite.

PBS–ALSS, Adult Learning Satellite Service

ALSS of PBS was established in spring 1988. It offers block feeds of telecourses, and special satellite teleconferences mostly geared to educators.

SCOLA, Satellite Communications for Learning, International

SCOLA's main headquarters is located on the Creighton University campus, Omaha, Nebraska. Its main goal is to import television foreign news. Live foreign world news from 10 different countries will be imported and relayed for distribution on the SCOLA satellite transmission system. News will be available in Russian, German, Scandinavian, Arabic, Portugese, Italian, Japanese, Chinese, Indian, and Korean. These programs will be made available through use of an uplink to a domestic satellite which will then be downlinked to the academic and instructional communities of the U.S.

4. POTENTIAL USES OF SATELLITE COMMUNICATION IN LEARNING

Reception of Specialized Cultural and Instructional Programs

In addition to educational and cultural programs available through educational satellite consortia, there is a wide variety of interesting and highly specialized programs available through satellite communication. These programs can be used to enrich educational offerings in history, science, communication, political science, Latin American studies, fine arts, and modern languages. For instance, the following networks carry programs of potential benefit to education.

- Healthcare Information Network
- C–SPAN—Live coverage of the House of Representatives
- Radio Television Italina—Italian
- Galavision—Spanish
- CBC (AnikD)—French
- BIZNET (American Business Network)—Financial news, business-related programming for the U.S. Chamber of Commerce
- CBC PARLIAMENTARY NETWORK—Canadian House of Commons proceedings in English or French
- FINANCIAL NEWS NETWORK (FNN)—Live business and financial news
- HOSPITAL SAT NETWORK—Medical programming, new technologies, educational and entertainment programs for hospitals throughout the nation, 24 hours a day, seven days a week; scrambled.
- DOW JONES CABLE NEWS—Text service featuring stock tapes and business news
- NEW YORK STOCK EXCHANGE—15 minute delayed stock tape
- REUTER NEWS-VIEW—Text service featuring financial news

(For more information on programs carried by satellites, please refer to ON–SAT, (7) a weekly magazine published by Triple D Publishing, Inc., 501 N. Washington Street, Shelby, NC 28150, Telephone (704) 482-9673.)

Distribution of School-Based
Television Programs on a Satellite Network

As a member of a satellite consortium, an educational institution can choose to send video-taped programs for satellite distribution to the uplink facilities of the consortium. There is a difference between producing a television program for distribution through open broadcast or cable television, and producing video programs for distribution through a satellite consortium. Open telecast distribution requires that the program should appeal to a relatively large audience. With satellite communication, programs can be designed to appeal to a narrower audience, yet reach a large population of that specific audience. For instance, a program featuring a new approach in teaching physics will not attract a public television audience; however, by telecasting the same program through a satellite consortium, it can attract a relatively large number of those concerned about teaching physics. Following is a sample of potentially feasible programs:

(1) Enrichment programs to public schools in science, mathematics, computers in education, and foreign languages.

(2) Special courses to schools which lack trained teachers, and required facilities. For instance, Arts and Sciences Teleconferencing Service (ASTS) of the College of Arts and Sciences of Oklahoma State University was established in 1984 to provide "equal access" to educational resources to rural high schools. Rural educators and the O.S.U. administration and faculty recognized that rural schools often could not offer foreign languages and upper level mathematics and science courses due to personnel, financial, and geographic restriction. Oklahoma State University's College of Arts and Sciences, the Oklahoma State Department of Education, the Oklahoma Legislature, and the Oklahoma rural superintendents of education across the state worked together to develop ASTS. The first course, German I by Satellite was broadcast in the fall of 1985. During 1987–88, ASTS served 170 schools across 14 states. Other courses have been added including

Physics by Satellite, Advanced Placement Calculus, Trigonometry, and German II by Satellite.
(3) In-service programs to teachers and administrators, and special programs focusing on new trends and problems facing education. Professionals within an educational institution will find satellite communication an attractive and efficient medium for sharing their expertise with other professionals in member institutions of the consortium.

In all of the above examples, providing the technology for feedback such as 800 telephone numbers can ensure the needed interaction between the originator of the program and the recipients of the program.

Participation in a Growing Teleconferencing Activity

Capitalizing on the expertise of faculty, administrators, and professional people within a university, college or school, video teleconferencing can be produced and transmitted for distribution to colleges and other teleconferencing sites through a satellite consortium.

The number of organizations and schools becoming interested in originating and distributing information through a satellite network is on the increase. Each consortium has its advantages. Which consortium would yield maximum benefit to one particular school has to be determined based on the needs of the school and available human expertise within the school.

To transmit a teleconference an uplink arrangement is needed. The uplink carries the signal from the originating site to a designated uplink facility to be distributed to the participating teleconference sites. Three uplink methods are possible. First, a transmitting dish could be rented for the day of the teleconference. Second, arrangements could be made with AT&T to carry the signal through its telecommunication system. Third, arrangements could be made with public television uplink facilities. Various factors have to be considered in deciding which method will be the most appropriate and economical. One of those factors is the determination of the receiving sites. Determination of the participating sites depends on which teleconferencing consortium a school joins, and on the topic of the teleconference. Most of the satellite consortia have coordinating offices which provide marketing surveys, program coordination and access to high-quality technical consultation at a reasonable cost. Usually they charge a fee to conduct a survey to determine interest in programs.

Typically, a recipient of a teleconference pays an amount ranging from $50.00 to a $100.00. It is important to plan topics which will attract enough people to cover the cost of the marketing survey, the cost of the print-related material, and the rental of an uplink device.

In addition to gaining exposure for the originating school on many campuses and corporate headquarters, students on campus would have free access to the teleconferencing. They would also gain exposure to some of the uses of telecommunication technology in education, business, and industry.

Becoming active in teleconferencing activities could be just in the form of being a recipient of teleconferences. Schools and universities ought to study the variety of teleconferences available through the afore-mentioned consortia to downlink the appropriate conferences for their needs. Acquiring the rights to video tape the conference can help increase the educational video collection of a school library.

Programming A Special Campus Channel

An entertainment and cultural channel can be programmed to carry entertainment and cultural programs especially selected for a specific student body. Programs can be either locally originated and/or received from different satellites, such as from Campus Network, Inc. Campus Network is a satellite communications company that provides video entertainment programming four hours a week to colleges and universities. National College Television (NCTV) is the weekly TV service distributed free of charge by Campus Network to campuses coast-to-coast. The transmission is taped by the affiliate and rebroadcast five times during the following week. Each affiliate establishes its own rebroadcast schedule.

NCTV is advertiser-supported. Advertisements on NCTV will not include tobacco, birth control, or hard liquor. The programs provide two minutes per hour of local advertising time for affiliates to utilize for ads and public announcements.

In addition to providing special cultural and entertainment programs for a specific student body, having a television channel on a campus provides the opportunity for students to gain firsthand experience in programming a television channel, and in marketing commercial spots.

5. INNOVATIVE USE OF
SATELLITE COMMUNICATION IN LEARNING

Examples of innovative use of satellite communication in learning are many. The following example is chosen to show how satellite communication can overcome the barriers of space and language to provide a vehicle for interaction among people from different cultures. This innovative utilization occurred in the spring of 1987 to bring interested American and Soviet Union parties to talk about how media affects the relationships between the two countries. *US/USSR SPACEBRIDGE: The Role of the Media in Current Relations,* was produced by the Center for Communication, and Gostelradio in conjunction with the American Society of Newspaper Editors. (8)

Originally the following material appeared in Instructional Development Newsletter, published by the Media Center of Fairfield University under the title "You Were There, . . . and Also Here," ID Newsletter, May 1987, Fairfield University. (9)

On April 8, 1987, the Media Center was the site of an exciting video teleconference between American and Russian journalists and university students. About fifty universities in the U.S.A. received the teleconference through satellite downlinks. In Connecticut, Fairfield University was the participating university in this venture. Fairfield University graduate and undergraduate students attended the teleconference, along with representative of news media.

This was not the first time a television program originated from two nations; however, it was one of the most exciting programs. Focusing on media in shaping US/USSR relationships, the telecommunication media was intelligently used.

How Did the System Work?

Each country had two interactive studios. All studios were interconnected allowing the person talking to be seen on receiving television sets. Set design and color schemes were complementary, yet different enough to allow viewers to identify immediately the location from which the person was speaking.

In the U.S.A. the main studio was in San Francisco, and the second interactive studio was in Boston. In the U.S.S.R., the main studio was in Moscow, and the second interactive studio was in Tbilisi, Georgia.

The Masonic Auditorium in San Francisco housed a five-camera mobile production unit. Peter Jennings moderated a panel of three American journalists: Stuart Loory, Senior Correspondent, Cable News Network; Seymour Topping, Director of Editorial Development, *The New York Times;* and Elizabeth Tucker, Staff Writer, *The Washington Post.*

On the other side, in the TV studio of Gostelradio (the USSR's State Committee for TV and Radio), Vladimir Pozner, a commentator for the Soviet State Television and Radio, moderated a panel of three Russian journalists: Alexander Shalnev, Commentator, *Izvestia* Newspaper; Tengiz Sulkhanishvilly, TV Correspondent, Tbilisi, Georgia; and Yurii Tschekochikhin, Staff Writer, *Literary Gazette.*

Each main studio received two signals, one from the interactive site in its country, and the feed that was sent from the other country.

At the same time, each main studio transmitted two signals. The first was its feed to the other country, and the second was its composite signal for broadcast in its own country. (See Figures IX-1 and IX-2.)

The two interactive sites in Boston and in Tbilisi transmitted one signal to their main studios via WESTAR IV, and Ghorizont respectively. They also received the broadcast composite signal through the same satellites on different channels.

Four satellites were involved in this event: WESTAR IV, SATCOM 1R, INTELSAT, and GHORIZONT. The first two are American domestic satellites. INTELSAT is an international satellite operated by INTELSAT Consortium, and GHORIZONT is a Russian domestic satellite.

The signal received by the viewers at teleconferencing sites travelled a half a million miles at the speed of light. Since the American TV signal is different from the European and Russian systems, en route to its destination, the American signal in NTSC was converted to SECAM standard, and the Russian signal in SECAM was converted to NTSC standard.

Figure IX-3 shows the complete route of all signals involved. From the Masonic Auditorium in San Francisco the American feed to Russia was transmitted via microwave to a SATCOM 1R uplink facility outside the city. The feed was be downlinked from SATCOM 1R by a Comsat earth station near Etam, West Virginia, and then was uplinked to an INTELSAT satellite.

The feed was then received by a Soviet earth station near Dubna, 150 miles from Moscow. There the signal was converted from the American television standard (NTSC) to the Russian format (SECAM) Finally the signal was transmitted to the Gostelradio television studios in Moscow.

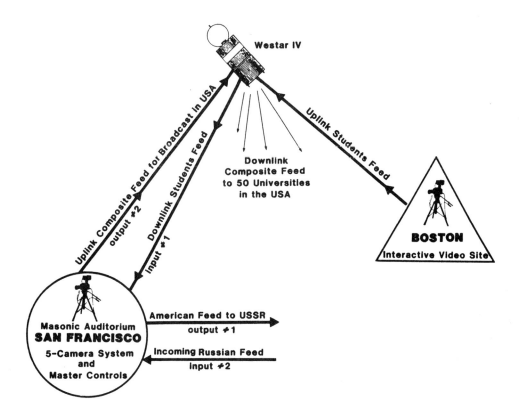

Figure IX-1 The American Site

The Russian feed to the U.S.A. followed the same route and was converted at Dubna from SECAM to NTSC standard.

The American composite signal was transmitted to WESTAR IV for downlinking at approximately 50 American universities in the U.S.A. The Russian composite signal was uplinked to Ghorizont for downlinking at Russian viewing sites.

In each main studio there were two directors. The lead director selected the shots for the composite signal for transmission on domestic satellites. This signal was recorded and edited into a one-hour program and given to PBS and commercial TV.

The second director selected the shots of the country's feed to the other country.

The producers and directors in the control rooms in San Francisco and Moscow had to be constantly in direct communication via an audio channel.

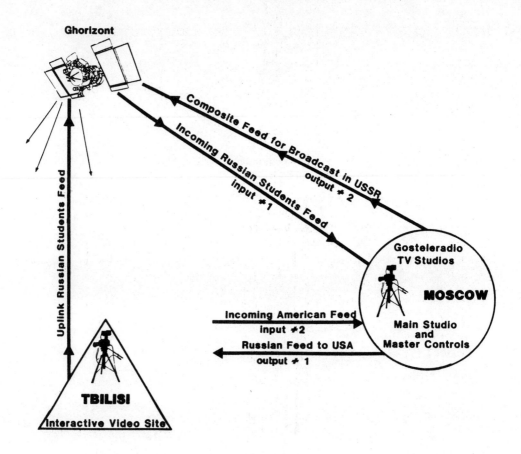

Figure IX-2 The Russian Site

Spacebridge technology has provided the channels through which nations can talk to each other. This is one of the bright sides of the new telecommunications technology.

CONCLUSION

Satellite communication is quickly becoming an important source of valuable teaching and learning programs unavailable through other sources of information. To summarize, satellite communication can:

• enrich educational offerings through the integration of highly specialized learning/teaching material unavailable on conventional channels;

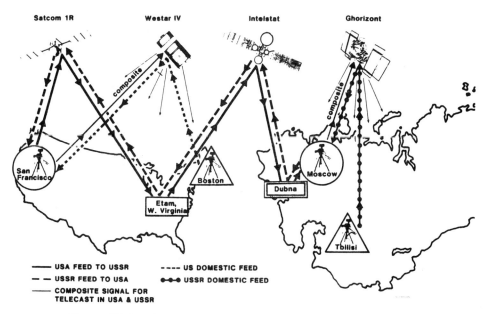

Figure IX-3. The Complete Route of US/USSR SPACEBRIDGE: The Role of the Media in Current Relations, Spring 1987.

- share educational experiences with other colleges, universities, and the corporate world;
- extend school boundaries to reach distant sites of learning and teaching;
- expose students and teachers to viable and cost-effective uses of tele-communication technology;
- provide students in communication with the opportunity to gain firsthand experience in television programming, and in marketing commercial spots; and
- open the classroom to the world through incorporating well-designed interactive teleconferences with other nations of the world.

REFERENCES

1. *The Futurist,* "Telefutures," April 1982, p. 62.
2. Long, Mark and Jeffrey Keating. THE WORLD OF SATELLITE TELEVISION. Mendocino, California: Quantum Publishing, Inc., 1986 Edition.
3. Whitehouse, George E. UNDERSTANDING THE NEW TECHNOLOGIES OF THE MASS MEDIA. Englewood, N.J.: Prentice-Hall, 1986.
4. Long, Mark. WORLD SATELLITE ALMANAC, THE COMPLETE GUIDE TO SATELLITE TRANSMISSION & TECHNOLOGY. Indianapolis, Indiana: Howard W. Sam & Company, Second Edition, 1987.

5. Long, Mark. THE DOWN TO EARTH GUIDE TO SATELLITE TV. Mendocino, California: Quantum Publishing, Inc., 1985.
6. Satellite Communication Research. SATELLITE EARTH STATION USE IN BUSINESS AND EDUCATION – SPECIAL REPORT, Tulsa, OK, 1820 S. Boulder Place, 74119: Satellite Communication Research.
7. *ON-SAT,* a weekly magazine published by Triple D Publishing, Inc., 501 N. Washington Street, Shelby, NC 28150, Telephone (704) 482-9673.
8. U.S.A./U.S.S.R. SPACEBRIDGE was produced by The Center for Communication, 1133 Avenue of The Americas, N.Y., N.Y., and Gostelradio, Moscow in conjunction with the American Society of Newspaper Editors. The SPACEBRIDGE PROJECT was funded by a grant from the John D. and Catherine T. McArthur Foundation. The Center for Communication, Inc. is a nonprofit organization that provides opportunities for university students and faculty to meet leading communication professionals. The Center sponsors seminars in all areas of communications including: advertising and marketing, television and radio, print and broadcast journalism, the new technologies, public relations, publishing, and examines current communication policy issues and conducts practical career development workshops. In November 1987, the U.S.A./U.S.S.R. SPACEBRIDGE was awarded First Prize Gold Medal by the International Teleconferencing Association.
9. "You Were Here.... and Also There," *Instructional Development Newsletter,* Media Center, Fairfield University, Fairfield, CT, May 1987.

PART IV
INTERACTIVE DATA BASES

Alfred Glossbrener wrote in *The Complete Handbook of Personal Communication* about our universe being an electronic universe, "in which messages and information streak across the continent or around the world at the speed of light. A place where you can find a fact or find a job, play a game, publish a poem, meet a friend, consult an encyclopedia, or do hundreds of other things without leaving your office or home." (p. xiii) That myriad of information is available through data banks and data bases, and can provide the learner with rich learning materials. One of the aims of education in the 21st century is to cultivate the learner who is capable of locating specific information, and of evaluating the pertinency of the information gathered and weighing it against other sources.

Two major types of these resources are available to the user. The first is data bases published on CD–ROM (Compact Disc Read-Only-Memory), and information utilities companies which can be accessed through the use of a personal computer and telephone line.

Chapter Ten, Interactive CD–ROM Databases, The Keys to Personal Information Access and Use, addresses the digital optical disc technology (DOD) with emphasis on CD–ROM data bases.

Appendix II, Information Utilities, lists some of the services available through some of the major information utilities companies.

Chapter Ten

INTERACTIVE CD-ROM DATABASES
The Keys to Personal Information Access and Use

FRANCIS A. HARVEY

INTRODUCTION

The amount of information which professionals in every field must deal with is growing almost exponentially. There are now thousands of professional journals in the fields of medicine, engineering, business and economics, and education. Clearly, it is impossible for a professional to keep track of this amount of information and to stay aware of the contents of this many journals, let alone read and understand them all.

To keep their knowledge current, professionals do not need to read every word produced in the literature of their discipline. It is essential, however, that they are able to identify and to locate relevant information on a particular topic *when they need it.* Some support mechanism is required which will allow professionals to ascertain which portions of the vast information available might be relevant to a particular question, then to examine that information and ultimately read just the portion of the literature which is truly relevant.

The task of organizing the contents of professional literature has traditionally been done by indexes. A variety of print indexes are available for the professional literature in specific fields. (1) In medicine, for example, the **MEDLINE** database covers more than 3,200 journals. The *Index of Economic Literature* covers 293 business and economics journals. *The Resources in Education* (RIE) and *Current Index to Journals in Education* (CIJE) indexes from ERIC cover more than 750 professional journals in education, as well as a large number of reports and other documents.

Indexes to professional literature became a much more useful tool when they were developed in online form. **MEDLINE, COMPENDEX,** and

ERIC are all available on mainframe computers which can be accessed via telephone lines by anyone with an account and a computer terminal or microcomputer equipped with a MODEM for phone communications.

Online databases, however, do have some limitations in terms of both cost and flexibility. The modem and communications software needed to establish communications between the mainframe computer adds additional cost for the user. In addition, a significant portion of the cost of use is directly proportional to the amount of time which the user is connected to the system. Since standard telephone lines will support communications of 1200 BAUD (120 characters/second) or 2400 BAUD (240 characters/second), costs for "connect time" can very quickly mount up. The cost of downloading, transmitting, the results of a complex search from the mainframe computer to the microcomputer at 120 characters per second can be prohibitive.

The user of an online database is also required to learn how to formulate a search query and provide other directions to the system (for example, concerning printing or transmitting the results of the search from the mainframe computer to the user) in the specific language used by that system. For the occasional or novice user, online systems can prove quite challenging and often frustrating. Online databases are further limited because the information contained in them is, in nearly all cases, restricted to text only.

Emerging digital optical disc storage technologies, DOD, hold the potential answer to the problems of information access. Microcomputer workstations equipped with digital optical disc storage devices and appropriate software can provide professionals with access to a large database of information in a manner which gives the professional extensive control and flexibility while providing considerable savings in cost, time, and efficiency.

Emerging DOD technologies could have as wide-ranging an impact on society, and particularly on education, as the introduction of the microcomputer in the later 1970s. Whereas the microcomputer helped bring about a revolutionary change in the degree to which people could manipulate data which was principally in the form of textual material and numerical data (and some relatively crude graphics, especially when compared with video), CD–ROM and other DOD technologies used in combination with microcomputers could bring about an "Information Revolution." Users could have immediate access to and control over:

1. a much larger amount of information;
2. a much wider range of types of information, including graphics, still video, motion video, and audio as well as textual and numerical information; and
3. more flexible and more powerful means of accessing, presenting, and manipulating this information.

Miller stated that:

These new technologies represent quantum leaps in technology. They do not simply improve on previous methods; rather, they open new doors and present opportunities never before available. We are only beginning to skim the surface of the potential represented by the marriage of optical disc formats with computers. Never before have we had at our disposal the vast amount of data or the large number of images now available through this combination. (2)

DIGITAL OPTICAL DISC TECHNOLOGY

An Overview

There are three major forms of digital optical disc technology:
1. **CD-ROM** (Compact Disc Read-Only- Memory),
2. **CD-I** (Compact Disc Interactive), and
3. **DVI** (Digital Video Interactive).

All of these forms are based on optical storage of digitally encoded information, using 12 centimeter (4.72 inch) diameter discs similar to CD–Audio discs. They differ significantly in the current state of their development, in the type of user for which they are being targeted, in the environments in which they are intended to be used, and in the types of applications which are being developed for them.

CD–ROM is a currently existing technology intended for use as a computer peripheral for mass data storage and retrieval. CD–ROM was introduced by Philips/SONY in 1984. Currently more than one hundred companies have licensed CD–ROM technology. (3)

CD–I is a proposed worldwide standard for a stand-alone system (with a built-in microprocessor) designed primarily for home use. It was originally expected to be available in 1988, and is now scheduled for release in late 1989. CD–I will be able to incorporate large amounts of high-quality sound, still video, and computer-generated and computer-manipulated graphics in an environment which is potentially very interactive.

DVI is a combination of proprietary hardware and software, still in the early development stages, which will be able to provide full-motion video in addition to most of the capabilities of CD–I. Several test sites for developing DVI applications were established at the end of 1988.

This chapter will focus on CD–ROM technology because that form was developed first, has the widest number of applications available, and seems to be evolving toward hardware and software standards which will allow it to grow quickly. CD–I and DVI will be discussed and compared at the end of this chapter. Emerging technologies such as multimedia CD–ROM applications and the use of hypermedia will also be discussed.

CD-ROM TECHNOLOGY

CD–ROM discs are designed for use as peripheral devices for storage of large amounts of digital data. One CD–ROM disc holds the equivalent of 1,500 MS–DOS microcomputer floppy disks (or over 3,000 Apple IIe disks). This corresponds to over 200,000 pages of single-spaced typewritten text—a stack of paper more than twenty feet tall. It would take one secretary typing ninety words per minute, eight hours a day more than eight years to type the amount of information which could be stored on one CD–ROM disc. A person reading one page per minute for twelve hours a day would take more than nine months to read the entire contents of one CD–ROM disc.

To produce a digital optical disc, digital information is encoded onto the plastic CD platter by burning tiny pits into the surface of a master disc using a high-powered laser. Each pit is 0.12 microns deep and 0.6 microns wide. One disc can store more than 550 million bytes of digitally-coded information in a spiral track beginning at the center of the disc and which, if it were stretched out in one long line, would be over three miles long. Since discs weigh less than 0.7 ounces, digital optical disc storage provides one of the densest information distribution media in terms of information per ounce.

Copies of the master disc are produced using technology similar to that used to produce phonograph records. The cost of mastering an optical digital disc is from two to five thousand dollars. The cost of producing copies in quantity can be less than a dollar each.

Compact disc players use a low-power laser beam to scan the surface of the spinning disc. A system of lenses and mirrors directs the light reflected from the pits and "lands" (the flat surfaces between the pits) on the disc into a series of light-sensitive diodes. Signal processing circuitry converts the light intensity reflected from the pits and lands to binary 1's or 0's and sends these bits to a computer or other device. The binary digit 1 is represented by a transition from a land to pit or vice versa. The number of digital 0's transmitted is proportional to the distance between pit/land or land/pit transitions. (4) Since the surface of the disc is never touched by anything but the laser beam, optical discs could in theory last forever.

The CD–ROM market is expanding rapidly. In 1985, less than 3,000 CD–ROM players were sold; it is projected that over 390,000 will be sold in 1989. (5, p. 14) Currently less than 2 percent of microcomputer storage uses CD–ROM, and by 1990 it is expected that this percentage will increase tenfold.

Advantages of CD–ROM

The major advantage of CD–ROM is its large capacity storage. Much more information can be provided to users in a much smaller space. This is important for libraries, for example, which must cope with ever-growing collections within a finite (usually fixed) space. Large capacity also makes it possible to include the full text of documents, rather than a citation and abstract, as in most print or online databases.

A second major advantage of CD–ROM is the permanent nature of its medium. Information, once put on the disc, can not be erased or changed, either accidentally by a naive user or intentionally by a knowledgeable (or malicious) user. For many applications, such as reference bases which are shared by several users or for archival information which does not change, this is desirable.

Since CD–ROM systems are microcomputer-based, they also provide a high degree of user control and accessibility. The information on a CD–ROM is available to the user at any time, without having to depend on phone lines, account numbers, or passwords for access to mainframe data base systems. Retrieval of information is much faster than the retrieval of the same amount and type of information by hand.

Other advantages of CD–ROM include their relatively low cost. CD–ROM discs use the same basic digital optical storage technology, although with additional software for error detection and correction, as the CD–Audio compact discs which have revolutionized the audio recording industry. The development costs of CD–ROM technology, therefore, were considerably lower than they would have been if the developmental base of CD–Audio were not available. CD–ROM discs are also durable, convenient, and flexible in terms of the variety of media which can be stored on them.

Limitations of CD–ROM

One advantage of CD–ROM, that the data cannot be changed, can in some applications be a disadvantage. Updating a CD–ROM disc involves remastering the entire disc with the old as well as new information. CD–ROM may not be the most appropriate format for data which changes rapidly, or for data to which users are constantly adding.

A second disadvantage is speed. Access time for CD–ROM discs, the time required to locate a particular piece of information on a disc, is relatively slow. Typically it takes about one second to locate a file on a CD–ROM disc and to position the laser beam for reading it, compared to one-tenth to three-tenths of a second for magnetic, floppy, or Winchester disk systems. The data transfer rate for CD–ROM, the speed at which the host computer reads data from a disc once the data are found, is approximately 150 kilobytes per second. This is much faster than the 31 kilobytes per second rate for data transfer from a magnetic floppy disk, but more than four times slower than a magnetic hard disk (625 kilobytes per second). (6) The slow speed of CD–ROM discs is most noticeable when large amounts of information are being transferred from the disc to the computer's memory, or when the information being transferred is located in many different parts of the disc. For most applications, the flexibility and extensive user control of a CD–ROM application more than compensate for its slow speed relative to magnetic storage media.

Equipment/Software Requirements

CD–ROM is designed to be used as a computer peripheral. A typical CD–ROM workstation consists of a microcomputer system such as an IBM–PC or XT to which a CD–ROM drive has been connected using a cable and interface card. The interface card, which is specific to the type of CD–ROM drive used, is placed in one of the microcomputer's internal slots and controls communications between the microcomputer and the CD–ROM drive. In June, 1988, Apple Computer Corporation began marketing a CD–ROM player for Macintosh Plus, SE, or Macintosh II microcomputers. The Apple CD–ROM player connects to the SCSI (Small Computer System Interface) port of Macintosh microcomputers; an additional interface card is not required. Newer, more complex CD–ROM applications may require more powerful microcomputers such as an IBM AT or PS/2 with extended memory (beyond 640K) and a Winchester hard disk drive; a Macintosh SE-30, or Macintosh II.

Hitachi, Philips, and Sony all market CD–ROM drives. Drives can be purchased either as stand-alone devices or as internal devices to be mounted within the microcomputer case as with built-in floppy disk drives. CD–ROM drives range in price from $700 to $1500; the price is dropping slowly as the market for drives expands.

Software for a CD–ROM system, in addition to the actual text or numerical information which comprises the database itself, consists of:

1. computer-based indexes to the database; and
2. application-specific software.

Typically, computer-based indexes are stored along with the database information on the CD–ROM disc itself. Application-specific software is usually provided either entirely on magnetic floppy disks or partially on floppy disks and partially on the CD–ROM disc itself. Application-specific software is usually designed so that it can be transferred and stored on hard disks (Winchester disks) for increased speed in actual use.

Computer-based indexes are used in searching and retrieving information from the database. They may consist, for example, of a list of every document contained in the CD–ROM database, the length of each document, and the location of each document on the disc. Another type of index frequently used is an inverted index, which alphabetically lists every word contained in the database and the locations in the database of every occurrence of each word. Indexes make possible the fast, flexible, and powerful searching which make CD–ROM databases useful information tools.

Application-specific software consists of the user interface and system utilities. The user interface controls screen displays, processes input from the user, and in general manages the exchange of information and instructions exchange between the microcomputer/CD–ROM system and the human user. System utilities manage the exchange of information between the CD–ROM disc and the microcomputer's memory, the manipulation and maintenance of index lists, the processing and maintenance of search specifications and search results, and the transfer of search results and search strategies from the computer to a printer or to magnetic disk storage.

The development of applications software is one of the fastest growing fields in CD–ROM. Newer applications have a wider variety of features than those found on earlier CD–ROM databases. For example, current applications generally provide enhanced support for electronic browsing, support more complex searching strategies, and allow far more flexibility in specifying the formats for saving or printing search results. Newer applications are much easier to use, and are considerably faster than applications developed even a few years ago. An emerging area of research interest in CD–ROM database development is the application of expert systems technology and other artificial intelligence techniques to specifying, locating, and utilizing information contained in a CD–ROM database.

CD-ROM and Interactivity

Digital optical disc technologies can be highly interactive, which has long been a goal of instructional designers. Han described interactive programs in this way:

> Interactive programs . . . distinguish themselves from other video programs and visual or text databases by having elements that are designed not only to facilitate the user's selections but also to "engage" the user. This goes beyond mere transparency or other ease of use. Designers of most computer-based programs have learned the value of removing obstacles to the user's direct input and rapid understanding. Engaging the user means, quite simply, that we begin with the assumption that the user must want to use the program—both in the overall sense, and at each point of input. (7, p. 16)

Han further suggested that designers of interactive programs and the programmers with which they work should begin with the attitude that the user must be satisfied at each step in the program and that the user must also feel a true sense of conversational "relationship" with the program.

CD-ROM APPLICATIONS

CD–ROM should be thought of a compact and powerful publication medium. Over 700 CD–ROM titles are now in print. (8) Many of these are special purpose discs designed for in-house use by large companies. A large number, however, are commercial products available to the general public. It is impossible to describe all CD–ROM products available here. Instead, representative examples of applications in several major categories: general reference, education, engineering, government, and medicine will be discussed. The reader is referred to the supplemental materials listed at the end of this chapter for more comprehensive information on CD–ROM applications.

CD-ROM Databases for General Reference

General reference CD–ROM databases include dictionaries, atlases, encyclopedias, general reference works such as style guides and thesauruses, newspapers and magazines, and databases of demographic or statistical data. The first mass market application of CD–ROM was the GROLIER ELECTRONIC ENCYCLOPEDIA in 1986. The GROLIER ELECTRONIC ENCYCLOPEDIA contains on one CD–ROM disc the entire text of the 20-volume, 10,000-page *Academic American Encyclopedia.* The text occupies over 50,000 bytes of disc space. The disc also contains a specially designed index which occupies 60,000 bytes on the disc. The index is used with the Knowledge Retrieval System (KRS) software developed by Activenture which is supplied on floppy disk with the **Grolier CD-ROM.** With this software, the user can search the encyclopedia by article title, by article text, or by bibliographies and tables. The user can ask to select all articles which contain a specific word, combination of words or phrases, or even partial words. Boolean search capabilities allow users to select articles based on combinations of words or phrases; for example, by specifying "red OR pink AND flowers" or "plants AND Pennsylvania BUT NOT steel." A "browse" capability is also included, which may be used to examine the alphabetical list of article titles.

Recently the GROLIER ELECTRONIC ENCYCLOPEDIA CD-ROM user interface has been completely revised and the contents of the disc updated. (9) The interface now makes extensive use of a mouse pointing device and features pull-down menus, which appear on the screen automatically when the user points at a specific word at the top of the screen such as "Search" or "Print." Other new features allow users to create their own linkages among the material reviewed or to create split screen displays to view two sections of a document or two separate documents simultaneously. The GROLIER ELECTRONIC ENCYCLOPEDIA is currently available for MS–DOS and Apple Macintosh microcomputer systems.

A general CD–ROM application which is unique in that it provides the user with both text and visual information is the **GEOdisc U.S. Atlas CD-ROM** and the **GEOdisc State Series** of **CD-ROM's** produced by GEOVISION. (10) The **U.S. Atlas** disc is a CD–ROM geographic database that contains a complete digital representation of the United States, including highways, waterways, political boundaries, railroads, federal land areas, and hydrological districts. A file of over one million places and landmarks, with coordinate information, is also included.

The **GEOdisc CD-ROM's** are designed to be used with Geovision's **Windows/On the World (WOW)** application software, which is written for the Microsoft's **MS Windows** environment. (**MS Windows** is a proprietary operating system developed by Microsoft Corporation for IBM and IBM-compatible microcomputers; it supports the use of a mouse pointing device, pull-down menus, and multiple screen windows). The **WOW** software allows the user to generate overlays of graphics, text, or symbols for maps generated from data on the CD–ROM disc. Information from external databases can be linked to the **GEOdisc** database, and the maps generated can be printed on a color printer or copied to documents generated by other MS Windows applications. The **GEOdisc CD-ROM** would be an excellent resource for students in geography or government classes in middle, secondary, or postsecondary schools.

MicroTrends, Inc. has produced the **LinguaTech Bilingual Dictionary CD-ROM** series. English/French, English/German, and English/Spanish versions are available.

The number of applications of CD–ROM technology available is growing rapidly. The rate of adoption of CD–ROM technology may increase even more rapidly as a result of the recent release of the **Microsoft Bookshelf**, a CD–ROM with the entire contents of the *American Heritage Dictionary, Roget's Thesaurus,* the *World Almanac and Book of Facts, Bartlett's Familiar Quotations,* the *Chicago Manual of Style,* a spelling verifier and corrector, and a variety of business forms and letters. (11) Some feel that the **Microsoft Bookshelf** could be the "VisiCalc of CD–ROM;" that is, the software product which makes acquiring CD–ROM hardware both desirable and respectable, just as the original **VisiCalc** spreadsheet program bestowed respectability on microcomputers. The **Microsoft Bookshelf** disc could be used in offices, in homes, or in middle and secondary school classes as a component of language arts and communications instruction.

An example of a general reference CD–ROM which creatively repackages existing information from a wide variety of sources into a comprehensive reference resource is the **Microsoft Small Business Consultant,** recently released by Microsoft. This CD–ROM contains the full text of over 200 publications from the Small Business Administration and other government agencies. Microsoft has also recently released the **Microsoft Stat Pack,** a compendium of social, political, economical, land use, business, and agricultural information from government sources. (12) In an attempt to broaden the market for CD–ROM technology, Microsoft has priced each of these CD–ROM's at $150 and $125, respectively.

A general reference CD–ROM application which is unique because of the type of information it contains is the **PC-SIG Library on CD-ROM.** (13) This disc contains thousands of shareware and public-domain software programs for MS–DOS computers, the equivalent of 1,000 floppy diskettes. The CD–ROM's extensive collection of educational programs for all levels of education, word processors, spreadsheets, databases managers, utility programs, games, and many special-use programs could be useful in a variety of settings.

Programs can easily, and legally be copied from the CD–ROM disc to floppy disks for general distribution. The well-organized directory structure allows users to select programs by browsing through program descriptions or searching by topic or program title. A CD–ROM player with the **PC-SIG Library** would be a useful and cost-effective resource for any organization.

Educational Applications of CD-ROM

CD-ROM Applications for Use by K-12 School Students

Most CD–ROM players in school settings are used for library applications. In Pennsylvania, for example, a statewide consortium of public, school district, and higher education libraries, in cooperation with Brodart Automation, have developed the **PA-Access CD-ROM** series, which is in effect a statewide union catalog of holdings of all the libraries in the consortium. Students in member schools can search for a book of interest based on title, grade or reading level, or subject matter. Over a million titles are included in the current version of the database. A student can use the CD–ROM disc to find out which libraries across the state have a particular book, then request it via interlibrary loan.

The CD–ROM vendor which has the widest range of products designed for the educational market is MicroTrends. They have produced the **BioLibe** series of biology teaching aids; **FastPast**, a world history tutorial; and **Versa Text**, a reading skills teaching aid, in addition to the bilingual dictionary series mentioned earlier.

CD–ROM Applications for Use by
K–12 School Teachers, Supervisors, and Administrators.

A CD–ROM application with specific relevance for middle school teachers and administrators is the **K-8 Science Helper** CD–ROM produced by Professor Mary Budd Rowe of the University of Florida. (14) This disc, a product of the Knowledge Utilization Project in Science, KUPS, at the University of Florida, Gainesville, is designed for use by teachers, curriculum planners, educational researchers, and publishers. The CD–ROM disc contains 918 science and mathematics lesson plans for grades K–8 selected from various elementary science curriculum development projects funded by the National Science Foundation during the 1960s and 1970s. The CD–ROM disc includes teacher-written abstracts of each lesson, the full contents of each lesson plan, summaries of the philosophy of each curriculum project, and comprehensive index and retrieval software which was designed and developed especially for this project. (15) System requirements are: an IBM PC/XT/AT or compatible computer with at least 256K RAM; a CD–ROM player; MS–DOS 3.1 or higher; and Microsoft's MS–DOS CD–ROM Extensions which are a set of software enhancements to the MS–DOS operating system to allow the system to handle very large files.

The retrieval software was designed for use by teachers who may not be familiar with database searching techniques, and is very easy to use. It makes extensive use of a hierarchical series of menus for selecting options; the user selects options by typing a single letter or by using the arrow keys to move a pointer to the desired menu item. A summary of the search strategy being used and the number of lesson plans which would be selected using this strategy are always displayed on the screen. This information is constantly updated as the search strategy evolves.

The user can select lesson plans based on a wide variety of criteria, including: grade level, curriculum programs (that is, the NSF-funded curriculum projects from which the sample lesson plans were taken), academic subjects, content themes, science processes, lesson titles, book titles (that is, the title of each specific teacher's guide), and vocabulary words or phrases.

The lesson plans used were selected from the following curriculum projects: **Conceptually-Oriented Program in Elementary Science (COPES), Elementary Science Study (ESS), Minnesota Mathematics and Science Teaching Project (MINNEMAST), Science: A Process Approach (S-APA), Science Curriculum Improvement Study (SCIS), and Unified Science and Mathematics for Elementary Schools (USMES).** Since the lessons were developed as part of funded National Science Foundation projects, and the contents of the lesson plans which are included on the CD–ROM were taken from trial editions developed by those projects, the lesson plans are in the public domain and may be copied freely by teachers or others for their use. In a thoughtful gesture of recognition of the original developers of the lesson plans used, the retrieval software allows the user to access, via the F10 function key, background information on the original teacher's guide, including the names of those who participated in its development.

The disc contains the complete contents of the 918 lesson plans. These were captured by scanning print versions of teacher's guides of the curriculum projects and capturing each page as a bit image; that is, a digitized "picture" of each page was developed. (15) While this approach made the data conversion process straightforward and relatively efficient, this efficiency was gained at some cost in flexibility and ease of use. If the text of each lesson plan had been entered as an ASCII file by retyping or by using optical character recognition (OCR) technology, a full-text retrieval system similar to that used by the **Grolier Electronic Encyclopedia CD-ROM** could have been developed. A full text retrieval system would allow teachers or other users to select lessons based on the occurrence of any word in the lesson plan, rather than being limited to the descriptors assigned to each lesson plan by the project developers. However, since the indexing system used by the retrieval software is very comprehensive, most users should have no difficulty in identifying and selecting lesson plans appropriate for specific students.

The **TESCOR First National Item Bank and Test Development System** (16) is a CD–ROM disc containing tens of thousands of validated test items for elementary schools. Each test item is linked to thousands of curriculum-related objectives. Teachers or administrators can use the disc to select appropriate test items for specified curriculum objectives. An added feature is the ability to have the computer format and print out the final version of a test constructed from the items selected.

Several state departments of education are utilizing CD–ROM technology. The Minnesota Department of Education depends on CD–ROM to distribute academic tests. (17, p. 49) The Texas State Department of Education and Quantum Access have produced the **State Education Encyclopedia.** (16, p. 53) This disc contains all state regulations and other official documents necessary for administering a school district in the state of Texas. The documents include the full text of relevant education legislation and departmental directives and regulations on student management, procurement, budgeting, personnel, and other administrative matters. A unique feature of this CD–ROM is the capability for the user to attach "notes" to a specific section of the text, for personal reference or for marking the text for use by colleagues.

CD–ROM Applications for Use by Educational Researchers

A variety of educational databases sponsored by the United States Department of Education, formerly available only via online searching using a modem attached to the computer, are now available on CD–ROM. Both **ERIC** data bases — **Resources in Education (RIE)** and **Current Index to Journals in Education (CIJE)** — are available from SilverPlatter and Dialog.

Engineering Applications

The **National Technical Information Service (NTIS)** database is distributed on CD–ROM by SilverPlatter. This database is comprised of documents from the U.S. Department of Energy, U.S. Department of Defense, National Aeronautics and Space Administration, and other federal, non-federal, and foreign agencies and sources. Topics covered include biotechnology, business and finance, communications, engineering, environment, robotics, and transportation. Over 70,000 completed reports are added to the NTIS database each year. (18, p. 1)

The National Institute of Building Sciences **Construction Criteria Base** CD–ROM provides the equivalent of an entire 60,000-page library of federal building guide specifications, standards, and manuals. Information includes the full text of guide specifications and design manuals of the Naval Facilities Engineering Command (NAVFAC), the Army Corps of Engineers, the National Aerospace Agency (NASA), and the Veterans Administration. Once identified, appropriate sections of information can be tagged and downloaded to a hard disk, then used in development of the actual specifications for a construction project. Use of the **Construction Criteria Base** CD–ROM is expected to significantly enhance quality control and productivity in preparing specifications for construction projects.

Other engineering-oriented CD–ROM applications are under development. McGraw-Hill is now testing and expects to make available in 1989 a CD–ROM version of **Sweet's Catalog**, the manufacturing product catalog which is a fundamental reference tool of the building industry.

Government Applications

Accessing the voluminous information produced by the federal government has been made simpler and faster by the introduction of the **Monthly Catalog of U.S. Government Publications** CD–ROM. (19) This CD–ROM version of an existing print catalog allows searches of technical reports, records of congressional hearings, catalogs, business and economic information, and other documents printed by the U.S. government. Documents may be selected by author, subject, title, report number, or keywords. The bibliographic records of the print version of the catalog back to 1976 are included, the equivalent of over 75 printed volumes.

Versions of the Government Printing Office catalog are also available on CD–ROM from other vendors. These include **GPO on SilverPlatter** produced by SilverPlatter and **LePac Government Documents Option** produced by Brodart Automation.

A variety of government agencies have produced CD–ROM applications utilizing their databases. The U.S. Census Bureau has produce **Census Test Disc #1**, which includes comprehensive census data indexed by zip codes. The U.S. Geological Survey has produced a prototype disc of geological information.

Medical Applications

MEDLINE, the National Library of Medicine Electronic Database which is recognized as the major index of biomedical literature, is available from Cambridge Scientific Abstracts on CD–ROM (20), and SilverPlatter (21). **MEDLINE CD-ROM** provides abstracts of articles and proceedings on biomedical research, clinical practice, administration, policy issues, and health care services from over 3,200 medical and biomedical journals from the United States and seventy other countries.

The **CANCER-CD CD-ROM** database (21) distributed by SilverPlatter contains references, abstracts, and commentaries of the world's literature on cancer and related subjects. The documents referenced in the database are drawn from Elsevier Science Publishers, Year Book Medical Publishers, and the National Cancer Institute in conjunction with the National Library of Medicine. Information covers documents from 1985 to the present, and is updated quarterly.

Information from professional journals in psychology and the behavioral sciences from the **PsycINFO** Department of the American Psychological Association is available on the PsychLit CD–ROM from SilverPlatter (21). The database covers entries from 1974 to the present, and is updated quarterly.

NEW DEVELOPMENTS AND TRENDS IN INFORMATION TECHNOLOGY

Technology for information access and use is changing rapidly. While CD–ROM has evolved into an accepted standard with a small but solid and growing base of users, new technologies based on digital optical storage technology are appearing almost daily. These new technologies can be expected to have significant impact on how we gain access to information, the range and types of information available to us, and how we use that information. Two emerging digital optical disc technologies which, like CD–ROM, are based on CD–Audio technology will be discussed in the following. Each, however, offers different advantages over CD–ROM, and each has limitations which might prevent its widespread acceptance. Also, an overview of hypermedia and its implications for creating and using information will be presented.

Emerging Digital Optical Technologies: CD-I and DVI

Compact Disc Interactive, CD-I

CD-I, Compact Disc Interactive, is a proposed standard format for storing and retrieving information on CD discs which was developed jointly by Philips and SONY, and which was first announced by them at the First Microsoft CD–ROM Conference in March, 1986. Several hundred companies have licensed CD–I technology and are developing applications.

The development of CD–I have taken much longer than originally expected; the first CD–I applications are now expected in 1989. On paper, the CD–I system is impressive. However, it is impossible to predict the compromises which may become necessary in developing CD–I and therefore the capabilities of the CD–I systems actually delivered.

CD–I represents a fusion of video, audio, text, data, and software storage and retrieval capabilities, all on one medium which shares a worldwide standard. All CD–I players and all CD–I software products should be compatible with each other. Lowe stated that "Philips and SONY believe that CD–I is the medium that will successfully mass-market interactivity to the electronic consumer . . . the object of CD–I is to set the standard for the generic home information and entertainment system of the future." (22)

A CD–I system will incorporate a compact disc player, a microprocessor, and a mouse or joystick input device. It will be designed to connect to a home TV set and stereo system. A computer is not required, although with the addition of a keyboard and appropriate software the CD–I system could incorporate the capabilities of a personal computer.

CD–I will provide four audio formats, from high-quality stereo to "speech mode" with quality equivalent to AM radio. Ten hours of stereo speech, twenty hours of monophonic speech, or 74 minutes of high quality stereo music can be stored on one disc. Sound formats can be mixed and matched on the same disc.

The video formats used in CD–I include natural video pictures, user-manipulable graphics, and quality graphics. Natural pictures will resemble high-quality video stills. User-manipulable graphics will be lower in quality, but will still provide very high resolution and a large number of colors. Quality graphics are more "cartoon-like;" however, they offer the capability of displaying full-screen animation, which could be combined with various sound tracks.

Text will resemble high quality text as seen on broadcast television rather than "computer screen text." Up to 600 million text characters can be stored on one disc. With the appropriate software on the disc, the user can search the text, retrieve and manipulate it.

Limitations of CD-I. CD–I uses digital, not analog, encoding of the information on the disc. Due to the speed of transferring such information from the disc and converting digital information to video, it will not be possible to produce true motion video with CD–I. Many instructional developers consider this a major drawback; others, however, feel that the other features of CD–I will allow instructional developers to overcome this limitation.

CD–I offers the promise of the ability to deliver vast amounts of informational or instructional material in many different modes. Using the sophisticated computer operating system which will be incorporated into CD–I applications, the user will be able to select portions of the informational or instructional material and interact with it in ways which are not possible with traditional materials. For example, the user may rearrange existing material, combine material from several different sources into one document, or add additional user-created information to existing information. The user can then print the new augmented information with a printer or save the new information on magnetic disk. Potentially, the user has more power to manipulate and modify the materials being presented than in any other technological system, and thus, in principle, learning with CD–I can be truly user-directed, active, and interactive learning.

DVI Technology

DVI, or Digital Video Interactive, was first introduced by RCA at the second international conference on CD–ROM in Seattle, Washington, in March, 1987. (23) DVI uses a standard CD–ROM disc and disc player. The major advantage of DVI is that it is capable of producing full-screen, full-motion video at a resolution equal to or exceeding standard broadcast video.

DVI achieves full-motion video capability through the use of a set of custom VLSI (Very Large Scale Integration) computer chips mounted on an expansion board in the microcomputer. The chips use specially developed compression/decompression programs which reconstruct images stored on the disc and produce motion video. A maximum of 72 minutes of motion video can be stored on one disc.

Demonstration applications of DVI include an interactive version of *Sesame Street; Palenque,* a tour of a Mayan historical site developed in cooperation with the Bank Street College of Education; a flight simulator; and a golf game.

DVI will be marketed initially as an expansion board for personal computers already equipped with regular CD–ROM drives, and eventually as a separate DVI player designed to be attached to a personal computer and as a separate, stand-alone integrated unit.

Limitations of DVI. DVI, like CD–I, is in the very early stages of development. It is marketed by a single company (Intel Corporation, which has purchased the original developers of DVI, RCA, and has expressed a commitment to continue its development), and may have more difficulty achieving wide acceptance than CD–I, which has been licensed to over one hundred developers. Initially, the cost of DVI will be prohibitive for most if not all K–12 applications.

CD–ROM, CD–I, and DVI are three different products aimed at separate and distinct markets, although there is considerable overlap in those markets, especially in the educational area. It is hoped that the three technologies will coexist and support each other, rather than compete with each other.

At present, the three technologies are at different stages of development, and it is difficult to predict whether one of these technologies, a combination of them, or some new as yet unknown version of digital optical disc will eventually become the "standard." It is safe to assume, however, that technologies with these capabilities will become commonplace in the near future, and that the technology which finally emerges as the "standard" (if one does) will be both digital and optical in nature. It may not, however, use the CD–Audio disc standard which, because of the relatively low access rate and data transfer rate, currently limits information utilization, especially of large amounts of data such as used for visual databases and full-motion video.

The demonstrations of the capabilities of DVI and the descriptions of the applications proposed for CD–I are indeed impressive. Widespread availability of such capabilities would significantly broaden the horizons of educational technology. Utilization of available CD–ROM applications, even in their present form, would greatly expand both the range of information available and the ease with which such information could be accessed.

Hypermedia

In addition to advances in optical disc technology (and to some extent because of these advances), increasing attention is being paid to:

1. how information is structured; and
2. the ways in which both producers of information and users of information are able to interact with that information and with each other.

One concept becoming increasingly popular is that of hypermedia, which is described by some of its proponents as Conklin, as "a computer-based medium for thinking and communication." (24, p. 32)

Hypermedia embodies three central concepts. The first is that information and communication use a wide variety of forms in addition to text; in other words, hypermedia is multimedia. The second central concept is the presentation and utilization of information in nonlinear, nonsequential form, as opposed to the traditional linear presentation of books, videotape, film, and most other media. The third central concept of hypermedia is that both the developer and the user of information should have the capability to create linkages among different parts of that information. In the following section, a brief overview of hypermedia and some of its implications for information access and use will be discussed.

Hypermedia is an extension of the concept of hypertext, a term first coined by Ted Nelson (1967) to denote nonsequential writing and reading. (25) Hypertext is nonsequential in that links can be created among any parts of the information in the document. Hypertext involves both writing and reading because in theory both the developer who "writes" the material, and the user who "reads" the material can create these links. Individual users, therefore, can organize the material in a way which makes sense to them.

Historically, the concept of hypertext was first described by Vannevar Bush in a 1945 article about a proposed system for organizing the complete body of scientific knowledge. (26) The hypothetical **Memex** supported browsing and making notes in a very large library containing on-line text and graphics information as well as personal notes, photographs, and sketches. It used multiple screens and included the capability for establishing labelled links between any two points in the library. Bush's vision is remarkable in that his article predates by several years the development of digital computers.

Nicole Yankelovich defines hypermedia in these terms: "We use the word **hypermedia** to denote the functionality of hypertext but with additional components such as two- and three-dimensional structured graphics, paint graphics, spreadsheets, video, sound, and animation. With hypermedia, an author can create links to complex diagrams, texts, photographs, video disks, audio recording and the like." (27)

Hypermedia, then, is a new computer-based way of using information which consists of both hardware and software. Because of the complexity, processing power, and display resolution required by hypermedia, most hypermedia software applications have been developed using mainframe computers, minicomputers, or powerful dedicated workstations. Commercial software packages currently available to support the development of hypermedia applications for microcomputers include **Guide**, developed by OWL International for both Macintosh and MS–DOS computers, and *HyperCard* from Apple Computer for the Macintosh. IBM has a hypermedia application for IBM microcomputers called **Linkways**, released in early 1989.

Current implementations of hypermedia for microcomputers are limited by the computing power and memory of their environments. A wide range of HyperCard applications, for example, has been introduced commercially or distributed as public domain or "shareware." These initial efforts, however, do not for the most part utilize the features of hypermedia which make it a unique delivery system. HyperCard, for example, requires the user to shift from a browsing mode to an authoring mode in order to establish new linkages among information, thus requiring skills more appropriate for a programmer than a user of a hypermedia application. For this reason, while HyperCard has demonstrated its usefulness as an authoring tool for multimedia data base design and for some instructional applications, not all HyperCard applications can be considered as true hypermedia.

In the following, two points will be presented. First, a description of several existing hypermedia applications developed on more powerful computers, as well as several hypermedia-like applications developed with HyperCard for Macintosh microcomputers. Second, a discussion of some specific features of hypermedia which impact most directly on the teaching and learning processes and the implications of those features for the future of teaching and learning.

Hypermedia Applications

Hypermedia Information Processing Applications

Researchers at the Xerox Palo Alto Research Center, PARC, have developed **NoteCards**. (28) NoteCards is designed as an information analyst's tool which supports collecting and organizing information. Information is stored as "cards" of which there are about fifty different types. The major card types include filebox cards as well as cards for text, tables, video, animation, graphics, and "actions," which are subprocedures implemented in Lisp.

The **Hyperties** (for Hyper*t*ext *I*nteractive *E*ncyclopedia *S*ystem) developed at the University of Maryland operates in the MS–DOS environment. (29) Short articles (50–1000 words each) are interconnected with Hyperties links. Each article has a short description to aid identification. The system includes a browser and supports the use of bookmarks. The user is able to add annotations to the information.

Hypermedia Instructional Applications

Larry Friedlander, a professor at Stanford University, has developed a hypermedia curriculum on Shakespeare. Students can read a scene from Hamlet, for example, then view a film version of the same scene. Students can freeze the action to consult the written text at any time, or switch among different performances by different companies. A student may change the audio track from the dialogue of the scene to an "interior monologue" which conveys the possible thoughts of a specific character. Students in theater classes may study acting styles by viewing all of the various entrances employed by the actors.

Researchers at Brown University, as part of the Intermedia project, have developed hypermedia applications for an introductory English literature course and an upper-level plant cell biology course. (30, p. 1) Intermedia is described as: (1) a tool for professors to organize and present lessons using a computer; and (2) an interactive medium for students to study materials and add their own annotations and reports to the material. Intermedia applications use text, timelines, computer graphics, video documentaries, music, and other materials interactively.

For example, a student studying Alexander Pope may access biographical information on Pope or use a timeline to study political events during Pope's life. Another student may compare Pope's use of satire with the satire techniques used by later authors.

Within the Intermedia environment, the instructor (and other students, if permitted) can read a student's paper, examine the reference materials used, and add personal annotation links including, for example, comments, criticism, and suggested revisions.

HyperCard Applications at Lehigh University

In February, 1989, Lehigh University was awarded a contract to develop a training curriculum and produce related training materials for Cities in Schools (CIS), Inc., a national nonprofit corporation recognized as a national leader in promoting and facilitating the coordinated delivery of existing health, social, education, and other support services for at-risk youth and their families. Three modules (out of an eventual total of eight modules) will be developed and tested during the first phase of the project (spring, 1989). These modules will cover:

- The history of Cities in Schools;
- The national, regional, and local organization of Cities in Schools;
- The CIS prototype replication process, which describes the specific steps taken to establish a local, operational CIS services delivery system.

Each module of the training materials will be accompanied by supplementary computer-based hypermedia materials. The author will have major responsibility for designing and developing these materials.

Researchers at Lehigh University have also developed *LaserGallery,* a HyperCard application using art images transferred to videodisc from the collection of the Allentown (Pa.) Art Museum. (31)

Other HyperCard Applications

Teachers at Lowell High School in San Francisco have worked with Apple Computer to develop **Grapevine,** a HyperCard treatment of Steinbeck's **Grapes of Wrath.** (32) A HyperCard stack (program) allows students to access a wide range of information, including segments of depression-era radio programs, Roosevelt's fireside chats and other speeches, music, photographs, films, demographic data, political and agricultural and economic data, and information on government activities and programs.

ABC News and Optical Data Corporation have announced the release of a HyperCard application to accompany their interactive videodisc **The '88 Vote** (ABC News Interactive, 1989). The two-sided videodisc includes material gathered from announcements from candidates, the party conventions, televised debates, political advertisements from the campaign, news commentary, and a wide range of other video and audio information about the 1988 presidential campaign.

Specific Hypermedia Features
Which Will Impact Learning and Teaching

Hypermedia applications provide a complex and potentially powerful delivery system utilizing the strengths of computers combined with the illustrative power of other media. Hypermedia is (1) computer controlled, (2) nonsequential, (3) multimedia, and (4) a new and unique medium in its own right. Each of these key elements of hypermedia presents special opportunities and challenges to instructional developers and educational researchers. Each will be discussed in turn.

Hypermedia is a Computer-Controlled Delivery System

Hypermedia applications would not be possible without the power of a computer to organize and manage the application. Hypermedia applications are by definition more complex than traditional computer-based applications. They must manage many overlapping, nonlinear linkages. For example, in an application consisting of just one hundred separate information items, or information "nodes," the theoretical number of possible linkages is 4,950! Furthermore, these linkages can be among different types of materials: text, graphics, digitized photographs or slides, audio, still video, or motion video. Each type of material may be supplied by a different device requiring a specific computer interface and display. This heightened complexity will greatly increase the need for programming expertise and a greater interaction between instructional developers and programmers. More powerful, therefore more expensive, computers and more sophisticated computer programming languages will also be needed in order to fully utilize the power of hypermedia.

Hypermedia is Nonsequential

Although hypermedia frees the user from linear constraints, the identification and delineation of potentially useful linkages will require considerable effort and a thorough understanding of the underlying conceptual structure of the material being presented. Sequencing and the impact of different sequencing will become much more important. Furthermore, since both the developers and users of hypermedia applications are able to specify linkages and paths, researchers will have to devise some method of tracking particular paths through material used by specific users. In the **Cities in Schools** hypermedia training materials, for example, current plans call for providing exit criteria for each module. The exit criteria submodule can be tried by the user at any time, even as the first activity in the module. However, if the user does not meet the exit criteria, a suggested path through the material is presented to the user, as a guide to organizing his or her own learning. Users may choose to follow the suggested path, or continue to explore on their own. When users, by whatever learning method, have met the exit criteria for a module, their accomplishment is automatically recorded by the system.

Hypermedia's flexibility of sequencing raises further research questions for researchers in educational technology. These questions include the issues of how learners use their increased power over the sequencing of material, whether the sequences selected by the user result in effective instruction, and the extent to which hypermedia users are bound by their acculturation to a "book technology" (that is, a linear, single-sequence technology).

Hypermedia is Multimedia

By definition, hypermedia is composed of elements of other media, including computer-generated text and graphics, videotape, videodisc, slides and photographs, audio materials, and other materials, and will require a large quantity of a wide range of material. This will mean new demands on the production of instructional materials, requiring much more of a team effort, and probably more subcontracting of production to facilities which specialize in a particular medium. The added layer of people and interactions will add considerably to the overall project cost and logistical overhead.

Since no hypermedia standards have been established, for the foreseeable future the question of incompatibility will present a challenge to developers. The conversion of existing print materials, through scanning and digitizing, to computer-usable form is currently both slow and expensive, and will be a major bottleneck in the development of new materials. Repurposing existing materials also will require the development team, the researcher, and the potential user to keep in mind the nonsequential nature of hypermedia and to avoid developing a "mindset" based on experience with linear media.

To develop effective hypermedia, more emphasis will need to be focussed on specific attributes of presentation rather than on the overall impact of the presentation. Formative research will become more important; the approaches of evaluative research and "pure" research will become more similar, and the two groups should benefit from a cross-fertilization of ideas about approaches and specific techniques.

Hypermedia is a New Medium in its Own Right

Hypermedia applications provide opportunities for examining, organizing, and utilizing information which were not previously available either to developers or to learners. A taxonomy of the components of hypermedia and the various ways in which these components interrelate would be of enormous benefit both to developers and researchers.

The separate subcomponents of hypermedia are clearly identified: they include text, tabular data, computer-generated graphics, digitized photographs or slides, audio (in the form of sound effects, music, or digitized speech), still video, and motion video. The properties of these subcomponents, when considered as separate entities, are well delineated. The properties of hypermedia which are not found in the separate components must be identified. Research is also needed to identify the properties of hypermedia applications themselves and to identify those specific combinations of media which together prove effective.

Implications of Hypermedia for
Teaching, Learning, and Educational Research

The introduction of hypermedia has considerably expanded the domain both of instructional development and of research on effective instruction. New roles, new opportunities, and new challenges are presented to both instructional developers and researchers. It is hoped that developers and researchers will both take advantage of these opportunities and move quickly to meet the challenges which hypermedia technology presents.

CONCLUSION

Technology users often spend unproductive time seeking a panacea, the ultimate technology which will, once developed, solve all of their problems. Gabriel Offiesh, in a discussion of the educational potential of DOD technologies, states that the challenge is to develop creatively the educational potential of current technologies, rather than to seek constantly for the newest and ultimately most powerful technological innovation. He holds that this will require a complete break with conventional wisdom. In his view, the "microcomputer revolution is on the same level as the Copernican revolution." (33, p. 300)

The real challenge, according to Offiesh, is determining where technology should go as opposed to where it can go. Research has the potential to play a central role in determining the future direction of educational technology. Such research should focus on how users conceptualize both a specific body of information and the identification and selection of specific information from that body, not just provide training in skills related to the mechanics of using a specific information system.

Digital optical storage technologies can play a major role in bringing about change. Current and evolving hypermedia applications indicate the direction such changes may lead in terms of what forms information takes, how it is created and communicated, and how the shared utilization of information takes place. The major challenge for the future will be to devise means for realizing the full potential of these technologies, in order to optimize the benefits of emerging technologies for the largest number of users.

REFERENCES

1. Johnson, J. Personal Communication. August 3, 1988.
2. Miller, Rockley E., "An Overview of the Interactive Market," In S. Lambert & J. Sallis (Eds.) CD–I and INTERACTIVE VIDEODISC TECHNOLOGY. Indianapolis: Sams, 1987, pp. 1–14.
3. McLaughlin, P, "CD–ROM for Educators," Syracuse, NY: ERIC Clearinghouse on Information Resources, 1987.

4. Roth, J. P. (Ed.) ESSENTIAL GUIDE TO CD-ROM. Westport, CT: Meckler, 1986, p. 28.

5. Myers, P., "Introduction to Optical Information Systems," In J. R. Roth (Ed.) PROCEEDINGS OF THE OPTICAL INFORMATION SYSTEMS 1987 CONFERENCE (OIS '87), New York. Westport, CT: Meckler, 11–37.

6. Einberger, J., "CD ROM Characteristics," In S. Ropiequet, J. Einberger, and B. Zoellick (Eds) CD ROM: OPTICAL PUBLISHING. Redmond, WA: Microsoft, 1987, p. 38.

7. Han, David, "Parameters for the Design of Interactive Programs," In S. Lambert & J. Sallis (Eds.) CD-I and INTERACTIVE VIDEODISC TECHNOLOGY. Indianapolis: Sams, 1987, pp. 15–28.

8. McFaul, J., "Systems and Hardware of the Future," National Science Foundation Workshop on CD-ROM, Washington, DC, 29 March – 1 April, 1988.

9. CD-ROM Review, Cole Leaves Grolier. *CD-ROM Review* 1988, 3(6), 7.

10. Hanley, E. Personal Communication. February 24, 1988.

11. Schlender, B. R. "Microsoft Will Sell Reference Library On a Compact Disk," *The Wall Street Journal,* 1987, March 4, p. x.

12. Stork, C. "Microsoft CD-ROM Publishing: Two Case Studies." Paper presented at the CD-ROM Developers' Seminar, New York, June, 14, 1988.

13. PC-SIG. "The PC-SIG library on CD-ROM," *Shareware,* 3(3), 1988, p. 27.

14. PC-SIG. SCIENCE HELPER K–8. Sunnyvale, CA: PC-SIG, Inc., 1988.

15. Britton, Ted. Personal Communication. July, 1988.

16. Tiampo, J. M. "CD-ROM Disc Titles," *CD-ROM Review,* 2 (5), 1987, pp. 48–55.

17. Smith, G. "World Movement Towards In-House CD-ROM Publishing," In J. R. Roth (Ed.) PROCEEDINGS OF THE OPTICAL INFORMATION SYSTEMS 1987 CONFERENCE (OIS '87), New York. Westport, CT: Meckler, 1987, pp. 48–54.

18. NTIS. NTIS BIBLIOGRAPHIC DARABASE ON CD/ROM: VENDOR INFORMATION. Springfield, VA: NTIS Office of Product Management, 1988.

19. Bowerman, R. Personal Communication. August, 1988.

20. Cambridge Scientific Abstracts. Compact Cambridge: MEDLINE on CD-ROM. Bethesda, Md: Cambridge Scientific Abstracts, 1988.

21. SilverPlatter Information Services, Wellesley Hills, MA: SilverPlatter Information, Inc., 1988.

22. Lowe, Larry D. "CD-I: The Medium of the Future," In S. Lambert & J. Sallis (Eds.) CD-I and INTERACTIVE VIDEODISC TECHNOLOGY. Indianapolis: Sams, 1987, pp. 118–37.

23. Strukhoff, R. "RCA Steals the Show," *CD-ROM Review,* 2(2), 1987, pp. 39–42.

24. Conklin, J. "Hypertext: An Introduction and Survey," *IEEE Computer,* 20(9), 1987, pp. 17–41.

25. Nelson, T. "Getting It Out Of Our System," In G. Schechter, (Ed.) INFORMATION RETRIEVAL: A CRITICAL REVIEW, Washington, DC: Thompson Books, 1967.

26. Bush, V. "As We May Think," *Atlantic Monthly,* July, 1945, pp. 101–8.

27. Yankelovich, N.; Meyrowitz, M.; and van Dam, A. "Reading and Writing the Electronic Book," *IEEE Computer,* October, 1985.
28. Halasz, F. G., Moran, T. P., and Trigg, T. H. "NoteCards In a Nutshell." Proc. of the ACM Conf. on Human Factors in Computing Systems, Toronto, Canada, April, 1987.
29. Yankelovich, N.; Landow, G.; and Heywood, P. "Designing Hypermedia "Ideabases"—the Intermedia Experience," IRIS TECHNICAL REPORT NO. 87-4, 1987, Providence, R.I.: Brown University.
30. Schneiderman, B., and Morariu, J. "The Interactive Encyclopedia System (TIES)." Department of Computer Science, University of Maryland, College Park, MD 20742, June, 1986.
31. Geyer, P. and Cushall, M. B. "Hypermedia, HyperCard, and Interactive Videodisc." Presented at the Apple Computer/Drexel University Hyper-Card Fair, Philadelphia, Pa., 31 March, 1988.
32. Rogers, M. "Here Comes Hypermedia," *Newsweek,* October 3, 1988, pp. 44–5.
33. Offiesh, Gabriel D. "The Seamless Carpet of Knowledge and Learning," In S. Lambert & S. Ropiequet (Eds) CD ROM: THE NEW PAPYRUS. Redmond, WA: Microsoft, 1986, pp. 299–319.

In addition to the above, the following periodicals focus on optical storage technology:

CD Data Report, Langley Publications, Inc. 6609 Rosecroft Place, Falls Church, VA 22043, (703) 241-2131

CD-I News, LINK Resources Corporation, 79 Fifth Avenue, New York, NY 10003, (212) 627-1500.

CD-ROM Applications Forum, 2101 Grandin Road, Cincinnati, OH 45208-3227, (513) 871-7767.

The IICS Journal, International Interactive Communications Society, Applied Communications Institute, College of Communications, California State College at Chico, Chico, CA 95926.

INFORM, Association for Information and Image Management Publications, Suite 1100, 1100 Wayne Avenue, Silver Spring, MD 20910, (301) 587-8202.

Information Today, Learned Information, Inc., 143 Old Marlton Pike, Medford, NJ 08055, (609) 654-6266.

Optical Information Systems Update, Department VV, P.O. Box 3000, Denville, NJ 07834,

Optical Memory News, Rothchild Consultants, 216 Laguna Honda Boulevard, San Francisco, CA 94116-1496, (415) 681-3700.

The Optical Memory Report, also published by Rothchild Consultants (See address above).

The Videodisc Monitor, P.O. Box 26, Falls Church, VA 22046-0026, (703) 241-1799.

A Discography of CD–ROM Applications Discussed in this Chapter

The following list includes information on the CD–ROM applications discussed in this chapter. The information is listed in the following format: Name of CD–ROM application, vendor name, address, and telephone; hardware/software requirements for version as supplied by vendor; contact person (where available); price. Subscription prices are listed with the subscription period; only current subscription prices are listed; contact the vendor for information on databases for previous years.

- Biolibe Series
  MicroTrends, Inc., 650 Woodfield Drive, Suite 730, Schaumberg, IL 60195, (312) 310-8928
  IBM–PC or compatibles, monochrome or CGA
  $199/disc

- CANCER CD
  SilverPlatter Information Services, Inc., 37 Walnut Street, Wellesley Hills, MA 02181, (617) 239-0306
  IBM–PC or compatibles, 512K (640K recommended), monochrome or CGA, hard drive or floppy, MS–DOS 2.1 or greater, printer (optional)
  $1,750/year

- Construction Criteria Base
  National Institute of Building Sciences, 1015 15th Street, N.W., Suite 700, Washington, DC 20005, (202) 347-5710
  IBM PC or compatibles; 512K, EGA graphics recommended, hard disk, MS–DOS 3.0 or greater, MS–DOS CD–ROM Extensions
  (Ms.) Terry Griffith, Computer Systems Manager
  $970/year with updates

- CD–ROM Prototype Disc
  U.S. Geological Survey, 804 National Center, Reston, VA 22092, (703) 648-4000
  IBM PC or compatibles; MS–DOS
  Jerry McFaul
  $35

- Census Test Disc #1
  U.S. Bureau of Census, Data Users Service
  Division, Washington, DC 20233, (202) 753-4100
  IBM PC or compatibles; MS–DOS
  $200

- Electronic Encyclopedia
  Grolier Electronic Publishing Inc., 95 Madison Avenue, Suite 1100, (212) 696-9750
  PC/XT/AT, or compatibles; 512K, monochrome or CGA (Apple Macintosh version expected by Fall, 1988)
  $299

- Electronic Sweets (Available first quarter 1989)
  McGraw-Hill Book Company, 11 West 19th Street, New York, NY 10011, (212) 512-2000
  IBM PC or compatibles, MS–DOS
  $115 (When purchased with print version of catalog)

- ERIC
  SilverPlatter Information Services, Inc., 37 Walnut Street,
  Wellesley Hills, MA 02181, (617) 239-0306
  IBM–PC or compatibles, 512K (640K recommended), monochrome or CGA, hard
    drive or floppy, MS–DOS 2.1 or greater, printer (optional)
  $1,750/year

- Dialog Information
  3460 Hillview Avenue, Palo Alto, CA
  94304, (800) 3-DIALOG
  IBM–PC or compatibles
  $950/year with updates

- FastPast
  MicroTrends, Inc., 650 Woodfield Drive, Suite 730,
  Schaumberg, IL 60195, (312) 310-8928
  IBM–PC or compatibles, monochrome or CGA
  $199

- First National Item Bank and Test Development System
  Tescor, Inc. 461 Carisle Drive, Herndon, VA 22070,
  (703) 435-9501
  IBM PC or compatibles
  $300–$800/month, depending on configuration

- GEOdisc U.S. Atlas; GEOdisc State Series
  Geovision, 270 Scientific Drive, Norcross, GA 30092,
  (404) 448-8224
  PS/2, PC/AT, or compatibles; 640K, EGA, hard drive,
  MS Windows
  Ed Hanley, Director of Sales
  $1500/series

- GPO on SilverPlatter
  SilverPlatter Information Services, Inc., 37 Walnut Street,
  Wellesley Hills, MA 02181, (617) 239-0306
  IBM–PC or compatibles, 512K (640K recommended), monochrome or CGA, hard
    drive or floppy, MS–DOS 2.1 or greater, printer (optional)
  $950/year

- K–8 Science Helper
  PC-SIG, Inc., 1030 East Duane Avenue, Suite D, Sunnyvale, CA 94086, (408) 730-9291
  PC/XT/AT, or compatibles; 256K, monochrome or CGA, MSDOS 3.1 or higher,
    MS–DOS CD–ROM Extensions
  Chuck Botsford, CD–ROM Product Manager
  $195

- LePac Government Documents Option
  Brodart Automation, 500 Arch Street, Williamsport, PA 17705, (717) 233-8467
  IBM/PC or compatibles
  $2,500/year with updates

- LinguaTech Bilingual Dictionaries
  MicroTrends, Inc., 650 Woodfield Drive, Suite 730,
  Schaumberg, IL 60195, (312) 310-8928
  IBM–PC or compatibles, monochrome or CGA
  $199/disc

- MEDLINE
  Cambridge Scientific Abstracts, 5161 River Road, Bethesda, MD 20816, (301) 951-1400
  PS/2, PC/XT/AT, or compatibles; 512K, monochrome or CGA, hard drive or
    740K floppy, MS–DOS 3.1
  $1,250/year

- SilverPlatter Information Services, Inc.
  37 Walnut Street, Wellesley Hills, MA 02181, (617) 239-0306
  IBM–PC or compatibles, 512K (640K recommended), monochrome or CGA, hard
    drive or floppy, MS–DOS 2.1 or greater, printer (optional)
  $900/year

- Dialog Information
  3460 Hillview Avenue, Palo Alto, CA 94304, (800) 3-DIALOG IBM–PC or
    compatibles
  Price TBA

- Microsoft Bookshelf
  Microsoft Corp., 16011 NE 36th Way, Box 97017, Redmond, WA
  98073-9717
  IBM PC or compatibles; 640K, monochrome or CGA, hard drive or two floppy
    drives, MS–DOS 3.1 or higher, MS–DOS CD–ROM
  Extensions
  $295

- Microsoft Small Business Consultant
  Microsoft Corp., 16011 NE 36th Way, Box 97017, Redmond, WA 98073-9717
  IBM pC or compatibles; 640K, monochrome or CGA, hard drive or two floppy
    drives, MS–DOS 3.1 or higher, MS–DOS CD–ROM Extensions
  $150

- Microsoft Stat Pack
  Microsoft Corp., 16011 NE 36th Way, Box 97017, Redmond, WA 98073-9717
  IBM PC or compatibles; 640K, monochrome or CGA, hard drive or two floppy
    drives, MS–DOS 3.1 or higher, MS–DOS CD–ROM Extensions
  $125

- Monthly Catalog of U.S. Government Publications
  Autographics, Pomona, CA
  IBM–PC or compatibles; 640K, monochrome or CGA
  $2500/year

- NTIS
  IBM–PC or compatibles, 512K (640K recommended), monochrome or CGA, hard
    drive or floppy, MS–DOS 2.1 or greater, printer (optional)

SilverPlatter Information Services, Inc., 37 Walnut Street,
Wellesley Hills, MA 02181, (617) 239-0306
$2,250/year

- PC–SIG Library
  PC–SIG, Inc., 1030 East Duane Avenue, Suite D, Sunnyvale, CA
  94086, (408) 730-9291
  PC/XT/AT, or compatibles; 256K, monochrome or CGA, MSDOS 3.1 or higher,
    MS–DOS CD–ROM Extensions
  Chuck Botsford, CD–ROM Product Manager
  $295

- PsycLIT
  IBM–PC or compatibles, 512K (640K recommended), monochrome or CGA, hard
    drive or floppy, MS–DOS 2.1 or greater, printer (optional)
  SilverPlatter Information Services, Inc., 37 Walnut Street,
  Wellesley Hills, MA 02181, (617) 239-0306
  $3,995/year

- Versa Text
  MicroTrends, Inc., 650 Woodfield Drive, Suite 730,
  Schaumberg, IL 60195, (312) 310-8928
  IBM–PC or compatibles, monochrome or CGA
  $199

SECTION III
SCHOOLS AND THE NEW LEARNING AND TELECOMMUNICATIONS TECHNOLOGIES

Without a comprehensive planning for the use of information age technologies in schools, education will continue to fall short of preparing the educated person for an effective living in a highly technological world. American schools must provide every student with access to comprehensive and rich educational experiences regardless of geographic location, town wealth, school size, or other economic or social factors.

To realize this end, five conditions must be met.

First, teachers should have a command of an extensive range of instructional resources and information necessary to meet their instructional planning and curriculum development needs, and the needs of their individual students.

Second, the effective use of the instructional technologies should be so infused into the teaching and learning process that the technologies become transparent.

Third, all elementary and secondary schools should be active participants in multi-information networks.

Fourth, school administrators and students should be confident, effective and comfortable in the information/technological world in which they will work.

Fifth, quality education is a shared responsibility among schools, parents, and the community at large, hence, there is a need to establish an effective partnership among these entities.

Since the first school library was established, there have been continued efforts to provide teachers and students with the resources necessary for well-rounded and meaningful teaching/learning experiences. Today, it is an accepted fact that the school library media is an instructional center of the school and that the role of the school library media specialist is three-fold: an information specialist, a teacher, and an instructional consultant.

Chapter Eleven, The School Library Media Center in the Information Age, focuses on the new roles of the school library, and the school media specialist.

Chapter Twelve, Epilogue: Effective Educational Utilization of the New Learning and Telecommunications Technologies, discusses teacher preparation and school media specialists programs with emphasis on those technologies, and the shared responsibilities among schools, parents, and the community to ensure quality education.

Chapter Eleven

THE SCHOOL LIBRARY MEDIA CENTER IN THE INFORMATION AGE

ROBERT HALE

INTRODUCTION

The world of the 21st century will be characterized by instant communication, rapid trans-global transportation systems and an interdependent world economy. A firm understanding of world cultures and the ability to communicate across traditional language and geographic barriers will be the norm rather than the exception.

World leaders of the 21st century will be those countries whose citizens have developed the facility to take full advantage of the available information and transportation technologies.

To establish the necessary firm foundation, our students must become productive citizens. American schools in the last decade of the 20th century must provide every student with access to comprehensive and appropriate educational experiences regardless of geographic location, town wealth, school size, or other economic or social factors. To realize this end, the following conditions are necessary:

1. Every teacher should have a command of an extensive range of instructional resources and information necessary to meet their instructional planning and curriculum development needs, and the needs of their individual students.
2. The effective use of appropriate technologies should be so infused into the teaching and learning process that the technologies are transparent.
3. All elementary and secondary schools should be active participants in multi-information networks.
4. Teachers, school administrators and students should be confident, effective and comfortable in the information/technological world in which they will work.

THE ROLE OF THE SCHOOL LIBRARY MEDIA CENTER

Since the first school library was established in the late 1800s there have been continued efforts on the part of school librarians (library media specialists) to provide teachers and students with the resources necessary for well-rounded and meaningful teaching/learning experiences. Early school libraries were the depositories and distribution centers for a vast resource of print materials. With the advent of lantern slides, motion pictures, audio recordings, and other audiovisual materials, the role of the school library began to change from one of a warehouse and distribution center to an instructional center. The change came about in response to the need on the part of students and teachers to learn more about accessing information from the expanded formats available from the school library.

Today, it is an accepted fact that the school library media is an instructional center of the school and that the role of the school library media specialist has an expanding role as information specialist, teacher, and instructional consultant. Moreover, the expectations of the school library media program are expanding to include the broad range of educational technologies.

DEFINITION OF EDUCATIONAL TECHNOLOGY

In order to build a common base for the application of technology in education, it is critical to have a common understanding of the definition of Educational Technology. The following definition is taken from EDUCATIONAL TECHNOLOGY: A GLOSSARY OF TERMS, published by the Association for Educational Communications and Technology, AECT.

Educational Technology is a complex, integrated process involving people, procedures, ideas, devices and organization, for analyzing problems, and devising, implementing, evaluating and managing solutions to those problems, involved in all aspects of human learning. In educational technology, the solutions to problems take the form of all the *Learning Resources* that are designed and/or selected and/or utilized to bring about learning; they are identified as Messages, People, Materials, Devices, Techniques, and Settings. The process for analyzing problems, and devising, implementing and evaluating these solutions are identified by the *Educational Development Functions* of Research-Theory, Design, Production, Evaluation-Selection, Logistics, Utilization, and Utilization-Dissemination. The processes of directing or coordinating one or more of these functions are identified by the *Educational Management Functions* of Organization Management and Personnel Management. The relationships among these elements are shown by the Domain of Educational Technology Model. (See Figure XI-1) (1)

Domain of Educational Technology Model

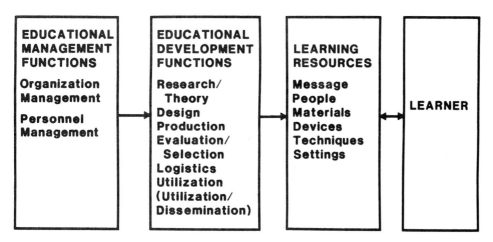

Figure XI - 1 Domain of Educational Technology Model

A somewhat simpler working definition, based on the AECT work, has been developed by the Connecticut Joint Committee on Educational Technology:

Educational Technology is that aspect of education involved in enhancing learning through the systematic identification, organization, utilization and management of a full range of learning resources. (2)

It is important to note that the above definitions address not only the hardware and software, but also the instructional strategies and delivery systems needed to assure that technology can further our country's educational goals.

POTENTIAL OF EDUCATIONAL TECHNOLOGY FOR ELEMENTARY AND SECONDARY EDUCATION

Achievement of the United States' vision for education for our children can be accelerated by the appropriate use of educational technology. Research indicates that the effective application of appropriate educational technology will make instruction more accessible, cost effective and efficient, immediate, productive, powerful, relevant, and responsive to special and individual needs.

Based on the potential of educational technology to improve learning opportunities for our students, the charge to the education community at all levels in the country must include the following:

1. Exercising leadership in the identification, acquisition and application of educational technology to meet the challenges of public elementary and secondary education.
2. Developing and implementing policies to assure that all students and teachers have equitable access to appropriate educational technologies.
3. Supporting research in and the application of educational technology to the teaching/learning process by:
   a. charging several state departments of education to undertake, in cooperation with institutions of higher education and other interested agencies, research activities in the area of educational technology;
   b. establishing, as a part of each state department of education, a state-wide clearinghouse for information related to educational technology;
   c. establishing educational technology demonstration centers in cooperation with higher education, regional education service centers, and public television agencies in their states to facilitate awareness of new and emerging technologies and their application to education in United States; and
   d. supporting the clearinghouse and demonstration center activities with fiscal, real, and human resources.
4. Assisting local school districts in the development and implementation of short- and long-range plans for educational technology.
5. Working to develop federal support to assist local school districts in the acquisition of equipment, materials and staff necessary to apply technology effectively to the teaching/learning process in our schools.
6. Requiring educational technology and its uses as a component of all teacher education programs.
7. Requiring faculty in teacher preparation programs to demonstrate competencies in educational technology.

8. Establishing a requirement that, to be eligible for teacher and administrative certification, an individual must be able to demonstrate ability to use educational technology.
9. Providing, as a part of renewable teacher certification, the development of a plan to assure appropriate professional development opportunities in the field of educational technology for current teachers and administrators.

It is further recommended that each chief state school officer develop an action plan to accomplish the goals and to report to their state board of education at least once each year on the progress of the action plan along with any recommendations for modification of the plan. Each of the above recommendations has implications for the school library media program.

Many components of the instructional plans used each day by teachers are based on tradition. As they work with our children to bring quality educational experiences to each and every learner, books, realia, maps, audio recordings, films, and a host of other materials and techniques, all considered traditional, are brought to bear on the task of teaching and learning. More recently, classroom television and computers have been added to the resources regularly employed by teachers. Today, we have the power of interactive technologies to add to our growing list of resources available to provide educational equity and excellence in instruction to all the students in our country.

A review of some of the emerging technologies now in the forefront in education serves to highlight the areas where school library media programs must expand in order to meet the primary mission as stated in *Information Power, Guidelines for School Library Media Programs,* "The mission of the library media program is to ensure that students and staff are effective users of ideas and information." (3) This mission encompasses a number of specific objectives to provide:

1. intellectual access to information;
2. physical access to information;
3. experiences that encourage users to become discriminating consumers and skilled creators of information;
4. leadership, instruction and consulting assistance in the use of instructional and information technology;
5. resources and activities that contribute to lifelong learning;

6. a facility that functions as the information center of the school; and
7. resources and learning activities.

It is not possible to plan for a fully integrated library media program without consideration of staff, curriculum, materials, facilities, intellectual access, and the hardware necessary for the end-user to take advantage of the program. Like any system, care must be taken to consider the individual components as they work independently and interact with each other as part of a system. When principles of instructional design include effective application of the full range of learning resources and technology appropriate to the identified instructional outcomes, education is enhanced. The responsibilities of the library media center staff are a key to the success of the effective use of educational technology.

There is unanimity in the library media community on the mission and the subsequent objectives. There is a need, however, to provide specific information as to the function of the library media program and the responsibilities of the library media specialist in the area of interactive technologies.

INTERACTIVE TELECOMMUNICATIONS COMMUNICATIONS TECHNOLOGIES

The use of the telephone, radio or television in our schools and classrooms is nothing new. For years we have expanded the opportunity of our students and teachers by the effective utilization of these basic technologies to provide home-bound instruction, participate in events at remote locations in real time and listen and/or see great performances as a part of our instructional program. The advent of the audio cassette and video cassette have made the use of both audio and video programs even more convenient and effective. More recently, the microcomputer and the MODEM (modulator/demodulator) as well as compressed video technologies using CODEC (coder/decoder) have expanded our opportunities even more.

We are all familiar with the traditional transmission systems currently in use as a part of the telecommunications technologies. These systems include: commercial and public broadcast television, radio, land-based telecommunications, telephone, cable television and leased lines, satellite, microwave, and Instructional Television Fixed Service (ITFS).

Each of these basic transmissions systems has variables which must be considered, such as the constraints imposed by topography, earth footprint and the like.

The library media specialists have the responsibility to constantly monitor the vast range of telecommunications technologies and keep themselves and the decision-makers they work with informed as to the potential for education.

The following are some examples of the application of telecommunications technologies to education.

SPECIFIC PROGRAMMATIC COMPONENTS REQUIRING TELECOMMUNICATIONS TECHNOLOGIES

Distance Education

What is the difference between what we have been doing and the concept of distance education? The following is a working definition of distance education: Distance education is the sharing of instruction among two or more sites using telecommunications technology while providing for interaction among the participants.

The important distinction between the traditional use of telecommunication technology and distance education is the provision for interaction among the participants. While distance education commonly employs these readily available technologies, it goes beyond the passive reception of information.

There is a place for the traditional use of instructional television, instructional radio, commercial broadcasting and now satellite broadcast in education. They are still a cost effective and convenient method to provide a vast range of learning resources and materials to our students and teachers.

The potential for distance education, with its capacity for interaction, is limited only by our imagination. The library media center staff has varying levels of responsibility, usually dependent on whether the local school is a program participant or a program originator. If the local school is the originator, the responsibilities for the library media staff cover the full range of considerations: needs analysis, instructional development, professional development activities, awareness activities and summative evaluation as appropriate. Following is a list of necessary components of distance education program.

Necessary Components of a Distance Education Program

- Policy considerations on the part of all participating agencies such as:
  - course credit
  - grading practices
  - student regulations
  - policies affecting teachers
  - calendars and schedules
  - evaluation of staff
  - fiscal responsibilities
  - homework
  - early dismissal and school closing
- Needs analysis
  - course offerings
  - curriculum
  - instructional materials
- Instructional development
  - selection of appropriate technology
  - course development appropriate to needs and technology selected
  - formative evaluation
  - selection, acquisition and/or preparation of instructional materials in print, nonprint and/or electronic formats
  - development of materials to determine student progress
- professional development activities for teachers and administrators necessary to make effective use of distance learning
- awareness activities for local decision-makers, parents, and students
- summative evaluation
- providing the necessary facilities, equipment, and telecommunication lines
- provide for the necessary contractual arrangements for the maintenance of equipment

Distance education can cut across all curriculum areas and most grade levels, although the most common application of formal distance learning programs is at the high school level.

Teleconferencing

The interactive teleconference, a less formal distance education application, is an excellent addition to the professional development opportunities available to educators. Agencies originating teleconferencing activities need to undertake many of the activities listed for distance education in the areas of policy, needs analysis, instructional design and evaluation. Although there is usually less involvement in the planning of teleconferences at the building or district level, there are still several areas of responsibility which must be addressed by the library media center staff. These responsibilities include:

- promotion of teleconference opportunities at the district and school level;
- providing the necessary facilities, equipment and telecommunication lines;
- scheduling of facilities;
- coordination of teleconferences;
- provision of necessary print, nonprint and/or electronic materials; and
- providing for the necessary contractual arrangements for the maintenance of equipment.

It is important to note that any telecommunications technology can be employed to implement distance education programs. The decision as to which technology is most appropriate is a part of the instructional design phase. Care must be taken to explore the advantages and disadvantages of each for the particular application. The library media center staff has to facilitate the use of technology for all forms of distance education.

Electronic Information Service

An electronic information service, such as E–Z Mail provided by the Connecticut State Department of Education, is designed to facilitate communication among schools, school districts, regional service centers, the Department and other interested members of the education community. As the needs of educators change, the electronic mail service can be expanded to meet those needs. Bulletin boards on the E–Z Mail system are designed to provide information to interested persons on a timely basis.

Responsibilities of library media center staff to facilitate the E–Z Mail service include:

- provide for training opportunities for student, teachers and administrators in the operation of the electronic information service;
- motivate the potential users of electronic information services to make effective and efficient use of the system;
- facilitate the acquisition of required hardware and software; and
- facilitate the installation of necessary telephone lines;

In addition it may well be that individual school districts will want to establish local electronic mail services to meet the needs of the students, teachers, and administrators in their schools. The library media center staff is the prime resource available to school districts to assist in development of services at the local level.

Searchable Remote Databases

The proliferation of information available through on-line databases has made instruction in the use of searching skills an important component of learning resources and technology programs at every level. Students, teachers and administrators will need to develop a high level of facility in the utilization of searchable databases.

Responsibilities of library media center staff to facilitate the use of searchable databases are to:

- provide for training opportunities for students, teachers and administrators in the use of searchable databases;
- facilitate the acquisition of required hardware and software;
- facilitate the installation of necessary telephone lines;
- ensure that copyright provisions are met; and
- provide for the necessary contractual arrangements with database providers.

Other Interactive Technologies

One of the benefits of the information age is the rapidity of development of new technologies or the expansion of existing technologies. In some cases the technologies, in use in few areas of education and training, are only waiting for appropriate courseware to be developed to extend their benefits to more students and teachers.

Among these new technologies are interactive videodisc and CD–ROM technologies. The responsibilities of the school library media staff regarding the implementation of these new technologies are to:

- research the available interactive videodisc materials to determine curriculum match;
- recommend specific materials;
- arrange demonstrations of interactive videodisc applications as necessary;
- facilitate the acquisition of required hardware and software;
- provide for training opportunities for students, teachers and administrators in the use of interactive videodisc instructional materials;
- ensure that copyright provisions are met;
- provide for the necessary contractual arrangements with CD–ROM providers to maintain currency of materials; and
- provide for the necessary contractual arrangements for the maintenance of equipment.

In addition to videodisc and CD–ROM, two new technologies are emerging: High Definition Television and Holography. High Definition Television has great promises to education since it can project enlarged and crisp images. Holography is a relatively new technology which also has great, yet still unexplored applications to education.

Library media staff should be aware of current developments in both fields. They ought to arrange for demonstrations of these new technologies to keep teachers and administrators apprised of their potential applications. Their long-term planning of equipment purchase should consider requirements of these new technologies, especially HDTV which appears to be invading the television industry in the very near future.

ONE-WAY TELECOMMUNICATION TECHNOLOGY

Although we have been concentrating on distance education and interactive technologies, it is important to reemphasize the role of the library media center staff in the utilization of instructional television, and satellite programming. Although considered "passive," the applications of these technologies to the teaching/learning process will remain an important source of up-to-date instructional materials for many years to come. It is important to note that, although the materials are considered passive, they are in reality a part of the interactive instructional process taking place on a day-to-day basis in the classroom.

Instructional Television

Instructional television (ITV) provides classroom teachers with materials which are selected to meet their specific goals and objectives. They are intended to be used by teachers as components of their instructional strategies. Instructional Television service is one of the methods which can be used to assist in providing equitable access to a wide range of quality instructional materials designed to support instruction in our schools.

Responsibilities of library media center staff to facilitate the Instructional Television service are to:

- provide for off-air recording of programs;
- catalog recorded programs for ease of access by students and teachers;
- ensure that copyright provisions are met;
- provide for professional development activities as necessary, e.g., utilization workshops on specific programs;
- provide for the distribution of the Instructional Television Schedule and Resource Guide;
- facilitate the acquisition and distribution of teacher guide materials;
- monitor broadcasts and report any problems to the agency originating the programs.

The instructional television service provided by the State Department of Education or your local public television station can make a significant impact on the instructional program of the school only if the library media center staff provides these necessary facilitating services.

Downlinking of Satellite Programming

More and more schools are installing satellite receivers (down-links) with the associated antenna, converter, amplifiers, and distributions system. Once the system is installed and ready for use, many of the schools then try to determine how they are going to use this "new technology," and where it fits into the instructional program. Just as in other technologies, the library media center staff has an important role in the effective use of satellite programming. It is necessary for them to:

- research the available satellite-delivered materials and programs to determine curriculum match;
- recommend specific materials and programs;
- arrange demonstrations of satellite applications as necessary;
- facilitate the acquisition of required hardware and software;
- provide for training opportunities for students, teachers and administrators in the use of the satellite system;
- ensure that copyright provisions are met;
- provide for the necessary contractual arrangements with program providers to maintain currency of materials; and
- provide for the necessary contractual arrangements for the maintenance of equipment.

CONCLUSION

Research in the area of learning resources and technology has revealed significant findings related to the improvement of educational practice. While it is not within the scope of this chapter to review all of the pertinent research in this area, the following are examples which support the need for effective use of educational technology in teaching. These examples are:

1. Results of a pilot program in Memphis Tennessee showed as much as a three year improvement on standardized tests in mathematics and language arts by students who were provided access to computers and appropriate software in school and at home. (4)
2. Dr. Elaine K. Didier, of the University of Michigan State University, found that the benefit of full-time library media specialists resulted in increased student attainment in reading and study skills, and the contribution of the library media specialists to the curriculum development process had a positive relationship to student achievement. (5)
3. The Delaware-Chenango BOCES in Norwich, New York, reports student performance in AP Calculus exceeded expectations as a result of offering the course over a distance learning system using computers and MODEMs which permit the simultaneous interactive

communication of both computer and voice over standard telephone lines. (6)

4. Mary Sceiford of the Corporation for Public Broadcasting reports in her publication, *The Effectiveness of Television for Learning: Highlights from Summaries of Research,* published in 1985, that both broadcast and recorded television are effective instructional tools. (7)

5. John Bransford and Ted Hasselbring of Vanderbilt University have conclusive evidence, as a result of a two-year project working with students at risk of school failure, that the effective use of "off-the-shelf" video and computer software makes a dramatic difference in student performance in mathematics and language arts. (4)

These examples of research concerning learning resources and technology not only support the effective use of educational technology, but also confirm the need for an informed, dedicated, and responsive staff committed to enhancing education through the appropriate and effective use of a full range of educational technology. The responsibilities of that staff include: policy considerations, needs analysis, instructional development, professional development activities for teachers and administrators, planning and executing awareness activities for local decision-makers, providing the necessary facilities needed for the implementation of a variety of instructional technologies, and providing for the necessary contractual arrangements.

Wouldn't it be great if:

- teachers could request a video program from a central library and have it the same day?
- every teacher who wanted to participate in a national teleconference could do so without leaving his/her district?
- speakers or presenters available in one school district could be available in any school district that needed or wanted the same presentation?
- teachers could share their innovative curriculum projects with their colleagues easily, quickly and with plenty of time for questions and answers?
- meetings of committees on critical education issues could be observed by interested persons all across the state, region, or the entire country?

- national and international teleconferences could be held and participants would not have to travel outside of their school districts?

All this and more is possible today. But school library media programs, computer education programs and distance learning programs working in isolation are not going to be able to meet these and other challenges facing education in our country. Only through the integration of these components of learning resources and technology, as well as planning for future technologies available to education, can we meet the needs of our students and teachers as well as the expectations of the citizens of the United States. Someone must take a leadership role in building comprehensive learning resources and technology programs. **Why not you?**

REFERENCES

1. AECT Task Force on Definition and Terminology. EDUCATIONAL TECHNOLOGY: A GLOSSARY OF TERMS. Washington, D.C.: Association for Educational Communications and Technology, 1977.
(2) "New Directions for Educational Technology, Recommendations of the Joint Committee on Educational Technology," prepared by Connecticut State Board of Education, Board of Governors for Higher Education, 1983.
(3) The American Association of School Librarians and Association for Educational Communications and Technology. INFORMATION POWER, Guidelines for School Library Media Programs. Washington D.C.: AECT, 1988.
(4) A Conference on Technology and Students at Risk of School Failure, June 28–30, 1987, Pheasant Run Resort, St. Charles, Illinois, Organized by Agency for Instructional Technology.
(5) Didier, Elaine K. Macklin. "Relationships between Student Achievement in Reading and Library Media Programs and Personnel," Ph.D. dissertation, University of Michigan, 1982; quoted in INFORMATION POWER, Guidelines for School Library Media Programs, p. 149.
(6) Galvin, Patrick. TELETRAINING AND AUDIOGRAPHICS: Four Case Studies. Ithaca, N.Y.: Cornell University, June 1987.
(7) Sceiford, Mary. "The Effectiveness of Television for Learning: Highlights From Summaries of Research," Washington D.C.: Corporation for Public Broadcasting, 1985.

Chapter Twelve

EPILOGUE:
EFFECTIVE EDUCATIONAL UTILIZATION OF
THE NEW LEARNING AND
TELECOMMUNICATIONS TECHNOLOGIES

IBRAHIM M. HEFZALLAH

INTRODUCTION

An essential element of the design of effective learning environments is ensuring the learner's interactivity with models of excellence, both in human resources and in learning materials. Very often, access to models of excellence can be achieved through mediated interaction. The technology of the information age provides students and teachers with the tools and vehicles through which models of excellence can be accessed. Availability of these tools is one side of the coin. Effective utilization is the second.

To implement effective utilization, first, school curricula have to be examined and restructured in the light of the goals of education with special attention to what the new learning and communications technologies can offer.

Second, teachers have to be educated in the use of the new learning and telecommunications technologies and their potential applications to education.

Third, there is a need to foster the new role of the school librarian in the information age. This new role is three-fold: an information specialist, a teacher, and an instructional consultant.

Fourth, there is a need to implement a partnership among schools, parents, and the community at large to provide for quality education for our nation's students.

Revision of school curricula is beyond the scope of this publication. This chapter will focus on the last three prerequisites for the effective utilization of the new learning and telecommunications technologies in education.

EDUCATING TEACHERS IN THE USE OF INFORMATION TECHNOLOGY

The new telecommunications and instructional technologies provide educators with the tools through which they can achieve quality education for all students of our country. However, prerequisites to reaping the benefits of these tools, are teachers who are competent in using these tools in their teaching.

Information technology encompasses print and electronic publications as well as a rich variety of media software. Familiarity with books and periodicals in one's field is no longer sufficient for a successful teaching career. However, the emphasis in education in colleges of education is still on one form of information: the printed page. To educate K–12 students in the viable uses of information technologies entails competent teachers in these aspects. To cultivate a competent K–12 teacher in the use of information technologies in teaching necessitates the following:

Competent College Professors in the Use of Information Technology in Teaching

There is a tendency among teachers to use methods of teaching through which they were taught. If teachers do not experience the effective use of information technology in their college and postcollege education, they will tend to practice traditional methods of teaching in their schools. For education to prepare the citizens for the information age, information technologies have to embedded in all of the course offerings in a teacher preparation program. However, due to lack of hardware and lack of awareness of effective software, college professors very often do not employ in their teaching what they are preaching to their students. As a result, information technology in education tends to be the practice of those who are interested in teaching about this field, instead of integrating it in every teaching experience schools of education offer. To make use of information technology in all of the course offerings of a teacher preparation program, faculty of colleges of education have to become competent in the use of information technology in teaching their own courses.

Staff development programs in colleges of education ought to address this issue. A professional development program for faculty could start with informing faculty about the new learning and telecommunications technologies and their potential applications to education. Providing the faculty with opportunities to examine a variety of software, media programs, and applications of the new technologies in teaching will help them in developing new insights in designing their courses and teaching plans.

Libraries, media centers, and computer centers in teacher preparation institutions have to cooperatively assume leadership and catalytic roles in educating the faculty in the implementation of the new technologies in college teaching. They also have the responsibility of providing a comprehensive and up-to-date sample of information technology applications and software designed for education K–12.

Libraries of Teacher Preparation Institutions Rich in Information Technology

When college professors become competent in the use of information technology in their research and teaching, exposing their students to a wide range of information resources becomes natural. They will ensure that comprehensive and up-to-date reference services are made available to their students. Taking that availability in mind, they plan their courses in which students use the library for a variety of reasons to fulfill course requirements. In addition, to resources needed to teach college courses, usually libraries of teacher preparation institutions maintain a K–12 curriculum collection. The curriculum collection has to be expanded to include, in addition to school textbooks and media programs, electronic publications designed for use with K–12 students.

New Requirements for Admission

A working knowledge of at least one word processor should be a requirement for enrollment in a teacher preparation program. If a student cannot meet this requirement, he ought to be given the opportunity to develop that competency without rewarding course credits. It is assumed that a student who has developed a working knowledge of a word processor posseses a minimum level of computer literacy and familiarity with basic operation of computers. Such background will be needed so that the student can use the computer to access information from data bases and information utilities.

Requiring an Introductory Course in Educational Technology From All Students Seeking a Teaching Certificate

An effective teacher preparation program should emphasize the right of every child to a rich learning environment. Today, children cannot be taught in the same fashion followed years ago. A visually and computer-oriented generation cannot be denied the right to use and interact with well-designed teaching materials presented through communications technology.

To graduate teachers capable of using the new learning and telecommunications technologies in education, teacher preparation institutions should require a basic course in the use of educational technology from all students seeking a teaching certification. A major objective of this course is developing preservice teachers' clear understanding of educational technology. As it was discussed in Chapter Two and Chapter Eleven, educational technology is more than machines and software, or a variety of teaching methods. Educational technology is a technology of the mind which may or may not use hardware or a highly technical teaching strategy to achieve the stated educational objectives. Its main goal is to achieve excellence in education. It requires systematic planning based on our knowledge of human learning, and the best methods of presenting information to involve the learner. It examines accessible communications and information technologies to determine those most appropriate for the achievement of the desired objective in a cost effective manner. The choice of technology of instruction is determined not only by economic considerations, but by the unique characteristics of each technology, the purpose of using it, with whom it will be used, and under what circumstances.

To be effective, a teaching system has to be designed and engineered with precision. Basic to the design of a teaching system is the proper use of information and communications technologies. Therefore, knowledge of these technologies and skills associated with their uses should be mastered by every teacher.

Teachers as Critical Consumers of Information

In the world of information abundance, it is crucial to develop the ability of every individual to judge the relevance of information. Different courses in a teacher preparation program encourage students to examine the information they retrieve. However, an area that is neglected in teacher education programs is developing their students' critical consumption ability of mass media. A critical consumer of the mass media is a person who can:

a. analyze the content of mass media;
b. distinguish between facts, fantasy, and assumptions;
c. make informed judgments and express a thoughtful evaluation of mass media material and programs; and
d. make intelligent use of leisure time in which exposure to mass media is one among other enjoyable activities. This is especially important when dealing with television viewing.

Critical consumption of mass media is an outcome of planned activities in which understanding the media and what it offers, and thinking about one's relationship with the media are underlined. It is a skill that can and should be taught to the young generation. However, before teachers can foster critical awareness of mass media in their students, they have to develop that awareness and wholly believe in its necessity to provide their students with models of intelligent use of media. Therefore, developing teachers' awareness of mass media is a significant and important goal of teacher preparation programs.

Emphasizing Educational Equity in Teacher Preparation Programs

In the information age, the educational gap between schools with adequate funds and resources and schools that lack these resources could increase. It is crucial to the establishment of harmony among members of our society regardless of their socioeconomic status to close this gap. In their preparation years, preservice teachers have to be made aware of this problem and ways of alleviating it. That awareness is best accomplished when students of teacher preparation institutions experience planned attempts of their institutions to reach out to underprivileged schools. These attempts ought to be a component of a master plan of schools of education to reach out to neighboring schools, especially underprivileged schools.

In developing this plan, consideration might be given to the establishment of a center for field services. Some of the goals of such a center are to:

a. establish strong relationships with schools and other institutions, and to assess their educational and training needs, which the school of education can offer;
b. recruit students from neighboring school systems;
c. help achieve educational equity for students in less than affluent school systems by providing them with communication links to the institution's resources (one should not overlook the possibilities of outside funds that might be allocated just to achieve this goal); and
d. provide the opportunities for the faculty and the students to work more closely with school personnel in a variety of settings.

THE SCHOOL MEDIA SPECIALIST

During the past two decades, the proliferation of information resources and new developments in information dissemination technologies have broadened the concept of the school library from a place of housing and distributing print materials to an instructional center of the school. Also, the role of the school librarian has expanded. Today, the school librarian has a new title: school media specialist. His/her role is three-fold: an information specialist, a teacher, and an instructional consultant.

Recently, two major national organizations, The American Association of School Librarians (AASL) and the Association of Educational Communications and Technology (AECT), addressed the mission and the challenges facing the school media libraries. Their findings and recommendations were published in 1988 under the title *Information Power.* (1) This publication will influence the educational practices for K–12 for many years to come. Colleges of education ought to examine this publication for the purpose of preparing teachers and school media specialists who can contribute to the fostering of their students' information power. Also, they ought to consider special programs for the preparation of professionals such as authors of learning materials, and producers of information packages who can contribute to widening the scope of information resources to learners in the 21st century.

Information Power identified the mission of the library media program as "to ensure that students and staff are effective users of ideas and information." It indicated that this mission encompasses a number of specific objectives:

1. **to provide intellectual access to information** through systematic learning activities which develop cognitive strategies for selecting, retrieving, analyzing, evaluating, synthesizing, and creating information at all age levels and in all curriculum content areas;
2. **to provide physical access to information through:**
    (a) a carefully selected and systematically organized collection of diverse learning resources, representing a wide range of subjects, levels of difficulty, communication formats, and technological delivery systems;
    (b) access to information and materials outside the library media center and the school building through such mechanisms as interlibrary loan, networking and other cooperative agreements, and online searching of databases; and
    (c) providing instruction in the operation of equipment necessary to use the information in any format.
3. **to provide learning experiences that encourage users to become discriminating consumers and skilled creators of information** through introduction to the full range of communications media and use of the new and emerging information technologies;
4. **to provide leadership, instruction, and consulting assistance in the use of instructional and information technology** and the use of sound instructional design principles;
5. **to provide resources and activities that contribute to lifelong learning** while accommodating a wide range of differences in teaching and learning styles and in instructional methods, interests, and capacities;
6. **to provide a facility that functions as the information center of the school,** as a locus for integrated, interdisciplinary, intergrade, and school-wide learning activities; and
7. **to provide resources and learning activities** that represent a diversity of experiences, opinions, social and cultural perspectives, supporting the concept that intellectual freedom and access to information are prerequisite to effective and responsible citizenship in a democracy.

Information Power also has identified five challenges that face the school library media specialists as they seek to fulfill the mission of the program. "The challenges result from a variety of influences and have the potential to radically reshape the services school library media specialists offer, the environment in which they work, and the profession to which they belong." (1, p. 2–3) These challenges are:

1. to provide intellectual and physical access to information and ideas for a diverse population whose needs are changing rapidly;
2. to ensure equity and freedom of access to information and ideas, unimpeded by social, cultural, economic, geographic, or technologic constraints;
3. to promote literacy and the enjoyment of reading, viewing, and listening for young people at all ages and stages of development;
4. to provide leadership and expertise in the use of information and instructional technologies; and
5. to participate in networks that enhance access to resources located outside the school (1, pp. 3–13)

"The school library media specialist will continue to be faced with complex challenges as expanding access to increasing amounts of information dictates the rethinking of traditional services and the provision of new services." (1, p. 13) Colleges of education preparing some of their students to assume the role of school media specialists have to focus on the expanding role of the school media library and the challenges which will face their graduates. Over the past decade, competencies needed to be mastered by school media specialists have been identified by state boards of education, professional organizations, and teacher training institutions. For instance, in the state of Connecticut, the following competencies are identified. The school media specialist should be capable of:

a. design, implementation, and evaluation of media programs. Media programs are defined as all the instructional and other services furnished to students and teachers by a media center and its staff;
b. evaluation, selection, acquisition, organization, production and retrieval of media, (print and nonprint);
c. teaching students, staff and faculty to utilize media and its accompanying technology by applying valid instructional methods and techniques;
d. assisting students in the interpretation of print and nonprint materials;
e. application of principles of administration and supervision for effective leadership and operation of the school library media center and program; and

f. formulation of the educational specifications and contribution to the design of school library media facilities.

Schools of education around the country have translated those and similar competencies into specific objectives of school media specialist programs. For instance, The Graduate School of Education and Allied Professions of Fairfield University developed the following as the specific objectives of its school media specialist program.

Specific Objectives of the School Media Specialist Program, Graduate School of Education and Allied Professions, Fairfield University

1. To further develop the student's understanding of the design of an effective learning environment in which the learner becomes motivated, interested and active.
2. To develop the student's ability to formulate realistic learning/teaching objectives and his/her ability to design a systematic approach to achieve those objectives.
3. To provide the opportunity for the student to develop a system approach for a unit of study in a chosen field of interest under the guidance of a faculty member.
4. To develop the student's sensitivity and appreciation of factors hindering effective student-teacher communication especially those related to the inappropriate selection and utilization of media.
5. To develop the student's understanding of the continuous process of evaluation and to develop his/her skill in using evaluation procedures in evaluating media programs and media hardware.
6. To develop the student's understanding of the leadership role of a school media specialist, especially in schools where a traditional approach in teaching is dominant.
7. To develop the student's understanding of the role of the media/library and its proper design to achieve the school objectives.
8. To develop the student's understanding of planning and conducting inservice training sessions to his/her school teachers.
9. To develop the student's understanding of the role of supportive personnel in the school media library.
10. To develop the student's ability and understanding of the process of selection and purchase of instructional materials and equipment to enhance the effectiveness of the learning/teaching process.

11. To develop the student's awareness of sources of information on available media and computer-assisted instruction programs.

12. To develop the student's skills in using library reference tools, and in training young people to retrieve information including the use of computers in conjunction with data banks and information utilities.

13. To develop the student's understanding and skills in basic cataloging procedures of both print and nonprint teaching materials.

14. To develop student's understanding and basic skills in using the microcomputer in the school library.

15. To develop the student's understanding of and familiarity with children and young adult literature presented in both print and nonprint media formats.

16. To introduce and train the student in the visual arts of communication to increase his level of visual literacy and his ability to express himself fluently through at least one form of visuals: still pictures, motion pictures, video, and/or computer generated visuals.

17. To develop the student's understanding of the principles and techniques of aural communication.

18. To train the students in basic production techniques and proper utilization of inexpensive teaching materials which can be made available to almost every classroom.

19. To develop the student's understanding of the state of instructional technology implementation in education and its projected development.

20. To develop the student's understanding of the present and future development in the field of telecommunications and computers and their potential effects on education.

21. To develop the student's understanding of current trends and needs in education and the potential application of instructional technology to serve educational needs.

22. To challenge the creativity of the student and to encourage him to experiment with new devices and new approaches in instruction including the use of computers in multimedia presentations.

23. To develop the student's understanding of the nature of research in educational media and to apply basic research principles to identify and test a proposed solution to an educational problem in one's field of interest.

To summarize, professional school media specialists can bring together people and resources and facilitate the use of those resources. They also can assume a three-fold role:

1. information specialists;
2. teachers; and
3. instructional consultants.

The need for those professional people is urgent if we are to provide rich, flexible, and interactive learning environments.

PARTNERSHIP AMONG SCHOOLS, PARENTS, AND THE COMMUNITY SNET/CONNECTICUT STATE DEPARTMENT OF EDUCATION TRAIL STUDY

Quality education is a shared responsibility among schools, parents, and the community at large. Our economic survival and leadership role in the free democratic world rest on the educated individuals of our nation. The need to improve the quality of education and to achieve educational equity for everyone is urgent.

There are many instances in which communities and corporations have worked together to improve education. To illustrate, the following is a description of a trial study, **SNET Links To Learning**, in which, for the first time, a telecommunications company sponsored an educational program using three communications technologies to promote quality education in one statewide effort.

In cooperation with Connecticut State Department of Education and a number of school districts across the state, **SNET Links To Learning Project** is a pioneering project employing the SNET public switched network to bring some of the latest information age technology to urban, suburban, and rural school districts in Connecticut. In the words of Walter H. Monteith, Jr., Chairman and CEO, Southern New England Telecommunications Corporation, October, 1988, "We are committed to enhancing education in Connecticut and to exploring uses of our network as an educational resource for all the people of our state." (2)

The SNET Links to Learning trail began in September, 1988 and will run through June 1990. Currently, it is comprised of three separate but related electronic technology trials. These technologies are: SNET Video Link, SNET Data Link, and SNET Voice Link.

SNET Video Link

SNET Video Link ties schools together with two-way audio and video. A teacher conducting class in one school can be seen and heard by students in one or more remote locations simultaneously. Students can respond to the teacher as if they were in the same classroom.

In 1987–88, North Haven and Hamden High schools were linked through two-way fiber optics for audio and video transmission and reception. During the 1988–89 school year, the system expanded to include Cheshire, Woodbridge and New Haven. In early 1989, another link was established between Hartford and West Hartford schools using compressed video technology. (Figure XII-1)

SNET Video Link can give school systems of all sizes the ability to share courses with other school systems. Students benefit from more options and schools benefit from a more enhanced selection of courses. Videotaping the presentation allows anyone who misses a lecture to watch it at a later date.

Professional development and extracurricular applications of SNET Video Link are other important values of the system. A renowned guest lecturer in one location can be seen, heard and appreciated by audiences in several other locations miles away. Remote video audiences can participate in question and answer segments.

SNET Data Link

SNET Data Link is being implemented in 15 different towns across the state from Bridgeport to Bloomfield and North Canaan to New London. The trial uses ConnNet, a statewide packet switched network and SNET MailPLUS, an electronic messaging service, to give these schools access to electronic mail and a number of on-line educational data bases. During the 1988–89 trail year, the Dow Jones News Services which features full text newspapers articles, and full text access to more than 80 national magazines; and the BRS search service including ERIC were included. For the 1989–90 trail year, DIALOG and Einstein services are being included also. (For more information on information utilities, please refer to Appendix II.)

SNET Data Link is simple to use. Most schools already own the computers they need, and support teams are always available for new

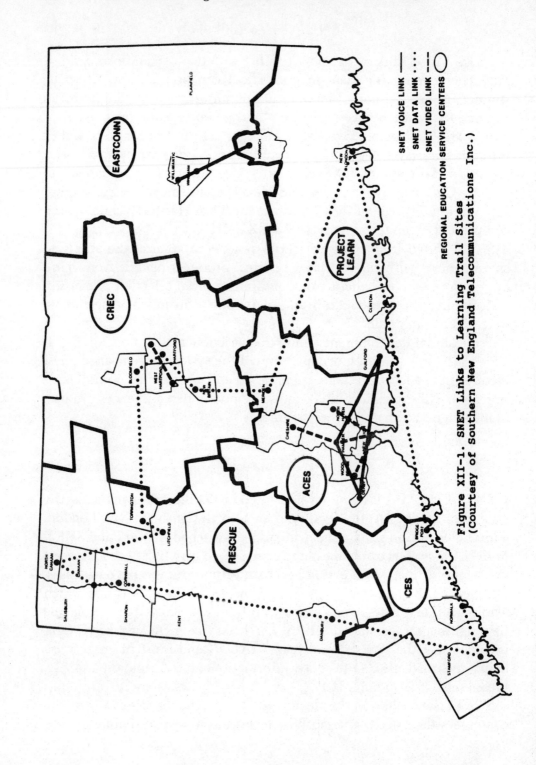

Figure XII-1. SNET Links to Learning Trail Sites
(Courtesy of Southern New England Telecommunications Inc.)

SNET Data Link applications, or to help teachers integrate the service into an existing lesson plan or curriculum.

Through this link students and teachers will have at their fingertips a wealth of the most current information to assist in learning a new subject, in supplementing classroom knowledge or in researching a special project.

Students are introduced to the excitement of electronic messaging via SNET MailPLUS. Using SNET MailPLUS students can exchange electronic mail with students across town or across the country. They can read and post items on electronic bulletin boards. They can even get up-to-the-minute stories on a topic for timely research or class discussion.

SNET MailPLUS can provide the following messaging services:

MAIL allows users to exchange electronic messages with one another.

NEWS provides access to the latest news on the AP Videotex News Service, UPI wire, OPEC News Agency news service, IMTS, USDA, Business Wire.

NEWS-TAB an electronic news clipping service that searches the news wires for stories of interest to the user 24 hours a day, 7 days a week. As stories related to a user-defined topic cross the news wire, they are automatically passed to the user via electronic mail.

PEN an information service which provides timely data on political campaigns, candidates, and elections in the United States.

SNET Voice Link

SNET Voice Link is an electronic messaging system which permits users to send and receive voice messages via the telecommunications network, and which teachers and parents can use to make their communication easier and more useful. Schools in Hamden, Derby, Guilford, Hampton, and Norwich are provided with this service. With it teachers can record messages and send them to the parents of every child in a particular class. They can receive messages from parents and other teachers as well.

Teachers can use it to update parents on their children's progress. From homework assignments to special announcements, parents can find out what their children are learning and how well they are learning. Then they can respond to the teacher, creating an ongoing dialogue. It is easier for parents to stay involved, because it is easier for them to stay in touch with the teacher. No more waiting for notes that might be accidentally forgotten or misplaced.

Principals and other administrators can increase efficiency and productivity, too. Messages can be left and returned efficiently. Meetings can be set, changed, and confirmed without the delays caused by return calling. A superintendent of schools can conduct an urgent meeting with five principals in five different locations.

To a new generation of parents who grew up with the phone and learned to spend long periods of time in telephone conversations with friends and in doing business, telephone communication is not a new tool. However, having interest in what the schools do and taking active participation in educating their children is an objective that schools have to strive to achieve. SNET Voice Link provides a medium through which schools can involve parents and encourage them to actively participate in educating their children.

To summarize, applications of SNET Voice Link include:

Home-to-school/teacher

- notify/verify absence
- request conferences
- inform of special students' needs
- access event/meeting/program dates

School-to-school

- request/notify other schools of information on inter-school events
- request policy information

School-to-community

- broadcast community interest news/event dates
- report specifics of event information

Teacher-to-home

- request conferences
- broadcast assignments
- assign work outside of class
- notify of events/field trips
- notify of attendance/behavior/attitude/academic issues

School-to-home

- notify of attendance problems
- inform of student obligations
- broadcast general interest items
- inform of school policy changes/issues

Observations

SNET Links to Learning is still in its trial period. Observations of the Project Team, teachers, and visitors to the schools participating in the system include:
SNET Video Link

- Students do as well or better in video classes.
- Higher level classes are well received and in demand.
- It allows for socialization among high school students, and allows for expanding social growth outside their school setting.
- Students see the opportunities to learn more beyond the required curriculum.
- There is enthusiasm to expand the use of the system. During 1987–88 North Haven and Hamden used the system to teach Algebra II. In 88–89 Cheshire and Amity Regional were added to the trial, and three more classes to the curriculum. By September 89, the plans call for offering up to twelve classes including Etymology, Chinese, Environmental Science, Russian, and Italian.

SNET Data Link

- It stimulates student interest by using computers as exciting interactive tools.
- It improves the computer literacy of students and teachers.
- It makes available the benefits of electronic mail, information data bases, full-text magazines and newspapers articles to all schools regardless of the community size.
- Classroom teachers and library media specialists report that it's easy to use SNET Data Link. They describe the training for the program as clear, interesting and complete. In their opinion, SNET Data Link becomes even easier to use the more it's applied. And the more familiar they become with its capabilities, the more innovative applications they find for them.

- Teachers note that SNET Data Link has increased their satisfaction with the nature and timeliness of the information they can obtain. Response indicates that they use SNET Data Link for almost all of their on-line data base and communications services.
- Teachers say that SNET Data Link is especially helpful for sharing information with teachers in other classes and other schools.
- Teachers use the program's information retrieval and electronic mail capabilities not only for enhancing lessons, but for professional development as well.
- Teachers report that students are more enthusiastic about school subjects, receive more enjoyment from the school experience, demonstrate more creativity on school projects and are able to do better quality work. (Table XII-1)
- Students report that SNET Data Link makes schoolwork more interesting.
- More than 90 percent of the students surveyed believe SNET Data Link helps them learn. Four out of five say they prefer using computer data bases to library books and other resources. Reasons cited include faster retrieval of information and the ability to find articles not contained in school or public libraries. Overall, students report that SNET Data Link makes schoolwork much more fun.

TEACHERS PERCEPTION of the EFFECT of SNET DATA LINK on STUDENT SCHOOL WORK

	Greatly increased	Somewhat increased	Had no impact
Creativity on school projects	24%	62%	14%
Enthusiasm in school subjects	24%	57%	19%
Student ability to do quality work	19%	62%	19%
Enjoyment of the school experience	24%	52%	24%
Motivation to pay attention to academic work	24%	33%	43%

Table XII-1. Teachers Perception of the Effect of SNET Data Link on Student School Work. (Courtesy of Southern New England Telecommunications Inc.)

SNET Voice Link

- It has successfully facilitated communication between the teachers and parents on the system.
- It has permitted parents and teachers to communicate at their own convenience.
- It has improved behavior and progress, especially with the more problem children.
- Training parents to use the system is highly recommended. Terminology and training should be geared for the parents in the simplest way possible. (3)

CONCLUSION

The route to achieving excellence in education is a multipath. The new learning and telecommunications technologies introduced by the information age offer vehicles through which excellence in education can be achieved. However, there is a need to study all aspects of educational practice including financial support for a cost-effective education; the preparation of teachers, school media specialists, and school administrators; professional development of school personnel; nourishing professional ties between faculty of colleges of education and schools; revision of school curricula to accommodate the needs of the new age; and the role of the school media library in education. Since quality education is a shared responsibility among schools, parents, and the community, there is a need to establish effective partnership among these entities.

Educational reform should not focus only on producing a skilled work force. It should target, as well, the cultivation of the educated person. In the concluding remarks in the television series Learning in America, Roger Mudd said:

> Much of the school reform appears to be driven by America's loss of her competitive economic edge and the threat to our jobs. Schooling, we would suggest, is not a preparation for earning a living. It is one of the objectives, it is not the main one. Learning is for the sake of learning and not for the sake of earning. Learning in America should not only enrich our spirit, powers, wisdom and inner-contentment, but also should enable our country to function and flourish, For a nation so diverse as ours to maintain itself, there must be intelligent discourse and common understanding. For that, education is the keystone. (4)

Our economic survival and leadership in the free democratic world rest on the educated individuals of our nation. The need to achieve excellence in education and educational equity for everyone is urgent. Only when our quest is multilateral and targets the student as a whole person will we realize excellence in education.

REFERENCES

1. The American Association of School Librarians and the Association for Educational Communications and Technology. INFORMATION POWER, Guidelines for School Library Media Programs. Washington D.C.: AECT, 1988.

2. Monteith, Walter H., SNET Links To Learning Conference, October 18, 1988, speech included in information package by Southern New England Telephone Company, SNET Links To Learning, 227 Church Street, New Haven, Connecticut, 05510.

3. SNET Links to Learning—Information Kit. For more information call SNET Links to Learning, 203-771-5116.

4. "Paying the Freight," the fifth and the last program in the television series LEARNING IN AMERICA, Produced by MacNeil/Lehrer Production and WETA, broadcast on PBS on April 24, 1989.

Appendix I

AUTHORING LANGUAGES
AND AUTHORING SYSTEMS

An **authoring language** is a special programming language developed to minimize the effort of authoring computer-assisted instruction (CAI) and computer-based education (CBE) programs (courseware). Authoring languages have authoring tools to create lessons using a variety of presentation techniques including text of different fonts, graphics, and full-motion video.

Knowledge and familiarity with programming are prerequisites for the efficient authoring of courseware using an authoring language. On the other hand, an **authoring system** is a tool that can be used by an instructor who has minimum knowledge of programming languages to create courseware. In the process of creating courseware with an authoring system, the instructor selects options from a menu and responds to screen messages. Sometimes, he may have to use short and simple commands.

An efficient authoring language or system offers the author the tools to produce graphics, to use text files created with other word processors, assistance in lesson design, satisfactory documentation, and access to help options all the time.

The quality of courseware depends not only on the flexibility and design options an authoring language or system offers, but also on the author's understanding of instructional design, his teaching experience, knowledge of subject matter, and his creative talents. A courseware team is usually recommended. The team includes programmers, instructional designers, subject matter specialists, graphic designers, and other creative talents.

The reader might chose to consult two references. The first is Kearsley, Greg. AUTHORING A GUIDE TO THE DESIGN OF INSTRUCTIONAL SOFTWARE. Reading, Massachusetts: Addison-Wesley Publishing Company, Inc., 1986. Among the topics discussed in this book are the authoring process; integrating software with other media; and guidelines for screen design, user control, response analysis, helps options, error handling, and revision to insure the quality of a program.

The second reference is Crowell, Peter. AUTHORING SYSTEMS. Westport, Connecticut: Meckler Corporation, 1988. According to Crowell, "There are about 200 authoring systems for Computer-Based-Training, and quite a few more that support videodiscs." (p. 87) Crowell developed an information database on interactive video authoring systems. It included information on about 60 interactive video authoring systems on the market today. He indicated that "Each one is . . . constantly being revised and upgraded." (p. 87)

The rest of this appendix presents a short account of two authoring system/languages: Digital's Courseware/DAL, and PC/PILOT/PROPI.

DIGITAL'S Courseware Authoring System (C.A.S.) (1)

DIGITAL'S Courseware Authoring System (C.A.S.) is a computer-based education system designed to make all the components of automated instruction available from a single software interface.

C.A.S. is an "enclosed environment" for teaching. This means that students or naive users of the system cannot wander around the computer's operating system. Rather, menus provide paths for both students and teachers through the system.

All the material to be learned is seen by students in the form of lessons. A student could choose a lesson from a program on mathematics, or history, or literature. Likewise, assignments are given in the form of lessons.

Digital Authoring Language (DAL) (1)

Lessons are built with authoring tools. Authoring tools are software tools used by authors to create and maintain lessons. Software tools include graphics editors, character set editors, text editors, and programming language. The programming language itself is the most important tool. It is called DAL, the Digital Authoring Language. This language is specially designed for authors of lessons and includes instructions and built-in functions and variables. The language is designed to work with C.A.S. to collect data, monitor student progress, and control lessons.

DAL offers features common to other VAX/VMS languages, including access to VAX/VMS system services and standard call interfaces to routines written in other computer languages. DAL is implemented as a native mode compiler under the VAX/VMS operating system. DAL produces object files that can be linked to produce native mode executable lessons, thus providing optimal system performance during lesson delivery.

PC/PILOT (2)

PILOT is an authoring language widely used with microcomputers. System requirements for this language include any model IBM PC or equivalent, 128K required, 256K recommended, DOS 2 or higher. Color Graphic adaptor or Extended Graphic adaptor are recommended, but not required.

PC/PILOT was created by Larry Kheriaty and George Gerhold, developers of PILOT for Sperry, IBM, NCR, Radio Shack, Apple and many other makers. It has an open architecture, and it can expand as the need arises.

Programs in other languages can be called directly within a PILOT program.

PC/PILOT supports external devices including mouse, touch screen, light pen, voice communications, compact disc, video tape, and video disc. It provides the designer with full screen and color control text or graphics modes, full and partial painted screen image graphics, special effects and wipes, turtle graphics, command vector graphics, sprite animation, multiple windows, and variable size and pitch character fonts.

The EZ TEXT EDITOR is a full screen text editor which is used to write PILOT program statements. It supports user-defined characters, character editor and macros.

PROPI Authoring System (2)

PROPI is a code generator which produces lessons written in the PC/PILOT language, although the author may never see anything which looks like PILOT code.

No authoring system of usable complexity can provide all the capabilities of a complete computer language. The choice is either to limit the applications of the authoring system, or to provide an easy way for the author to modify the results of an editing session and to add segments written in a suitable computer language. PROPI has a seamless integration with PILOT. It also can provide for the integration of program segments written in other languages.

PROPI tools include tools for screen design, and animation, peripheral hardware control, answer analysis, computation, record keeping, and—at a somewhat higher level—lesson design and documentation.

REFERENCES

(1) For more information please refer to:
Digital Equipment Corporation, INTRODUCTION TO COMPUTER-BASED EDUCATION, 1984, Digital Equipment Corporation, Education Computer Systems, MR03-2/E7, Three Results Way, Marlborough, Massachusetts 01752-9103

(2) For more information write to Washington Computer Services, 2601 North Shore Road, Bellingham, Washington 98226.
Telephone: (206) 734-8248

INFORMATION UTILITIES

T his appendix includes brief descriptions of services available on seven major databanks. For more information on these services, the reader might choose to write or call the selected utility. For more information on retrieval of information from data banks, two reference books by Alfred Glossbrener are recommended: *THE COMPLETE HANDBOOK OF PERSONAL COMPUTER COMMUNICATIONS,* and *How To Look It Up Online,* both published by St. Martin's Press, N.Y., N.Y., 1985 and 1987 respectively.

Usually, a personal computer, a modem, a communication software for the computer, and a phone line are standard equipment needed for reaping the benefits of the vast and varied information available on databanks. Adding a printer allows the use to produce a hardcopy of the retrieved information.

BRS INFORMATION TECHNOLOGIES

1200 Route 7
Latham, New York 12110-9976
518-783-1161
Fax # 518-783-1160
Telex # 710 444 4965

The following information on BRS was furnished by Peter C. Bonner, Director of Marketing, BRS Information Technologies.

Available Services:

BRS/SEARCH SERVICE. BRS provides a full range of information search and retrieval services. BRS provides access to 150 databases on a variety of subject areas. You can search BRS using the command driven method or MENUS, making it user-friendly.

BRS/AFTER DARK. Your own university library online at home! BRS/After Dark offers access to millions of journals, books, government studies and research and technical reports via your microcomputer. For as little as $6 per hour you can access one of the world's leading information sources and locate information on business, education, finance, medicine, and psychology, to mention just a few of the subject areas available.

BRS/COLLEAGUE. The personal, computerized medical knowledge system for the clinician. Colleague provides immediate, indepth literature review of comprehensive complete-text and bibliographic libraries via computerized databases of

234

notable books, journals and other pertinent medical knowledge. Colleague is menu-driven making it even easier to search.

BRS/EDUCATOR and BRS/INSTRUCTOR offer discounted subscription plans for schools to use microcomputers connected through telephone lines to search databases like ERIC, and PsycINFO.

BRS/ONSITE. BRS/OnSite can help you maximize the utility of your area network and build a state-of-the-art, electronically unified campus (or corporation). With BRS/OnSite you can choose from among approximately a dozen major biblio-graphic databases in a variety of areas—weekly or monthly. Thus, your users will have local access to the most current information in their fields at a fixed cost.

BRS/COLLEAGUE DISC. BRS/Colleague Disc combines the most prestigious medical database with the leading search software and the latest storage technology to create the complete desktop reference system for medical education. The database, English-language citations from the National Library of Medicine's MEDLINE database in convenient one-year segments from 1986 to the present.

COMPUSERVE INFORMATION SERVICE

Corporate Headquarters
5000 Arlington Centre Boulevard
P.O. Box 20212
Columbus, Ohio

The following brief description of the services offered on the CompuServe Information Service was furnished by Jo Ann Ivne, Public Relations Intern.

The Compuserve Information Service is the world's largest online information service for microcomputer users, both in terms of the number of members and the amount and scope of information offered. More than 500,000 members can now access the service by a local phone call in more than 600 cities across North America and in over 100 foreign countries.

The CompuServe Information Service was designed for instantaneous communication and information retrieval in the home, school, or office. To access CompuServe, members need a microcomputer, terminal, or communicating word processor; a modem (a device connecting the computer to the telephone), communications software, and a telephone.

Members of the CompuServe Information Service can choose from a selection of more than 1,000 subject areas including:

• CompuServe forums allow members to attend online conferences, exchange information on forums' message boards and in the libraries, and benefit from the expertise and enthusiasm of other members who share a common interest.

Forums of interest to educators and students include the Education Forum, Computer Training Forum, Foreign Language Forum, Education Research Forum, Science/Math Education Forum, Space Education Forum, Disabilities Forum, and the IBM/Special Needs Forum.

Students might be especially interested in the Students' Forum where members meet to discuss topics of interest, including term papers, course offerings, scholarships, and current events. Some students become electronic pen pals with CompuServe members from other areas of the country and the world.

• CompuServe members may communicate through EasyPlex electronic mail, which allows members to send and receive messages 24 hours a day, regardless of distance or time zone. Over 600,000 electronic mailboxes are linked through EasyPlex. The CB Simulator is an online interactive communication service that allows members to chat electronically with others across the country via "live" online dialogue.

• Several education and reference services are available on CompuServe. IQuest allows access to over 800 article reference and full-text databases. The Grolier's Academic American Encyclopedia is a comprehensive online reference source of more than 31,000 articles, fact boxes and bibliographies, accessible by a simple keyword search. Through Paperchase, CompuServe members have access to over 5 million references from 4,000 medical journals dating from 1966. Computer Database Plus provides current, comprehensive summaries or complete text articles from over 130 major computer industry publications.

• News services provided by the Associated Press, The Washington Post, Reuters, McGraw-Hill, and the OTC NewsAlert are available on CompuServe. The Executive News Service allows members to define a keyboard, and any story on the specified wires that contains that keyword is saved for the member in a special folder.

• Travel services, such as TRAVELSHOPPER, the Official Airline Guide Electronic Edition (OAG), and EAASY SABRE provide continually updated information on schedules and fares for virtually every published airline in the world.

• The Electronic Mall allows members to shop in over 100 online stores, including Bloomingdale's, Brooks Brothers, and Waldenbooks. Products can be ordered with a few simple keystrokes from the comfort of home or office.

• A broad range of investment data is available on CompuServe, including information on stocks, mutual funds, bonds, options, commodities, and the money market. Members use this information to research companies and plan investment strategies.

• A variety of games are available on CompuServe, including multi-player, trivia, word and adventure games. Word games, a tough IQ test, and a history game challenge the skills and knowledge of players of all ages.

• The Handicapped Users Database provides material for and about the handicapped on a broad range of topics, including specially designed computer hardware and software, rehabilitation research, and relevant nonprofit and commercial organizations. For many members with speech or mobility impairments, CompuServe's two forums for handicapped users—as well as other special interest forums and the CB simulator—greatly facilitate communication with other members across the nation.

• The CompuServe Information Service is growing constantly as new services are added and existing ones are expanded and enhanced. In spite of the vast amount of information available, however, no computer experience is necessary to master the system. A simple, concise menu format guides the new user through a series of choices until the desired information is found. The experienced user can save time by using quick reference words and the "GO" commands to bypass menus.

A comprehensive and detailed Users Guide offers step-by-step instructions for all areas and capabilities of the CompuServe Information Service. The guide, User ID and initial password necessary to access CompuServe are all included in the subscription kit, which can be purchased at retail outlets such as Waldenbooks, Radio Shack, Sears Business Centers, and ComputerLand or directly from CompuServe by calling (800) 848-8199.

DIALOG INFORMATION SERVICES, INC.

3460 Hillview Avenue
Palo Alto, CA 94304
Telephone 800-334-2564
FAX 415-858-7069

The following brief description of the services available on Dialog Information Services was furnished by Katherine S. Mulvey, Marketing Communications.

The story of the online industry is the story of Dialog Information Services, Inc. In part this reflects the company's size—Dialog has more than 175 million items online and 98,000 customers—but, more significantly, its emergence at the dawn of information retrieval.

Dialog grew out of a Lockheed Missiles and Space Company research and development program begun in 1963. Contracts with government agencies such as NASA and the U.S. Office of Education followed, beginning in 1968. In 1972, Dialog was established as a commercial search service, and in 1981 became a wholly owned subsidiary of Lockheed Corporation.

Dialog was purchased by Knight-Ridder Business Information Services, Inc. in August, 1988. It is headquartered in Palo Alto, Calif., with offices in Boston, New York, Philadelphia, Washington, Chicago, Houston, and Los Angeles. Dialog serves customers in 89 countries, with representatives in Canada, Japan, Korea, Mexico, Australia, Brazil, Argentina, and throughout Europe.

Those customers include over 75 percent of Fortune 500 companies, along with government agencies, business consultants, libraries, universities, and research institutions around the world.

The Dialog product line includes the DIALOG (r) Information Retrieval Service, KNOWLEDGE INDEX (R), DIALOG Business Connection (sm), DIALOG Medical Connection (sm), and DIALOG OnDisc (tm) CDROM products. Dialog also provides DIALMAIL (sm), an electronic mail service; and DIALNET (r), a telecommunications network.

As the world's largest and most comprehensive online databank, DIALOG offers more than 320 databases covering virtually every discipline, with especially strong offerings in business, science and technology. Information on more than 12 million companies from such sources as Dun & Bradstreet, Standard & Poor, and Moody is available through DIALOG databases. DIALOG users have access to information on 14 million patents in over 50 countries, summaries of articles from more than 100,000 journals, and complete text from 700 journals and newsletters. DIALOG's online information includes directory entries, journal articles, conference papers, patents, books, trademarks and statistics. *PC World* magazine described DIALOG as "the ultimate online library."

Dialog has been offering information retrieval services to the educational community since 1972. Dr. Roger Summit, Dialog's president, strongly believes that database suppliers and service vendors must play a vital role in bringing online retrieval training into schools across the country and should work closely with educators to do so.

The online instruction program was conceived in 1976 when Dialog was approached by library science educators who expressed a need to expose library schools and students to online searching in a cost effective manner. This resulted in Dialog's first Classroom Instruction Program (CIP).

In an effort to extend the instructional concept to other academic areas, Dialog has, within the past two years, introduced two new Instruction Programs: DIALOG Classmate (sm) and DIALOG Business CIP.

DIALOG Classmate introduces online information retrieval to students in elementary schools, high school and undergraduate institutions. It provides access to over 80 scientific and general interest databases including MAGAZINE INDEX, ACADEMIC AMERICAN ENCYCLOPEDIA, AMERICA: HISTORY AND LIFE and NATIONAL NEWSPAPER INDEX.

DIALOG Business CIP introduces business applications to students in undergraduate and graduate programs. Applications include acquisitions planning, corporate intelligence, competitive analysis, market research and planning, and financial screening for investment management.

Both Classmate and DIALOG business CIP uniquely provide complete curriculum-supporting materials to facilitate their integration into students' daily courses or studies. Classmate includes a student workbook and a teaching guide containing the student workbook, masters for creating instructional overhead transparencies, a curriculum of in-class activities, readings, and lectures from text materials assignments, tests, and discussion sections.

The Classmate student workbooks are priced at $5 each for quantities of ten or more and $8 each for quantities under ten.

DIALOG Business CIP includes instructional case studies for finance, marketing and strategic planning, student practice exercises, sample lesson plans, and support materials. Subscribers to DIALOG Business CIP may also purchase a complete self-instructional user's guide and DIALOGLINK communications software at a special price of $45. Both Classmate and DIALOG Business CIP can be accessed for only $15 per connect hour including telecommunications charges.

DOW JONES NEWS/RETRIEVAL SERVICE

P.O. BOX 300
Princeton, N.J. 08543-0300
Telephone 609-520-4065
FAX 609-520-4072

Dow Jones News/Retrieval is an electronic source for business information. Powerful yet easy to use, it provides business with timely and detailed facts, figures, analyses, and insights into the business world.

Financial analyses, reports and data are frequently updated. The user has access to the most current information as soon as 90 seconds after breaking on the Dow Jones News Service®. The news alert feature, along with current quotes databases, automatically lets the user know when the companies he/she is watching are making the headlines.

With News/Retrieval's detailed business and financial information on companies, industries and the economy the user can:

- Review reports from leading analysts and detailed corporate profiles.
- Monitor prospects, customers and competition
- Study expert opinions and forecasts on the U.S. economy and foreign markets.
- Retrieve real-time, same-day and historical quotes.
- Follow the commodities and financial futures markets.
- Make transactions online through an independent broker during the business day, at night, and on weekends — and have the broker manage the portfolio.

Using the news database, the user can:

- Read the latest world and national business and general news from *The Wall Street Journal*® reporters and the Dow Jones News Service.
- Get daily business and economic news on any industry or region worldwide, for example: Japan.
- Review historical information or today's news and financial stories.

Reference databases let the user search and retrieve background business information from *The Wall Street Journal*, Dow Jones^{SM} News, *Barron's*®, *The Washington Post*, major business publications, and specialized journals and newspapers published in the U.S., Canada, and Japan.

News/Retrieval also offers a full complement of databases that can help the user throughout the day into leisure hours. For instance one can:

- Send and receive electronic mail across the U.S.;
- Plan a trip and purchase flight tickets. Purchasing tickets is blocked from the Official Airline Guide, OAG, for academic customers. They can view OAG but they cannot make reservations;
- Purchase business products;
- Scan book and movie reviews;
- Check the standings of favorite sports teams or athletes

The information in News/Retrieval is gathered through the considerable resources of Dow Jones & Company, Inc., and from the opinions, analyses, and research of many of the country's most learned and renowned business analysts and investment firms. SEC filings, Standard & Poor's reports, and Dun's Financial Records^{SM} give the user details needed for business decisions (Dun's Financial Records^{SM} is blocked from academic customers).

Following is a summary of available services.

• Dow Jones News^{SM}: Stories from *The Wall Street Journal, Barron's* and Dow Jones Service recent as 90 seconds, as far back as 90 days.

• Dow Jones Capital Markets Report^{SM}: Newswire providing continuously updated, comprehensive coverage of fixed-income and financial futures markets around the world. Use four-digit codes to retrieve information on key U.S. government securities; bond trading; all facets of the Eurobond market, Ginnie Maes, and corporate and municipal bonds.

Text-Search Services^{SM}: Text-Search Services is optional to academic customers and a flat rate payment plan is an additional $.25/minute. It includes:

> • The Wall Street Journal Full-Text Version: All news articles published or scheduled to appear in *The Wall Street Journal* since January, 1984.
> • Dow Jones News: Selected stories from *The Wall Street Journal, Barron's,* and the Dow Jones News Service since June, 1979.
> • Barron's: Full text of articles from January, 1987. The Washington Post Full-Text Version: Full text of selected stories from *The Washington Post* since January, 1984.
> • Business Week: Full text of all articles from *Business Week* back to January 1985.
> • The Business Library: The full text of the PR Newswire and the Japan Economic Newswire plus selected articles from *Forbes, Fortune, Inc., Money, Financial World, American Demographics.*
> • Business Dateline: Full text of selected articles from 150 regional business publications from January, 1985. DataTimes: Full text of articles from 24 regional newspapers, two AP wires, the *Congressional Quarterly,* Gannett News Service and *USA Today* (DataTimes is not included in the ALL command).

• Business and Finance Report: Continuously updated business and financial news culled from the Dow Jones News Service, other newswires, and *The Wall Street Journal.* Detailed cross references to related information.

• Dow Jones QuickSearch^{SM}: One command generates a complete corporate report drawing information from multiple News/Retrieval sources. Provides the latest news, current stock quote, financial overview, company vs. industry performance, income statements, and more.

• Media General Financial Services: Financial and statistical information on 5,400 companies and 180 industries. Compare company versus industry, company versus company, and industry versus industry. For example:

KO   detailed corporate financial information on Coca-
            Cola (KO) with comparative industry data on the
            same screen

KO/PEP	comparative corporate financial information on Coca-Cola (KO) and PepsiCO (PEP) on the same screen
332/400	Comparative information on the soft drink industry and food chain industry

• Zacks Corporate Earnings Estimator[SM]: Consensus earnings-per-share estimates and P/E ratio forecasts for over 4,800 companies. Industries earnings estimates and five-year growth rates.

• Innovest Technical Analysis Reports: Technical opinions based on computer analysis of over 4,500 stocks trading on New York and American exchanges and over-the-counter.

• Investext®: (Blocked from academic Customers). Full text of over 20,000 research reports on more than 5,000 U.S. and foreign companies and 50 industries.

• Disclosure Database®: 10-K extracts, company profiles, and other detailed data on over 12,000 held companies from reports filed with the SEC and other sources.

• Dun's Financial Records[SM]: (Blocked from academic Customers). Financial reports and business information from Dun & Bradstreet over 750,000 private and public companies.

Insider Trading Monitor[SM]: (Blocked from academic Customers). Insider trading information on over 6,500 publicly held companies and 60,000 individuals (corporate directors, officers and shareholders with more than 10% ownership). Reports transactions of 100 shares or more. Updated daily.

• Standard & Poor's Online®: Concise profiles of 4,700 companies containing current and historical earnings and estimates, dividend and market figures.

• MMS Weekly Market Analysis[SM]: Weekly survey of U.S. money market and foreign exchange trends. Median forecasts of monetary and economic indicators.

• Dow Jones News/Retrieval World Report[SM]: Continuously updated national and international news from the Associated Press, the Dow Jones News Service, and broadcast media. Corporate Canada Online: News and detailed financial and market information on 2,200 public, private, and crown (government-owned) Canadian companies from Canada's national newspaper *The Globe and Mail.*

• Japan Economic Daily[SM]: Same-day coverage of major business, financial market, and political news from the Kyodo News Service in Japan.

• Wall Street Week[SM] Online: Transcripts of the public broadcasting program "Wall Street Week."

• Words of Wall Street[SM]: Over 2,000 financial and investment terms defined.

Quotes & Market Averages

• Dow Jones Enhanced Current Quotes[SM]: Quotes on common and preferred stocks (with News Alert feature), corporate and foreign bonds, mutual funds, U.S. Treasury issues and options. (Quotes minimum 15-minute delayed during market hours.)

• Dow Jones Enhanced Current Quotes[SM]: Real-time stock quotes. (Additional agreements must be completed for the use of RealTime Quotes. Contact Customer Service for details.)

Dow Jones Historical Quotes[SM]: Historical quotes for common and preferred stocks including daily quotes available for the trailing trading year, monthly summaries back to 1979 and quarterly summaries back to 1978.

• Tradeline^SM: (Blocked from academic Customers). Historical information on stocks, bonds, mutual funds & indexes back 15 years. Historical data on options back one year. Screen for issues that fit your investment requirements. Securities snapshot of market performance and background data. Find cash dividends, splits and interest payments.

• Dow Jones Futures Quotes^SM: Current (10–30 minute delay) and historical quotes for 80 contracts from the major exchanges. Updated continuously during market hours.

Historical Dow Jones Averages^SM: Historical averages including daily high, low close and volume available for industrials, transportation, utilities and 65-stock composite averages for the trailing trading year.

General Services:

• OAG Electronic Edition® Travel Service: Airline schedules and fares, hotel/motel information. Make flight reservations online.

• MCI Mail®: (Academic customers cannot access through MCI). Mail service for sending printed and electronic communications next door or world-wide.

• Academic American Encyclopedia®: Contains over 32,000 carefully researched and concisely written articles covering industry, finance, and academic subject areas. Updated quarterly.

• Peterson's College Selection Service^SM: Peterson's guide to two- and four-year U.S. and Canadian colleges and universities.

• Comp-u-store OnLine^SM: An electronic shopping service for over 250,000 discounted brand-name products.

Cineman Movies Reviews: Reviews of the latest releases as well as thousands of movies back to 1926.

• Magill Book Reviews: Reviews of many recent fiction and nonfiction works with new titles added weekly.

• Dow Jones News/Retrieval Sports Report^SM: Scores, stats, standings, schedules and stories for most major sports. Updated continuously.

• Dow Jones News/Retrieval Weather Report^SM: Three-day Accu-Weather forecasts for over 100 U.S. and foreign cities. Using Dow Jones News/Retrieval.

For Your Information: FREE online newsletter covering database enhancements, new databases, rate changes, free-time offers, and other important information. Check //FYI regularly for announcements.

• Master Menu: Complete listing of the information contained in the service, along with detailed access instructions.

Dow Jones News/Retrieval Symbols Directory: A comprehensive online listing of the symbols and codes used with Dow Jones News/Retrieval databases. Updated daily.

MEAD DATA CENTRAL

9393 Springboro Pike
Post Office Box 933
Dayton, Ohio 45401
Telephone 513-865-6800

The following description of Mead Data Central's services was furnished by Sharon Peake Williamson.

The LEXIS® Service

Law firms, corporations, courts and government agencies find the Mead Data Central, Inc.'s LEXIS service is a valuable tool for quick access to full-text, online information.

LEXIS is the world's leading computer-assisted legal research service, with extensive files of federal and state case law, codes, regulations, and dozens of specialized libraries of law, including tax, securities, insurance, and labor. LEXIS also includes English and French law, and Shepard's® and Auto-Cite® citation services.

Mead Data Central also offers the NEXIS® service with full-text articles from more than 350 leading newspapers, magazines, and wire services; the LEXIS® Financial Information™ service, with SEC filings and security analysts reports from dozens of top brokerage firms; the LEXIS® Country Information™ service, with country analysis reports and international news; the MEDIS® medical information service; the LEXPAT® patent service; and the NAARS accounting database, made available by agreement with the American Institute of Certified Public Accountants.

The NEXIS® Service

Mead Data Central, Inc.'s NEXIS® service provides quick access to critical business information to help professionals make informed, timely decisions. NEXIS is a computer-assisted general news, business, and company information service that offers full-text articles from more than 350 news sources.

These sources include leading newspapers (e.g., *The New York Times, Financial Times, The Boston Globe* and *Chicago Tribune*), business and financial magazines (e.g., *Fortune, Institutional Investor, Business Week, Automotive News®* and *Advertising Age®*), newsletters covering a wide variety of industries and topics, and foreign and domestic wire services, including the Associated Press, UPI, and Reuters.

Mead Data Central also offers the LEXIS® Financial Information™ service, with SEC filings and security analyst reports from dozens of top brokerage firms; the LEXIS® Country Information™ service, with country analysis reports and international news; the MEDIS® medical information service; and the LEXPAT® patent service.

NEWSNET

945 Haverford Road,
Bryn Mawr, PA 19010
215-527-8030

The following information on NewsNet was furnished by Patricia A. McParland, Marketing Communications Specialist, NewsNet.

NewsNet is a full-text newsletter database. NewsNet offers access to over 350 industry-specific business newsletters—covering 30 industry groups such as defense, aerospace, telecommunications, and electronics and computers—and 11 major newswires, including wires from United Press International, the Associated Press, and Reuter. All of the services carried on NewsNet are full-text, and each can be read or downloaded in its entirety, searched for specific terms, or monitored using NewsNet's exclusive electronic clipping service, NewsFlash. In most cases, the information available on NewsNet is available online before it's released in print.

NewsNet subscribers are also connected to several special gateway services. Without having to dial another phone number or remember another sign-on protocol, users can access such databases as *TRW Business Profiles,* which offers in-depth credit reports and analysis on over 13 million U.S. business addresses; *Vu/Quote Stock and Commodity Quotes,* with stock and commodity quotes from the New York Stock Exchange, NASDAQ, and AMEX exchanges; and the *Official Airline Guide,* which allows you to make and review airline reservations, as well as providing travel and frequent flyer information.

NewsNet is especially useful as a current awareness database. Over half of the information in the database is updated at least daily. The newswires are updated constantly throughout the day, and there is no time embargo associated with these wirefeeds. Articles from the wires can be read as soon as they are received by NewsNet, and most of them (with the exception of the wires from the United Press International) are completely keyword searchable within an hour of release.

NewsFlash, NewsNet's exclusive electronic clipping service is an extremely powerful current awareness tool. NewsFlash will monitor the entire database—or selected parts of it—for keywords chosen by the user. Twenty-four hours a day, incoming articles will be scanned for specified topics of interest, and those articles clipped and saved for automatic delivery to the user's NewsNet account. There is no online searching involved—just the assurance that NewsFlash is catching breaking stories as they break.

The commands used to access the NewsNet system are logical and easy to learn—although training classes are offered on a regular basis, the system is straightforward enough that even a novice can soon move around comfortably. System commands are common-sense English words, and reflect their functions: to scan the headlines of a newsletter, for example, the command SCAN is used.

NewsNet's command structure combines the flexibility of a command-driven system with the ease of a menu-driven system, without the user having to learn innumerable commands or wade through endless menus. A main command (SCAN, for example) is required at the main command prompt to begin a process, but once a main command has been entered, the system will prompt you for the remainder of your input.

For the user who needs help, NewsNet offers online help messages that are accessible from any point in the database. Each customer is also provided with complete user documentation, free of charge.

For more information about NewsNet, call 800-345-1301 (215-527-8030 outside the U.S.).

VU/TEXT INFORMATION SERVICES, INC.

325 Chestnut Street
Suite 1300
Philadelphia, PA 19106
Telephone 215-574-4400
A Knight-Ridder Company
The following description of available services on VU/TEXT was extracted from information furnished by Donna S. Willmann, Director of Marketing.

Types of Databases Available on VU/TEXT

The following is a list of the major categories of databases within the VU/TEXT databank. All of these are full text. A complete and current list is available online.

1. NEWSPAPERS—40 Total and Still Growing

- Washington Post
- Boston Globe
- Chicago Tribune
- Detroit Free Press
- Miami Herald
- L.A. Times
- Philadelphia Inquirer
- Houston Post

2. NEWSWIRES—News, Press Releases, and Financial Information

- Associated Press
- KNT Newswire
- Knight-Ridder Financial Wire
- PR Newswire
- Business Wire
- AP Political Wire

3. MAGAZINES—News, Business and Celebrities

- Time
- Sports Illustrated
- People
- Fortune
- Money
- Life

4. BUSINESS JOURNALS—Selected articles from over 180 journals

- Crain's New York
- Philadelphia Business Journal
- Kansas City Business Journal
- Silicon Valley
- South Florida Business Journal

5. TRANSPORTATION INDUSTRY FILES—Worldwide Maritime Information

- Journal of Commerce
- Transportation News Ticker
- ECS Marine Report
- FISYS Ship Characteristics

6. INTERNATIONAL DATABASES—Available through PROFILE

- Financial Times
- The Economist

- The Banker
- Times of London
- Spearhead & Celex EC Trade Legis
- McCarthy's Int'l Press Clippings
- Financial Times Business Reports

VU/TEXT offers a VIE (VU/TEXT in Education) program to schools that provide instruction in online retrieval. The program offers an opportunity to the students to learn full text searching and retrieval. Through this program students can have access to

- The entire written content of 40 regional newspapers (36 are exclusive)—from Boston to Los Angeles, Seattle to Miami
- Full text selected articles from more than 180 regional business journals from the U.S. and Canada, including—Atlanta Business Chronicle, The Denver Business Journal, & Crain's New York Business
- TIME, FORTUNE, MONEY, LIFE, SPORTS ILLUSTRATED, and PEOPLE magazines in full text
- Newswires, including—PR Newswire, Business Wire, and AP Political File
- The Journal of Commerce, FISYS (Information Systems) Ship Characteristics, and a transportation ticker (all three exclusive).

VU/TEXT IN EDUCATION provides each instructor with a teaching guide that includes an outline and a biography to support classroom teaching of VU/TEXT:

- History of Databases
- History of VU/TEXT
- Descriptions of VU/TEXT Databases
- Using VU/TEXT as a Professional.

The instructor receives the bi-monthly VU/TEXT newsletter, *Newsline,* to keep the instructor and the students informed of the latest databases and software enhancements available on VU/TEXT.

Individual support services of VU/TEXT IN EDUCATION include:

- one person may attend any of the regular regional VU/TEXT training sessions free of charge
- support through customer service 800 telephone number (800-258-8080)
- VU/TEXT personnel available for classroom demonstration in some areas
- VU/TEXT User Guide

- two copies of the VU/TEXT Mini-Guide for use in the library
- a Ready Reference Guide for each student
- a list of all databases
- a monthly printout of each student's use of VU/TEXT (if the students use individual passwords).

INDEX